CW01096187

TECHNOL   **EST**

In this groundbreaking work, Haochen Sun analyzes the
ethical crisis unfolding at the intersection of technology
and the public interest. He examines technology companies' growing power and their increasing disregard for the
public interest. To tackle this asymmetry of power and
responsibility, he argues that we must reexamine the nature
and scope of the right to technology and dynamically protect it as a human right under international law, a collective
right under domestic civil rights law, and potentially a
fundamental right under domestic constitutional law.
He also develops the concept of fundamental corporate
responsibility requiring technology companies to reciprocate for users' contributions, assume an active role responsibility in upholding the public interest, and counter
injustices caused by technological developments.

Haochen Sun is Associate Professor of Law at the
University of Hong Kong. He has published numerous
articles and co-edited books on intellectual property and
technology law. His opinions about intellectual property
and technology law have appeared in many media outlets
such as *Forbes, The Los Angeles Times, The New York Times,
South China Morning Post,* and *The Wall Street Journal.*

Technology and the Public Interest

Haochen Sun

University of Hong Kong, Faculty of Law

CAMBRIDGE
UNIVERSITY PRESS

University Printing House, Cambridge CB2 8BS, United Kingdom

One Liberty Plaza, 20th Floor, New York, NY 10006, USA

477 Williamstown Road, Port Melbourne, VIC 3207, Australia

314–321, 3rd Floor, Plot 3, Splendor Forum, Jasola District Centre, New Delhi – 110025, India

103 Penang Road, #05–06/07, Visioncrest Commercial, Singapore 238467

Cambridge University Press is part of the University of Cambridge.

It furthers the University's mission by disseminating knowledge in the pursuit of education, learning, and research at the highest international levels of excellence.

www.cambridge.org
Information on this title: www.cambridge.org/9781108416962
DOI: 10.1017/9781108255905

© Haochen Sun 2022

First published 2022

A catalogue record for this publication is available from the British Library.

ISBN 978-1-108-41696-2 Hardback
ISBN 978-1-108-40348-1 Paperback

Cambridge University Press has no responsibility for the persistence or accuracy of URLs for external or third-party internet websites referred to in this publication and does not guarantee that any content on such websites is, or will remain, accurate or appropriate.

CONTENTS

INTRODUCTION

A PROBLEMS WITH TECHNOLOGICAL DETERMINISM

Technology has the amazing power to change lives. Many years ago, I came across the exciting news that laser technology was being adopted in eye surgery to cure near-sightedness. As I was quite troubled by near-sightedness in my left eye, I enthusiastically consulted an eye doctor in my city to see whether such surgery could effect a major change in my life. She was a famous doctor who had received post-doctoral training in eye surgery at Harvard Medical School. After examining my eyes, she encouraged me to have laser surgery and not to worry about the potential side effects. I can still vividly recall her quick response to my concerns: "You don't need to worry about side effects. Technology always advances. It will cure side effects in the future." This response did not assuage my concerns. Instead, I asked a follow-up question: what if technological advancement was unable to eliminate side effects? The doctor immediately responded: "Please believe in technology!" Our conversation ended there, and I left the consultation room deciding not to have the surgery.

In January 2019, I was celebrating with Professor Barton Beebe a public lecture on technology and legal futurism that he had just delivered at the University of Hong Kong. During the lecture, he had shared with the audience a range of thought-provoking ideas about how technologies, from the Internet, to 3D printing, to space technology, shape the law. Enjoying the spectacular night view of Hong Kong across Victoria Harbor as we continued the discussion, I had a flash of insight. I told him that it seemed to me that any project concerned with how technology changes the world must also deal with the ways in which it can bring about pain and death and even the end of the world. I worried about the very real potential for technologies to be egregiously misused by human beings. After all, we have already produced technologies such as nuclear weapons that can destroy the planet, bringing humanity to an end.

I am sure that many readers will think that I am overly concerned with technology's harms. Why not have followed that famous doctor's advice all those years ago and enjoyed the correction of my near-sightedness by laser technology? Why not just focus on technology's transformative power in improving the quality of human life without thinking about pain and death? After all, technology is no evil monster. It is a necessary and inevitable force that transforms not only individual lives but the whole world.

Indeed, humanity's past is a history of the invention of tools and techniques that have transformed individual lives and the world as a whole.[1] Our Stone Age ancestors figured out how to make stone tools, fire, clothing, and shelters, thereby securing their survival. From the ancient to medieval to early modern periods, human beings have strived to utilize metal tools, wind power, and water resources to improve agricultural and manufacturing productivity, promote trade, and facilitate transportation. The two Industrial Revolutions spanning from the mid-seventeenth to early nineteenth centuries ushered in new technologies such as steam engines, chemical products, electricity, and petroleum-powered machines that massively boosted productivity and transformed lifestyles. The twentieth century saw the rapid development of even more innovative technologies, including automobiles, telephones, radio, television, and computers. Technology changes the material conditions of human existence. It also improves the quality of life by promoting cultural and political aspects of society. For example, the invention of the printing press and the Internet greatly facilitated the dissemination of knowledge and, in turn, the development of political institutions.

Where technology permeates individual lives and the fabric of society, technological determinism comes to the fore.[2] Many scholars and policymakers have elevated technology to a governing force in

[1] *See* HANNAH ARENDT, THE HUMAN CONDITION 144–53 (2d ed. 1998) (examining the history of technological developments related to human activities such as labor and work).
[2] Gaia Bernstein, *When New Technologies Are Still New: Windows of Opportunity for Privacy Protection*, 51 VILL. L. REV. 921, 929 (2006) ("Technological determinism is the view of

society, with technological development determining historic progress and social change. For example, Karl Marx expected the construction of railways in India to dissolve the caste system,[3] and Thorstein Veblen asserted that "the machine throws out anthropomorphic habits of thought."[4] Jacques Ellul concluded that "[n]o social, human, or spiritual fact is so important as the fact of techn[ology] in the modern world."[5] Following technological determinism, many people overwhelmingly support the faster and greater supply of technology as a panacea for their problems and for social ills. The historian Charles Beard captures the essence of such popular support for technological determinism in his statement that "[t]echnology marches in seven-league boots from one ruthless, revolutionary conquest to another, tearing down old factories and industries, flinging up new processes with terrifying rapidity."[6]

However, in their embrace of ever faster and greater development, adherents of technological determinism have turned a blind eye to the ethical issues and even humanitarian crises brought about by technology's use. Martin Heidegger once cautioned that technology's dominance in human society is "*danger* in the highest sense."[7] In reality, the history of technology is synonymous with a history of pain, despair, and death.

Powered by technology, the weapons deployed in war have killed countless individuals and caused massive damage and destruction of public facilities and private property. In the case of World War I and World War II, this devastation was on an almost inconceivable scale. Although nuclear technology promised to generate a range of energy and health benefits, the 1986 Chernobyl disaster caused a nightmare for the people affected and horrifying damage to the environment. The pervasive use of various technologies in manufacture and consumption

---

technology as an autonomous entity that develops according to an internal logic and direction of its own, resulting in determinate impacts on society.").

[3] *See* KARL MARX, ON COLONIALISM 85 (1974).

[4] THORSTEIN VEBLEN, THE THEORY OF BUSINESS ENTERPRISE 105 (1904).

[5] JACQUES ELLUL, THE TECHNOLOGICAL SOCIETY 3 (1964).

[6] Charles A. Beard, *Time, Technology, and the Creative Spirit in Political Science*, 21 AM. POL. SCI. REV. 1, 5 (1927).

[7] MARTIN HEIDEGGER, THE QUESTION CONCERNING TECHNOLOGY, AND OTHER ESSAYS 28 (1977) (emphasis in original).

has led to a global environmental crisis. Climate change, for example, is the defining crisis of our time, and it is happening even more quickly than we feared. Human activity is producing greenhouse gas emissions at record highs, accelerating global warming and its catastrophic effects.

How should we deal with these ethical crises so as to develop and apply technology in the public interest? Back in 1962, Rachel Carson was already warning us of technology's harmful effects on the public interest in her book *Silent Spring*. She revealed the adverse environmental effects of the indiscriminate use of pesticides and accused the chemical industry of spreading disinformation, and public officials of accepting the industry's marketing claims unquestioningly. Carson offered one of the leading lessons she had learned from the crisis:

> No responsible person contends that insect-borne disease should be ignored. The question that has now urgently presented itself is whether it is either wise or responsible to attack the problem by methods that are rapidly making it worse. The world has heard much of the triumphant war against disease through the control of insect vectors of infection, but it has heard little of the other side of the story – the defeats, the short-lived triumphs that now strongly support the alarming view that the insect enemy has been made actually stronger by our efforts. Even worse, we may have destroyed our very means of fighting.[8]

Carson's thoughts remind us that we must take a broad-based assessment of how technology should be developed and applied in the public interest. The public has the right to be assured that technologies promote societal interests in environmental protection. Technology companies must take corresponding responsibilities seriously. To deal with the problems Carson warned of sixty years ago, I believe that the public should be bestowed with a right to technology. This right would empower the public to enjoy technological benefits with minimal harmful effects upon the environment. Technology companies must also take responsibility for informing the public of those harmful effects and for taking proactive steps to minimize them.

---

[8] Rachel Carson, Silent Spring 266 (1962).

However, these public interest-oriented measures have not yet come to fruition. Rapid technological development has created new and even more formidable problems and challenges for our society. For example, unethical uses of digital and health technologies are harming the public interest in unprecedented ways.

In this digital age, technology companies reign supreme. In collecting enormous amounts of data from the public, technology companies have gained ownership of one of the world's most valuable resources.[9] They also regulate all kinds of speech activities on their platforms, operating as governors of social communication in the digital age.[10] They have developed new technologies such as artificial intelligence, acting as decision-makers for the future of humanity. However, the powers gained by leading technology companies far exceed the responsibilities they have assumed. They have thus far reaped their rewards with impunity, demonstrating no commitment to a conception of corporate responsibility commensurate with the nature and extent of their ever-expanding powers.

The major technology companies have been accused of being even more irresponsible than the financial institutions that caused the 2008 financial crisis.[11] While the public has invested their trust and support in technology companies such as Facebook, these companies have ignored their attendant responsibilities. Instead, they have created a "black box society"[12] and new forms of oppression.[13] Privacy breaches have become routine in the technology sector.[14] Tax evasion or avoidance by technology companies is occurring more frequently and on a larger scale than ever before, with Apple being named one of

---

[9] *The World's Most Valuable Resource Is No Longer Oil, but Data*, ECONOMIST (May 6, 2017).

[10] *See* Kate Klonick, *The New Governors: The People, Rules, and Processes Governing Online Speech*, 131 HARV. L. REV. 1598, 1603 (2018).

[11] Saqib Shah, *Banks Behind Financial Crash Were Better Behaved Than Facebook, Says Ex-Goldman Sachs President Gary Cohn*, SUN (Aug. 7, 2018) ("[B]anks were more responsible citizens in '08 than some of the social-media companies are today. And it affects everyone in the world. The banks have never had that much pull.").

[12] FRANK PASQUALE, THE BLACK BOX SOCIETY: THE SECRET ALGORITHMS THAT CONTROL MONEY AND INFORMATION 191 (2015).

[13] Stephen Hawking concluded that "[a]longside the benefits, AI will also bring dangers like powerful autonomous weapons or new ways for the few to oppress the many." *Stephen Hawking Launches Centre for the Future of Intelligence*, U. CAMBRIDGE (Oct. 19, 2016).

[14] Andrew Rossow, *Why Data Breaches Are Becoming More Frequent and What You Need to Do*, FORBES (May 23, 2018).

the largest tax avoiders in the United States[15] and Amazon paying no income tax whatsoever.

Meanwhile, unequal access to technological benefits has become a pressing social justice issue.[16] Recent studies show that even in the United States, a technologically advanced country, access to technology has become a determining factor in the knowledge divide between rich and poor youths.[17] It is time to decide whether the general public or a small group of elites has the final say over how the benefits of technological progress are distributed. Moreover, it is also a matter of urgency that we deal with the new forms of racial and gender discrimination being facilitated by new technologies across the globe.[18] However, digital technology companies have to date done very little to deal with the unjust distribution of technological benefits.

The COVID-19 pandemic has exposed another ethical crisis resulting from health technology. Major pharmaceutical companies possess the know-how to manufacture medicines and vaccines and own numerous medical patents, the rights to which must be exercised in a socially responsible manner. In the face of this unprecedented global public health crisis, a public policy priority should be ensuring that technology companies assume responsibility for swiftly and expansively benefiting the public through their medical innovations in COVID-19 research. In doing so, they should attach less importance to their existing or potential patent rights over those innovations.

However, major pharmaceutical companies have failed to react to the global call for greater responsibility. To accelerate and broaden global access to vaccines, treatments, and diagnostics, an international group of scientists, entrepreneurs, and lawyers launched the Open

---

[15] *Apple "Among Largest Tax Avoiders in US" – Senate Committee*, BBC (May 21, 2013).

[16] *See* Haochen Sun, *Can Louis Vuitton Dance with Hiphone? Rethinking the Idea of Social Justice in Intellectual Property Law*, 15 U. PA. J.L. & SOC. CHANGE 389, 409 (2012) ("Despite a series of breakthroughs in areas such as information technology and biological research, the past few decades have witnessed a deeply uneven distribution of the benefits from such development."); Sonia K. Katyal, *Technoheritage*, 105 CAL. L. REV. 1111, 1114 (2017); VIRGINIA EUBANKS, AUTOMATING INEQUALITY: HOW HIGH-TECH TOOLS PROFILE, POLICE, AND PUNISH THE POOR 38 (2018).

[17] *See* Meghan Murphy, *Technology as a Basic Need: The Impact of the Access Gap in Poverty*, 1776 (Apr. 2, 2015), https://bit.ly/3F2ubPT.

[18] *See* RUHA BENJAMIN, RACE AFTER TECHNOLOGY: ABOLITIONIST TOOLS FOR THE NEW JIM CODE (2019).

COVID Pledge (OCP) in April 2020, and the World Health Organization launched the COVID-19 Technology Access Pool (C-TAP) in May 2020. The OCP and C-TAP urge patent holders to responsibly share their patented technologies in the public interest by altering their dedication to exclusive rights protection. As the key institutions in bringing an end to the pandemic, the major pharmaceutical companies have yet to take part in either initiative. The OCP has engaged many companies, including IBM, Facebook, and Uber,[19] and has obtained over 250,000 pledged patents,[20] none of which are owned by the major pharmaceutical companies.[21] The C-TAP has not yet started to function because "no technology or treatments have been shared,"[22] and no pharmaceutical companies had voluntarily joined it as of March 2021.[23]

B HOW TO DEVELOP AND APPLY TECHNOLOGY IN THE PUBLIC INTEREST

Amid these ethical crises, a profound question arises: how should technology be developed and applied in the public interest? In my opinion, this is one of the most important yet difficult issues facing the current and future operations of humanity. Few would doubt the fundamental importance of this issue as technology has already become the driving force of economic, social, and political development in our society. But why is it so exceedingly difficult to tackle the relationship between technology and the public interest?

[19] *See* Charlotte Kilpatrick, *Tech Companies Promote Benefits of Open Covid Pledge* (Sept. 24, 2020).

[20] *See* Michael S. Horikawa, *The Open COVID Pledge – Don't Say "I Do" Till You Think It Through* (Jun. 24, 2020), https://www.pillsburylaw.com/en/news-and-insights/open-covid-pledge-ip-diligence.html.

[21] *Id.* ("However, the Pledge has not yet seen wide adoption in certain key industries. For example, it does not appear that the Open COVID Pledge has been embraced by the pharmaceutical or medical device industries.").

[22] Michael Safi, *WHO Platform for Pharmaceutical Firms Unused Since Pandemic Began,* GUARDIAN (Jan. 22, 2021).

[23] Selam Gebrekidan and Matt Apuzzo, *Rich Countries Signed Away a Chance to Vaccinate the World,* N.Y. TIMES (Mar. 21, 2021) ("Not a single vaccine company has signed up [for the C-TAP].").

The first difficulty arises from the fact that "the public interest" is itself one of the most perplexing concepts. Technology is already a complicated concept,[24] and determining the nature and scope of the public interest is a much more daunting task. Synonymous with concepts such as the common good, general welfare, and public values, the public interest is one of the most-used concepts in public discourse[25] and is deemed vital in the making of public policy.[26] Nonetheless, the public interest has been criticized as "semantic chaos,"[27] "vague [and] impalpable",[28] "the least defined and the least understood,"[29] and even dismissed as "vacuous, deceptive, and generally useless."[30] Therefore, there are concerns that the public interest is vulnerable to misuse and even manipulation by those in power.[31]

Three main factors contribute to the elusiveness of "the public interest" and the concept's lack of universally acceptable philosophical and practical foundation.[32] First, it lacks a single theoretical formula to define its nature and scope. It has been understood as the common interests of all members of a polity,[33] a theory which, assuming interests of all are compatible, suggests "the fulfillment of all human persons and communities now and in future,"[34] exercise of governmental power "only for the public good,"[35] and promotion of justice for "the

---

[24] ERIC SCHATZBERG, TECHNOLOGY: CRITICAL HISTORY OF A CONCEPT 1 (2018) (pointing out that "the definition of *technology* is a mess") (emphasis in original).

[25] Chris Wheeler, *The Public Interest Revisited: We know it's Important but Do We Know What It Means?*, at 34, AIAL FORUM No. 72 (2013).

[26] BARRY BOZEMAN, PUBLIC VALUES AND PUBLIC INTEREST: COUNTERBALANCING ECONOMIC INDIVIDUALISM 84 (2007).

[27] Frank Sorauf, *The Conceptual Muddle, in* NOMOS V: THE PUBLIC INTEREST 183, 190 (Carl J Friedrich ed., 1962).

[28] FELIX FRANKFURTER & HARLAN B PHILLIPS, FELIX FRANKFURTER REMINISCES 72 (1960).

[29] Wheeler, *supra* note 25, at 34.

[30] VIRGINIA HELD, THE PUBLIC INTEREST AND INDIVIDUAL INTERESTS 1 (1970).

[31] *See* Rebecca Giblin & Kimberlee Weatherall, *If We Redesigned Copyright From Scratch, What Might it Look Like?*, *in* WHAT IF WE COULD REIMAGINE COPYRIGHT? 1, 4 (Giblin & Weatherall eds., 2017).

[32] *See* ISABELLA ALEXANDER, COPYRIGHT LAW AND THE PUBLIC INTEREST IN THE NINETEENTH CENTURY 298 (2010) (arguing that "the concept of public interest . . . lack[s] a universally accepted, morally sustainable and philosophically consistent foundation.").

[33] HELD, *supra* note 30, at 44.

[34] John Finnis, *Aquinas' Moral, Political, and Legal Philosophy, in* STANFORD ENCYCLOPEDIA OF PHILOSOPHY (2021), https://stanford.io/3xUxMMM.

[35] JOHN LOCKE, THE SECOND TREATISE OF CIVIL GOVERNMENT 4 (2005).

common good."[36] Utilitarianism, however, defines the public interest as "the sum of the interests of the several members who compose it."[37] Through aggregating of interests, it prioritizes interests of the majority of people in a society.[38] Second, public interests may be competing with each other, making it difficult to protect them as a clearly defined concept.[39] When it comes to the Trump administration's decision to shut down the operations of TikTok and WeChat in the United States, freedom of information promoted by these social media outlets as a public interest conflicts with national security invoked as a public interest ground on which to penalize those outlets.[40] Third, public interests may vary among societies and countries.[41] People with different religions, ethnicities, or classes may support totally different and even conflicting groups and societal or national interests.

The other major difficulty in promoting technology in the public interest stems from the "wealth maximization" mentality that positions technology companies to put their profits before the public interest. In the past ten years or so, major technology companies have become the world's richest and most politically powerful corporate institutions.[42] Given that they are institutionally designed to maximize wealth for their shareholders, technology companies may make every effort to forestall any legal reforms that seek to properly tighten regulation of their businesses for the public interest. Meanwhile, this wealth

---

[36] JEAN JACQUES ROUSSEAU, THE SOCIAL CONTRACT (Book II) (1762), https://bit.ly/3DmEb4x ("If the object is to give the State consistency, bring the two extremes as near to each other as possible; allow neither rich men nor beggars. These two estates, which are naturally inseparable, are equally fatal to the common good."); JOHN RAWLS, THE LAW OF PEOPLES 44 (1993) ("[B]asic social institutions satisfy a conception of justice expressing an appropriate conception of the common good.").

[37] JEREMY BENTHAM, AN INTRODUCTION TO THE PRINCIPLES OF MORALS AND LEGISLATION 5 (1789).

[38] See MIKE FEINTUCK, 'THE PUBLIC INTEREST' IN REGULATION 11 (2004).

[39] See JOHN DEWEY LIBERALISM AND SOCIAL ACTION 81 (2000) ("Of course, there are conflicting interests; otherwise there would be no social problems.").

[40] See Anupam Chander & Haochen Sun, Sovereignty 2.0, 55 VAND. J. TRANSNAT'L L. (forthcoming 2022).

[41] See JANE JOHNSTON, PUBLIC RELATIONS AND THE PUBLIC INTEREST 1 (2016).

[42] See JAMIE BARTLETT, THE PEOPLE VS TECH: HOW THE INTERNET IS KILLING DEMOCRACY (AND HOW WE SAVE IT) 1 (2018); Stephen Johnston, Largest Companies 2008 vs. 2018, a Lot Has Changed, MILFORD (Jan. 31, 2018), ("Technology companies not only dominate our daily lives (how many times have you checked your iPhone today?) but also the ranking of world's biggest companies.").

maximizing posture has won a lot of popular support. The powers held by technology companies far exceed any responsibilities they have assumed in promotion of the public interest. Rather than interrogating the responsibilities of technology companies, there has been a far greater media focus on celebrating the astounding wealth they have amassed from stock markets and users through the exercise of their power.

Despite these difficulties, I present the "rights and responsibilities" ethos as a new ethical approach to promoting the development and application of technologies in the public interest. The approach strives to dynamically protect the right to technology and enforce the responsibility of technological companies. The fusion of this right and responsibility, as I will show, would generate a thorough, forward-looking understanding of the nature and scope of public interests that should be promoted by the development and application of technology. Instead of wrestling with a theoretical definition of the public interest in the first place, this ethical approach starts from setting systematic agendas for promoting the public interest through protection of the right to technology and enforcement of technology companies' responsibilities. Therefore, this approach first sets in motion a dynamic protection of the public interest and then attempts to ascertain the nature and scope of the public interest related to the development and application of technology.

In applying this approach, I refute the sole reliance on technological determinism and its resultant silence on the ethical issues posed by technology. Instead, I argue that the answer to technology does not lie in technology. Single-minded reliance on technology's power – without any consideration of the public rights and private responsibilities attached to it – is not the path toward a better future for humankind. Rather, the development and application of technology must be subject to an ethical examination of how to protect the public's right to technology and to enforce technology companies' responsibility.

Concerning the right to technology, I suggest that we must examine how this right could be effectively protected as a human right under international law, as a collective right under domestic civil rights law, and as potentially a fundamental right under domestic constitutional law. The right to technology derives from Article 27 of the Universal Declaration of Human Rights (UDHR), which states that "[e]veryone has the right . . . to share in scientific advancement and its benefits." [43]

For the sake of brevity, I refer to this human right as "the right to technology."[44] "Technology," in my opinion, captures the essence of both phrasings in the UDHR's "scientific advancement and its benefits" as well as the "benefits of scientific progress and its applications" protected by the International Covenant on Economic, Social and Cultural Rights.[45] Both are concerned with the practical use of scientific discoveries[46] rather than the academic process of scientific discovery itself. In other words, they manifest the utilitarian function of technology in transforming the knowledge outputs of scientific research into products that solve problems and improve our lives.[47] The UN Committee on Economic, Social and Cultural Rights has affirmed that this human right focuses on "the particular implementation of science to the specific concerns and needs of the population" facilitated by "the technology deriving from scientific knowledge, such as the medical applications, the industrial or agricultural applications, or information and communications technology."[48] From this perspective, referring to the human right in question as "the right to

---

[43] Universal Declaration of Human Rights, G.A. Res. 217, U.N. GAOR, 3d Sess., U.N. Doc. A/810 (1948), art. 27.

[44] Some scholars term this human right "the right to enjoy the benefits of scientific progress and its application." In my opinion, this name is too long. *See, for example,* Audrey R. Chapman, *Towards an Understanding of the Right to Enjoy the Benefits of Scientific Progress and Its Applications,* 8 J. HUM. RTS. 1, 4 (2009); William A. Schabas, *Study of the Right to Enjoy the Benefits of Scientific and Technological Progress and Its Applications, in* HUMAN RIGHTS IN EDUCATION, SCIENCE AND CULTURE: LEGAL DEVELOPMENTS AND CHALLENGES 273, 274 (Yvonne Donders & Vladimir Volodin eds., 2007).

[45] International Covenant on Economic, Social and Cultural Rights, Dec. 16, 1966, S. Treaty Doc. No. 95-19, 993 U.N.T.S. 3, 6 I.L.M. 360 (1967), art. 15.1(b).

[46] *See* JOHANNES MORSINK, THE UNIVERSAL DECLARATION OF HUMAN RIGHTS: ORIGINS, DRAFTING AND INTENT 219 (1999) (reporting that delegates to the UDHR drafting meetings "stressed that the task of science was to work for the advancement of peaceful aims and to make human life better").

[47] ERIC SCHATZBERG, TECHNOLOGY: CRITICAL HISTORY OF A CONCEPT 1 (2018) ("In many ways, technology has displaced science as the main concept for making sense of modern material culture, as seen in phrases such as 'information, bio-, and nanotechnology.'").

[48] UN Committee on Economic, Social and Cultural Rights, *General Comment No. 25 (2020) on Science and Economic, Social and Cultural Rights (article 15 (1) (b), (2), (3) and (4) of the International Covenant on Economic, Social and Cultural Rights,* Apr. 30, 2020, E/C.12/GC/ 25, para.7.

science"[49] would not be appropriate because "science" refers to an academic research process and not the practical application of knowledge outputs.[50]

Working in tandem with the right to technology would be a more robust enforcement of technological companies' responsibility. I put forth the concept of fundamental corporate responsibility, demonstrating how and why three responsibilities should be imposed on technology companies. Specifically, these responsibilities are to: reciprocate for users' contributions; play a positive role; and counter the injustices caused by technological developments. Fulfillment of these fundamental corporate responsibilities should be a core mission of technology company managers. When developing new technologies, collecting data, regulating speech, and protecting intellectual property, they must act responsibly in the public interest. Conventionally, the public interest is a concept used to evaluate the performance of the government.[51] The ethical approach I present in this book would add a new function to public interest considerations: to evaluate validity of corporate decisions concerning the development and application of technologies.

In Chapter 1, I explore why the right to technology is a forgotten human right despite its pivotal importance. In 1948, the UDHR framers created this human right in response to the wholesale destruction wrought by technologically advanced weapons in World War II. The right to technology embodies one of the most profound lessons the UDHR framers learned from that war: Technology must benefit humanity rather than harm it. It has now been more than seventy years since the UDHR's adoption, and technology has advanced at a rapid pace to become more important than ever before in our daily lives. Yet in this age of technology, the right to technology remains obscure, dormant, and ineffective. No other human right has received

---

[49] According to some scholars, article 27 of the UDHR recognizes the right to science. *See, for example,* Lea Shaver, *The Right to Science and Culture,* 10 Wis. L. Rev. 121, 124 (2010); Jessica M. Wyndham & Margaret Weigers Vitullo, *Define the Human Right to Science,* 362 Science 975 (2018).

[50] *See* Thomas Kuhn, The Structure of Scientific Revolutions 37 (1970) (discussing why science is essentially non-utilitarian).

[51] Held, *supra* note 30, at 9–10 (arguing that concepts such as the public interest are indispensable in evaluating government decisions).

such scant attention, and the right to technology has indeed become an "orphan" in the international human rights regime. The chapter traces the origins of society's disregard for the right and attributes it to the confluence of three main contributing factors: (1) the right's inherent obscurity, (2) the ineffective human rights enforcement system, and (3) the international community's overemphasis on intellectual property protection. The current human rights regime is unable to address these complex factors, because it remains deeply rooted in the individual rights system and lacks a full-fledged distributive justice vision.

In Chapter 2, I seek to reinvigorate the right to technology by recommending its protection as a collective right. The chapter considers how and why the right to technology should be redefined as a collective right that entitles people to enjoy the benefits of technological progress and minimizes the harms that such progress may cause. A collective right to technology can protect larger societal interests in maintaining public freedom and dignity, as well as specific group interests in guarding against the use of technologies to prejudice group freedom and dignity. This new understanding of the right to technology, therefore, sets a distributive justice agenda for promoting the development of intellectual property law in the public interest. The chapter suggests that domestic courts' protection of the collective right to technology as a civil liberty would provide a new avenue for better achieving distributive justice in relation to the enjoyment of technological benefits. To this end, it explores how courts could apply this right to reinterpret the nature and scope of copyright fair use and the IP Clause of the US Constitution in the public interest.

In Chapter 3, I explore how the right to technology could be protected as a fundamental right under the US Constitution. The COVID-19 pandemic has exposed the extreme inequities in internet access throughout the United States. Given the scale of this social problem and the urgent need to address it, the chapter suggests that it is time to recognize a new fundamental right to technology as a liberty protected by the Fourteenth Amendment to the US Constitution. The new right would expand technological benefits such as internet access by triggering proactive governmental measures and enhanced judicial protection. This proposal is made in the hope that other countries will also recognize this fundamental right in constitutional law, ensuring global protection of the right to technology.

Based upon the discussion of the right to technology in the first three chapters, I consider in the remainder of the book how and why technology companies should assume three fundamental corporate responsibilities. In Chapter 4, I examine the causes of technology companies' evasion of their responsibilities. In today's digital age, technology companies reign supreme. However, the power they hold far exceeds the responsibilities they have assumed. The ongoing privacy concerns and "fake news" scandals swirling around Facebook demonstrate the shocking asymmetry of power and responsibility where these companies are concerned. The legal reforms that have taken place in the United States in the past twenty years or so have failed to correct this asymmetry. The US Congress has enacted major statutes that have actually minimized the legal liabilities of technology companies with respect to online infringing acts, privacy protection, and the payment of taxes. Although these statutes have promoted innovation, they have also had the unintended effect of breeding irresponsibility among technology companies.

To deal with the ethical crises created by technology companies, I put forward in Chapter 5 the concept of corporate fundamental responsibility as an ethical and legal foundation for imposing three distinct responsibilities upon technology companies: a responsibility to reciprocate for users' contributions, a responsibility to play a positive role, and a responsibility to confront injustices created by technological development. The chapter further considers how these responsibilities could be applied to strengthen the protection of private data and encourage the responsible exercise of intellectual property rights by technology companies. I build this conception of fundamental corporate responsibility upon the ethical theories of reciprocity, role responsibility, and social justice. Therefore, fundamental corporate responsibility paves the way for technology law to embrace ethics wholeheartedly, creating new legal and ethical guidance for the benevolent behavior of technology companies. In developing technologies, collecting data, and regulating speech, the managers of these companies must act responsibly in the public interest.

Finally, in Chapter 6, I apply the tripartite conception of corporate fundamental responsibility to technology companies that are also the holders of patent rights. Patent law protects a bundle of strong rights to incentivize investment in innovation. Beyond protecting the rights of patent holders, should patent law also impose responsibilities upon them? As I will reveal in Chapter 6, the COVID-19 pandemic has also revealed that the legal power conferred upon technology companies by patent law far exceeds the responsibilities they have assumed. This asymmetry of rights and responsibilities has undermined collaborative efforts to develop testing methods, medicines, and vaccines to contain the pandemic. In this final chapter of the book, I present the first comprehensive theoretical study of patent holders' responsibilities. Examining COVID-19-related innovations, I show how prevailing rights-focused patent law has failed to reflect the social nature of innovation. I argue for the reform of patent law to ensure that it not only effectively protects patent holders' exclusive rights but also adequately enforces their responsibilities. Based on ethics and political theories, I propose that these new responsibilities require patent holders to reciprocate for public contributions, fulfill their innovator role responsibly, and confront injustices caused by patent protection.

1   THE HUMAN RIGHT TO TECHNOLOGY

Alfred Nobel, the inventor of dynamite and other explosives, suffered from severe depression following a French newspaper's erroneous publication of his obituary in 1888. The obituary condemned him as a "merchant of death" who had become wealthy by inventing new technologies designed to "kill more people faster than ever before."[1] Many other newspapers worldwide followed the obituary's lead in celebrating Nobel's supposed demise, which later proved to be what we would today call "fake news." Devastated by the international media's accusations, Nobel began to reevaluate his fame and fortune, both of which derived from his invention and patenting of deadly technologies, although those technologies had also facilitated construction work ranging from rock blasting to the building of canals. This reevaluation led him to denounce the widespread use of weapons in wars as "the horror of all horrors and the greatest of all crimes"[2] and to dedicate most of his wealth to funding the establishment of Nobel prizes in a variety of fields, earning him a posthumous reputation for promoting peace and knowledge growth.

In a similar vein, international leaders gathered in the wake of World War II to seek avenues for ensuring that technologies would henceforth be used for the benefit of humanity. In response to the wholesale destruction wrought by technologically advanced weapons in World

---

[1] *See* Marc Preel, *How "Merchant of Death" Alfred Nobel Became a Champion of Peace* (Oct. 4, 2010), https://www.thelocal.se/20101004/29406.

[2] *See* Kenne Fant, Alfred Nobel: A Biography 265 (1993).

War II, they created the right to technology[3] in 1948 as a human right under the Universal Declaration of Human Rights (UDHR).[4] Article 27 of the UDHR states that "[e]veryone has the right ... to share in scientific advancement and its benefits." This human right embodies one of the most profound lessons that the framers of the UDHR learned from World War II.

Although Alfred Nobel's individual effort to ensure that technology was used in the public interest yielded enormous positive effects, international leaders' collective endeavor to achieve the same has largely failed to deliver the intended effects. It has been more than seventy years since the adoption of the UDHR, and technology has become more integrated into our daily lives than ever before. In an age of technology, what human right could be more important than the right to technology? Yet this right remains obscure, dormant, and ineffective, leading some to lament that it is a "sleeping beauty."[5] Indeed, no other human right has received such scant attention. Lacking institutional guardians or advocates, the right to technology has become an "orphan" in the international human rights system.

In this chapter, I first examine how international human rights treaties gave birth to the right to technology, which reflects one of the most profound lessons of World War II: technology must be utilized for the benefit of humankind. I then discuss how and why this right has become an orphan in the global human rights system based on the confluence of three main contributing factors: (1) the right's inherent obscurity, (2) the ineffective human rights enforcement system, and (3) the international community's overemphasis on intellectual property (IP) protection. The current global human rights regime is unable to sufficiently address these complex factors, as it remains in large part deeply rooted in the individual rights system and lacks a full-fledged distributive justice vision.

---

[3] The introductory chapter states the reasons why this human right should be termed as "the right to technology." *See* Introduction, notes 42–50 and accompanying text.

[4] Universal Declaration of Human Rights, G.A. Res. 217, U.N. GAOR, 3d Sess., U.N. Doc. A/810 (1948).

[5] Eibe Riedel, *Sleeping Beauty or Let Sleeping Dogs Lie? The Right of Everyone to Enjoy the Benefits of Scientific Progress and Its Applications (REBSPA)*, in 1 COEXISTENCE, COOPERATION AND SOLIDARITY 503 (Holger P. Hestermeyer et al. eds., 2012).

A THE BIRTH OF THE RIGHT TO TECHNOLOGY

1 The UDHR

The Second Industrial Revolution, spanning the latter part of the nineteenth century and early part of the twentieth, represented a massive technological and social shift that boosted the efficiency of both industry and ordinary households to a tremendous degree. More efficient production facilities resulted in mass production, while the improved availability and affordability of common household goods enhanced the quality of life and productivity of the average citizen. Improved steel production led to massively expanded railway networks and increased mobility, electricity and associated technologies (such as light bulbs and telephones) enhanced communications and lengthened working hours,[6] and the internal combustion engine revolutionized transportation.[7]

At the same time, technological advancements contributed to the most catastrophic damage to people and property that the world had ever seen. The combatants in World War II deployed devastating new weapons that resulted in sixty million deaths and unprecedented destruction.[8] Both the German and Japanese armies wielded new technologies to perpetrate massacres on a scale hitherto unseen, with the Holocaust and Nanjing Massacre among the most atrocious crimes against humanity in modern history.[9] The atomic bombs dropped by the United States[10] resulted in tremendous suffering and loss of life and the leveling of two Japanese cities.

The trauma of World War II prompted the international community to tackle the double-edged sword of technological advancement. After the United Nations (UN) was founded in 1945, a key agenda

---

[6] *See* Kenneth E. Hendrickson Jr., *Electricity, in* ENCYCLOPEDIA OF THE INDUSTRIAL REVOLUTION IN WORLD HISTORY 268, 293 (Kenneth E. Hendrickson III ed., 2014).

[7] *See* Justin Corfield, *Internal Combustion Engine, in* ENCYCLOPEDIA OF THE INDUSTRIAL REVOLUTION IN WORLD HISTORY 268, 473 (Kenneth E. Hendrickson III ed., 2014).

[8] *See* UNITED STATES HISTORY, *World War II*, https://www.u-s-history.com/pages/h1661 .html (last visited Dec. 1, 2019).

[9] RICHARD CLAUDE, SCIENCE IN THE SERVICE OF HUMAN RIGHTS 16–17 (2002).

[10] HISTORY.COM, *Bombing of Hiroshima and Nagasaki* (Nov. 18, 2009), https://bit.ly /3C8lWzC.

item was the creation of a global bill of rights, leading to the adoption of the UDHR at the 1948 UN General Assembly.[11] The UDHR framers reached an agreement to "disregard and contempt for human rights have resulted in barbarous acts which have outraged the conscience of mankind."[12] The first draft of the UDHR in 1947, which was prepared by John Peters Humphrey, reflected this dedication to protecting human rights. One groundbreaking move was to identify the right to technology as a new human right that had not hitherto been recognized by any national law. Under this new right to technology, the draft stated, "[e]veryone has the right . . . to share in scientific advancement and its benefits."[13]

Humphrey's draft kindled heated debate and profound reflection on the nature of scientific advancement among the UDHR framers. A motion to inject politics into the right to technology was vehemently rejected. Alexei Pavlov, the Soviet Union's delegate, asserted that the draft provision concerning the right to technology should be revised to reflect the need for the right to be protected "in the service of progress and democracy"[14] and for "the cause of peace and international cooperation,"[15] an assertion that was met with resounding opposition from his fellow delegates. Eleanor Roosevelt, who served as chairperson of the UN Commission on Human Rights from 1946 to 1951, offered the rebuttal that "[t]he words 'progress' and 'democracy' apply to abstract ideas, and for these ideas no uniform interpretation exists."[16] She then asserted that Pavlov's proposal would lead to the "enslavement of science" because it would subject the right to technology to ideological struggle and political manipulation.[17] Delegates from Australia, Belgium, and Britain echoed Roosevelt's opinions,

---

[11] CLAUDE, *supra* note 9, at 16–17 ("The Universal Declaration of Human Rights was a global response to the devastating confrontations of World War II.")

[12] UDHR, pmbl.

[13] Humphrey drew on Article 13(1) of the 1948 American Declaration of the Rights and Duties of Man, which states that "[e]very person has the right to take part in the cultural life of the community, to enjoy the arts, and to participate in the benefits that result from intellectual progress, especially scientific discoveries." *See* JOHANNES MORSINK, THE UNIVERSAL DECLARATION OF HUMAN RIGHTS: ORIGINS, DRAFTING AND INTENT 218(1999)

[14] CLAUDE, *supra* note 9, at 33.

[15] *Id.*

[16] *Id.*

[17] *Id.*

stating, respectively, that "progress" was an ideological concept that had been applied by propagandists who "bestow[ed] racial superiority upon Germany,"[18] that Pavlov's proposal "assign[ed] to science a political mission,"[19] and that "the sole aim of science could only be the quest for truth."[20]

Although the Soviet attempt to politicize the right to technology was resoundingly rejected, the framers reached agreement that science by nature should serve the common good of humanity. They did debate, however, whether the right to technology should entitle everyone to share in "scientific advancement" alone or "scientific advancement and its benefits." Following several rounds of deliberation, the framers reached a consensus to opt for the latter, thereby finalizing the first part of Article 27 of the UDHR, which states that "[e]veryone has the right ... to share in scientific advancement and its benefits."

The drafting process of UDHR Article 27 reflected the framers' dedication to capitalizing on this new human right to ensure that technologies would henceforth be utilized in the public interest.[21] For instance, Pavlov boldly asserted that "the benefits of science [are] not the property of a chosen few, but the heritage of mankind."[22] P. C. Chang, the Chinese delegate, argued that science should be treated as a social enterprise that energized both research developments by experts and the enjoyment of the benefits of such developments by the public. According to Confucianism, he explained, the aesthetic enjoyment of the arts and letters had dual dimensions: passive enjoyment through the appreciation of beauty and active enjoyment through the creation of new artistic works. He then likened science to the humanities, contending that the right to technology should protect both active and passive enjoyment. In his opinion, it was not appropriate merely to protect experts' active enjoyment of scientific advancement via their research endeavors. Instead, the public's passive enjoyment of the benefits of scientific advancement should be protected as well. René Cassin firmly

[18] *Id.*
[19] *Id.*
[20] *Id.*
[21] *See* MORSINK, *supra* note 13, at 219 (reporting that delegates to the UDHR drafting meetings "stressed that the task of science was to work for the advancement of peaceful aims and to make human life better").
[22] *Id.* at 219.

supported Chang's view and convinced the delegates to arrive at a consensus concerning the need to protect the public's right to share in the benefits of scientific advancement.[23]

Meanwhile, the framers also saw the right to technology as a vehicle for promoting equal and universal access to technological benefits.[24] Roosevelt stressed that the right's creation was intended to "stress the universality" of technological benefits.[25] Pérez Cisneros, the Cuban delegate, explained that the specific reason for including technological benefits in the right was that "not everyone was sufficiently gifted to play a part in scientific advancement."[26] Cassin, who won the 1968 Nobel Peace Prize for his crucial contribution to the UDHR, firmly supported that broader inclusion. In his opinion, "even if all persons could not play an equal part in scientific progress, they should indisputably be able to participate in the benefits derived from it."[27] Although members of the public, according to Cisneros and Cassin, might not necessarily have the expertise to participate in scientific progress as scientists do, they should still be entitled to receive its benefits, such as access to affordable medicine.[28]

2 ICESCR

When it adopted the UDHR, the UN General Assembly also decided to complete the drafting of a new convention laying out legally binding standards and commitments for UN member states. Growing Cold War tensions, however, slowed down the drafting process,[29] and it was

---

[23] CLAUDE, *supra* note 9, at 36.

[24] Farida Shaheed (Special Rapporteur),*Report of the Special Rapporteur in the Field of Cultural Rights: The Right to Enjoy the Benefits of Scientific Progress and Its Applications*, at 6, U.N. Doc. A/HRC/20/26 (May 14, 2012) (discussing the relationship between the right to technology and the realization of other relevant human rights) ("The preparatory work on the Universal Declaration of Human Rights ... reflected the intention of the drafters to include a provision promoting universal access to science and culture.").

[25] Comm. on Human Rights, Working Group on the Declaration of Human Rights, 2nd Sess., *Summary Record of the Ninth Meeting*, at 3, U.N. Doc. E/CN.4/AC.2/SR.9 (Dec. 10, 1947).

[26] *Report of the Special Rapporteur, supra* note 24.

[27] MORSINK, *supra* note 13, at 219.

[28] MORSINK, *supra* note 13, at 219 (interpreting the implication of the unanimous adoption of "and its benefits" so as to realize the need "[t]o participate in the benefits").

[29] *See* JEFFREY L. DUNOFF ET AL., INTERNATIONAL LAW: NORMS, ACTORS, PROCESS 338 (2020).

not until 1966 that the UN General Assembly adopted the International Covenant on Economic, Social and Cultural Rights (ICESCR).[30] Article 15 of the ICESCR also recognizes the right to technology, entitling everyone to "enjoy the benefits of scientific progress and its applications."[31]

The ICESCR strengthened protection of the right to technology in three major ways. First, it improved the right's definition. During the ICESCR drafting process, members of the UN Human Rights Commission expressed concerns about the UDHR's definition of the right to technology as a right "to share in scientific advancement and its benefits."[32] In their opinion, this definition made it difficult to impose concrete legal obligations on states to specify in their domestic laws how everyone can share in scientific advancement and its benefits. "Enjoy" better captured the nature of the right to technology, they believed, because it entitles everyone to receive such benefits without requiring states to determine how to apportion them.[33] Moreover, "enjoy" also had the advantage of connoting that technologies should be developed and applied in a manner beneficial, rather than harmful, to the public interest.[34] The ICESCR's definition therefore entitles everyone to enjoy the beneficial effects of technologies and also requires states to prevent or rectify their harmful effects.

Second, the ICESCR drafting process expressly echoed the egalitarian ethos of the right to technology, as expressed by the framers of the UDHR. While the ICESCR was being drafted, the UN Educational, Scientific and Cultural Organization (UNESCO) proposed a definition of the right to technology that envisioned it as "the determining factor for the exercise by mankind as a whole of many other rights."[35] After the ICESCR had been drafted, but before it was adopted, the UN passed a resolution setting out the principles and

---

[30] International Covenant on Economic, Social and Cultural Rights, Dec. 16, 1966, S. Treaty Doc. No. 95-19, 993 U.N.T.S. 3, 6 I.L.M. 360 (1967) [hereinafter ICESCR].

[31] *Id.* art. 15.1(b).

[32] CLAUDE, *supra* note 9, at 43.

[33] *See* BEN SAUL et al., THE INTERNATIONAL COVENANT ON ECONOMIC, SOCIAL AND CULTURAL RIGHTS: COMMENTARY, CASES, AND MATERIALS 1218 (2014).

[34] CLAUDE, *supra* note 9, at 43.

[35] Maria Green, *Drafting History of the Article 15(1)(c) of the International Covenant on Economic, Social and Cultural Rights*, at 7, U.N. Doc. E/C.12/2000/15 (Oct. 9, 2000).

agenda for achieving global social progress and development consistent with the ICESCR, emphasizing the role that technology can play in "meeting the needs common to all humanity."[36]

Third, the ICESCR further stipulates three obligations arising from the right to technology: (1) an obligation to promote the conservation, development, and diffusion of science; (2) an obligation to respect the freedom that is indispensable for scientific research and creative activity; and (3) an obligation to recognize the benefits that can be derived from the encouragement and development of international contacts and cooperation in various scientific fields.[37] The first obligation implies that states should adopt dynamic, broad-based measures ranging from the conservation and development of science and technology to their diffusion. The second obligation adds a new dimension to the right to technology by ensuring freedom of scientific research and communication.[38] The third obligation emphasizes the importance of international collaboration among state governments, thereby actualizing the delegates' appeal that "scientific discoveries should benefit not only all individuals but all nations, regardless of their degree of development."[39] It also encourages communication and information exchange among scientific experts from different countries as extensively and freely as possible.[40]

B THE ORPHANING OF THE RIGHT TO TECHNOLOGY

Although the UDHR and ICESCR wholeheartedly support the right to technology on paper, neither provides for any specific organization that can pursue effective strategies and measures to enforce the right in practice.[41] Such institutional support is necessary to provide concrete

---

[36] G.A. Res. 2542, Declaration on Social Progress and Development, pmbl. (Dec. 11, 1969).
[37] Id., art. 15.
[38] SAUL ET AL., supra note 33, at 1216; CLAUDE, supra note 9, at 44–45.
[39] CLAUDE, supra note 9, at 43.
[40] SAUL ET AL., supra note 34, at 1222–23.
[41] See UNESCO, The Right to Enjoy the Benefits of Scientific Progress and Its Applications at 7 (2009), https://unesdoc.unesco.org/ark:/48223/pf0000185558 (pointing out that the right to technology is ineffective "due to the bland wording of Article 15(1)(b) ICESCR and to the lack of Committee practice in dealing with this right").

guidance and constructive standards for protecting the right both domestically and internationally. In addition, many of the international organizations that could have assumed a guardianship role have simply overlooked the right to technology. For example, among the key missions of UNESCO, which was founded in 1946, are promoting human rights and encouraging scientific collaboration.[42] However, after submitting its proposal for defining the right to technology to the ICESCR drafting committee in 1951, UNESCO failed to set up any schemes dedicated exclusively to protecting that right. Moreover, it neglected technology as a core issue for state compliance with the ICESCR. For decades, UNESCO excluded the enjoyment of basic technologies from the ICESCR's core minimum requirements, stating only that "a State Party in which any significant number of individuals are deprived of essential foodstuffs, essential primary health care, basic shelter and housing, or the most basic forms of education is, *prima facie*, failing to discharge its obligations under the Covenant."[43] It was not until 2009 that UNESCO's Expert Committee finally adopted the Venice Statement on the Right to Enjoy the Benefits of Scientific Progress and Its Applications.[44]

The UN Human Rights Council (UNHCR) initiated no protection measures for the right to technology until 2012 when it appointed a Special Rapporteur in the Field of Cultural Rights.[45] The Special Rapporteur later submitted three reports, one on the nature of the right to technology,[46] another one on its relationship with copyright, and the third one on its relationship with patents.[47] Since then, however, the UNHCR has adopted no further resolutions responding to the reports or considering

---

[42] UNESCO, *UNESCO and the Universal Declaration on Human Rights*, https://en.unesco.org/udhr.

[43] UNESCO, *Sharing Scientific Knowledge Through Publications: What Do Developing Countries Have to Offer?* (2000), https://unesdoc.unesco.org/ark:/48223/pf0000120879.

[44] UNESCO, *The Right to Enjoy the Benefits of Scientific Progress and Its Applications* [hereinafter Venice Statement], U.N. Doc. SHS/RSP/HRS-GED/2009/PI/H/1 (July 17, 2009).

[45] Human Rights Council Res. 19/6, U.N. Doc. A/HRC/19/L.18 (Apr. 3, 2012).

[46] *Report of the Special Rapporteur, supra* note 24.

[47] Farida Shaheed (Special Rapporteur), *Report of the Special Rapporteur in the Field of Cultural Rights: Copyright Policy and the Right to Science and Culture*, U.N. Doc. A/HRC/28/57 (Dec. 24, 2014); Farida Shaheed (Special Rapporteur), *Report of the Special Rapporteur in the Field of Cultural Rights: Patent Policy and the Right to Science and Culture*, U.N. Doc. A/70/279 (Aug. 4, 2015).

issues that go beyond copyright and patents. It still holds the view that the right to technology is a "largely neglected" human right.[48]

In addition to the Venice Statement, other statements and reports have been issued over the years, including the American Association for the Advancement of Science's Statement on the Human Right to the Benefits of Scientific Progress.[49] However, statements and reports of this kind have only a very limited effect in practice. They are neither legally binding on any parties nor exert any effective influence on the policymaking process at the international and national levels.[50]

Worse still, even in the face of humanitarian crises that have led to the large-scale deprivation of human lives, the right to technology has not been directly invoked to protect those affected. In response to the HIV epidemic and famines in Africa, the international community has called for concerted efforts to protect the rights of those affected to health and food.[51] For example, in November 2001, the World Trade Organization (WTO) adopted the Doha Declaration on the TRIPS Agreement and Public Health[52] to protect the right to health by expanding affordable access to patented drugs, particularly for HIV-infected patients. Without referring to the right to technology, the declaration neglects the need to fairly distribute the benefits of medical innovation as a means of promoting public health. [53]

Although a 2016 report by the UN High-Level Panel on Access to Medicines acknowledged the importance of the right to technology for

---

[48] United Nations High Commissioner for Human Rights, *Report on the Seminar on the Right to Enjoy the Benefits of Scientific Progress and its Applications* 13, A/HRC/26/19 (2014) ("The right to enjoy the benefits of scientific progress is a largely neglected right despite its importance for the enjoyment of other human rights and fundamental freedoms in the modern world.").

[49] AAAS, *Statement of the Board of Directors of the American Association for the Advancement of Science on the Human Rights to the Benefits of Scientific Progress* (Apr. 16, 2010).

[50] *See* LAURENCE R. HELFER & GRAEME W. AUSTIN, HUMAN RIGHTS AND INTELLECTUAL PROPERTY: MAPPING THE GLOBAL INTERFACE 238 (2011).

[51] *See, e.g.*, UN HUMAN RIGHTS OFFICE OF THE HIGH COMMISSIONER, *States Must Act Now to Fulfil Famine Victims' Right to Food–UN Expert* (Oct. 23, 2017), https://bit.ly/2VIpB7G.

[52] World Trade Organization, Declaration on the TRIPS Agreement and Public Health of 14 November 2001, ¶ 4, WTO Doc. WT/MIN(01)/DEC/2, 41 I.L.M. 755.

[53] It was not until recently that a few expert reports and research papers began to briefly examine the relationship between the right to technology and the treatment of HIV. *See, e.g.*, African Commission on Human and Peoples' Rights, *HIV, the Law and Human Rights in the African Human Rights System: Key Challenges and Opportunities for Rights-Based Responses to HIV* 49 (2019).

public access to health technologies alongside the right to health, it merely mentions the existence of the former right without any further consideration of how it should be protected.[54] Instead, it only evaluates problems in the context of the right to health, thereby suggesting tailor-made solutions to protecting that right.[55] The COVID-19 pandemic prompted the UN Committee on Economic, Social and Cultural Rights to declare that the right to technology requires equitable sharing of innovations in effective medicines and vaccines.[56] However, this statement and subsequent scholarly commentary[57] have so far received little attention, resulting in minimal impact.

At the same time, the right to technology has also never been invoked to deal with important matters that enrich human lives, such as facilitating the creation and dissemination of knowledge. Given that the right is supposed to entitle everyone to technological benefits, it follows that everyone is entitled to the benefits of advances in digital technology, including access to and the use of digital libraries. However, no legal expert or human rights organization has yet asserted that the right to technology has any role to play in allowing the public to enjoy the technological benefits derived from the creation of public digital libraries. Ostensibly, such libraries benefit everyone by providing convenient and affordable means of disseminating and accessing information and knowledge. However, the international community has largely grounded discussions of digital libraries in terms of access-limiting intellectual property[58] without any consideration of the access-expanding role the right to technology should have.

---

[54] *Report of the United Nations Secretary-General's High-Level Panel on Access to Medicines: Promoting Innovation and Access to Health Technologies* 12 & 20 (2016).

[55] *See, e.g., id.* at 7.

[56] UN Committee on Economic, Social and Cultural Rights, General Comment No. 25 (2020) on Science and Economic, Social and Cultural Rights (article 15 (1) (b), (2), (3) and (4) of the International Covenant on Economic, Social and Cultural Rights, Apr. 30, 2020, E/C.12/GC/25, para. 82 ("If a pandemic develops, sharing the best scientific knowledge and its applications, especially in the medical field, becomes crucial to mitigate the impact of the disease and to expedite the discovery of effective treatments and vaccines.").

[57] *See, e.g.,* Marco Perduca, *The Universal Right to Science,* NATURE (Feb.10, 2021).

[58] The US courts upheld the legality of the Google Books library, allowing users to make full-text searches of the copyrighted books that Google has scanned and to subsequently enjoy snippet views of those books. However, the Chinese courts ruled that Google Books violated Chinese copyright law, and a French court also held Google liable for violating

   The Manifesto for Digital Libraries reflects the global silence on the
relevance of the right to technology. Drafted by the International
Federation of Library Associations and Institutions (IFLA), the manifesto presents the digital library initiative as an important step toward
realizing the UN's Millennium Development Goals.[59] However, despite being expressly based on a human rights approach, the manifesto
makes no reference to the right to technology. This could be seen as an
inadvertent omission by IFLA, a professional association, but less
excusable is that the manifesto was endorsed by UNESCO. This is
because UNESCO did not invoke the right to technology, although
merely recognized the potential role of digital libraries in disseminating
information and knowledge and narrowing the digital divide.[60] No
government, organization, or activist to date has advocated for digital
libraries in service of the right to technology. Without referring to right
to technology, academics and policymakers have considered only how
digital libraries can promote education[61] and freedom of expression.[62]

C WHY THE RIGHT WAS ORPHANED

What caused the orphaning of the right to technology? I argue in this
section that the right has failed to take effect because of its obscurity,
the innate weakness of the human rights system, and the international
community's overemphasis on intellectual property (IP) protection.

1 Obscurity of the Right to Technology

The right to technology is arguably the most obscure of all human
rights, with the result that it is severely underapplied in practice. One

   French copyright law. *See* Haochen Sun, *Copyright Law as an Engine of Public Interest Protection*, 16 Nw. J. Tech. & Intell. Prop. 123, 186 (2019).

[59] International Federation of Library Associations and Institutions, *IFLA/UNESCO Manifesto for Digital Libraries* (July 13, 2018), https://bit.ly/3Ee69AP.

[60] UNESCO General Conference, *Digital Library Manifesto of the International Federation of Library Associations and Institutions (IFLA)*, ¶ 7.3, U.N. Doc. 36 C/20 (Oct. 6, 2011).

[61] *See* Susan Perry & Claudia Roda, Human Rights and Digital Technology: Digital Tightrope 163 (2017).

[62] *See* Eric Goldman, *Why Google's Fair Use Victory In Google Books Suit Is A Big Deal – And Why It Isn't*, Forbes (Nov. 14, 2013), https://bit.ly/3A7lhOb.

hindrance to the right's full application appears to be the difficulty of defining such abstract terms as "scientific progress" and "the benefits" of that progress. Given that these terms are exceedingly difficult for science and technology experts to define,[63] it is no wonder that human rights experts and activists have not attempted to elucidate them.[64]

More puzzling still is how the benefits of scientific progress can be shared in or enjoyed, as the UDHR and ICESCR mandate. Are there any principles or standards for determining the scope of technological benefits that can be shared in or enjoyed? Have any human rights treaties prescribed them, or is this a job best left to national governments? Unfortunately, neither human rights treaties nor national governments have ever attempted to tackle these questions. Of course, the rapid development of technology itself also complicates any attempts to define these concepts in a meaningful way. Scientists and policymakers often appear baffled as to how technologies can be developed ethically and how the positive and negative functions of a particular technology can be differentiated.

By contrast, concerted efforts have been made over time to delineate the contours of other major human rights, rendering them easier to understand and apply in practice. Take the rights to free speech and property as examples. In general, these rights are largely treated as negative liberties[65] that prevent governments from unduly interfering with the exercise of freedom of expression and private control of property, respectively. The First Amendment to the US Constitution, for instance, states that "Congress shall make no law … abridging the freedom of speech."[66] Similarly, the Fifth Amendment mandates that "private property [shall not] be taken for public use, without just

---

[63] ERIC SCHATZBERG, TECHNOLOGY: CRITICAL HISTORY OF A CONCEPT 1 (2018)(observing that the "definition of *technology* is a mess").

[64] *See* Audrey R. Chapman, *Towards an Understanding of the Right to Enjoy the Benefits of Scientific Progress and Its Applications*, 8 J. HUM. RTS. 1, 1 (2009) ("[T]his right is so obscure and its interpretation so neglected that the overwhelming majority of human rights advocates, governments, and international human rights bodies appear to be oblivious to its existence.").

[65] *See* Isaiah Berlin, *Two Concepts of Liberty*, in LIBERTY 166, 169 (Henry Hardy ed., 2d ed. 2002) ("The defence of liberty consists in the 'negative' goal of warding off interference.").

[66] US CONST. amend. I.

compensation."[67] Subsequent to these two amendments, numerous judicial hearings, policy debates, and academic texts have wrestled with the proper protection of free speech and property rights. Such efforts have shed light on the nature and scope of these rights, thereby making the public aware of them and, in turn, encouraging the public to take legal action to defend them.

Owing to its obscurity, the right to technology has seen very little substantive practical application or theoretical exploration of its nature and scope,[68] a situation that has further marginalized it in human rights practice and policy consideration. The result is a vicious circle: the less the right to technology is invoked and protected, the less likely that its obscurity will be alleviated in the minds of human rights experts and laypersons alike.

2 Ineffective Human Rights Enforcement System

The human rights system itself lacks effectiveness in practice,[69] which is another factor rendering the right to technology particularly feeble. Most of the regional human rights treaties adopted in the past few decades have turned a blind eye to the right's protection. Nowhere in the European Convention on Human Rights, for example, is there any provision recognizing the right to technology, and nothing in the African Charter on Human and Peoples' Rights protects that right for Africans, who arguably need the benefits of technological progress more than their counterparts on other continents.[70] There are several reasons for these omissions.

First, the legal status of major international human rights treaties at the national level remains unclear. Although it has been argued that the UDHR has become binding on national governments as part of

---

[67] US CONST. amend. V.

[68] *See* Lea Shaver, *The Right to Science and Culture*, 10 WIS. L. REV. 121, 152 (2010) ("The passage of six decades has produced very little in the way of scholarly interpretation and even less in terms of national jurisprudence.").

[69] *See generally* JACK L. GOLDSMITH & ERIC A. POSNER, THE LIMITS OF INTERNATIONAL LAW 119–26 (2005); ERIC POSNER, THE TWILIGHT OF HUMAN RIGHTS LAW 7 (2014); Oona A. Hathaway, *Do Human Rights Treaties Make a Difference?*, 111 YALE L.J. 1935, 2004 (2002).

[70] *See* William A. Schabas, *Study of the Right to Enjoy the Benefits of Scientific and Technological Progress and Its Applications*, in HUMAN RIGHTS IN EDUCATION, SCIENCE AND CULTURE: LEGAL DEVELOPMENTS AND CHALLENGES 273, 289 (Yvonne Donders & Vladimir Volodin eds., 2007).

customary international law, given that countries have regularly invoked it for more than fifty years, a number of countries continue to deny that it has automatic binding force with respect to their governments. In *Sosa* v. *Alvarez-Machain*,[71] for example, the US Supreme Court ruled that the UDHR "does not of its own force impose obligations as a matter of international law."[72] The courts of several other countries have followed suit, deciding that the UDHR is not in and of itself part of their domestic laws and cannot be enforced except through recourse to domestic implementing legislation. With respect to the ICESCR, the United States has signed but not yet ratified it, which has served to weaken the protection of human rights in the United States.

Second, the major human rights treaties lack the teeth to effectively protect rights in countries that fail to fulfill their obligations. The UN Security Council is the only UN body with the authority to issue resolutions that are binding on member states. Where "threats to the peace, breaches of the peace, or acts of aggression" occur, the Security Council can impose economic sanctions or even use force to intervene.[73] However, it does not hand down binding resolutions on general violations of human rights obligations, and nor is there any other human rights body in the UN vested with the authority to do so. The UNHRC operates a complaint procedure that allows consistent patterns of gross and reliably attested violations of human rights to be reported. However, that procedure is merely a confidential petition system that imposes no binding sanctions upon countries that are found to have committed violations.

Third, in any case, major human rights treaties are not legally applicable to corporations. In today's globalized world, an increasing number of corporations are both violating human rights and facilitating the protection of those rights. Without holding corporations – particularly those that wield more economic power than many nation states – accountable, it will be virtually impossible to strengthen the global human rights system in any meaningful way.[74] Worse still, corporations

---

[71] 542 U.S. 692 (2004).

[72] *Id.* at 734.

[73] U.N. Charter, arts. 41–42.

[74] *See* Pierre Thielbörger & Tobias Ackermann, *A Treaty on Enforcing Human Rights against Business: Closing the Loophole or Getting Stuck in a Loop?*, 24 IND. J. GLOBAL LEGAL STUD. 43, 46–51 (2017).

are playing an increasingly important role in developing new technologies and determining who shares the benefits of technological progress, and the inability of the present global human rights system to legally engage corporations is a major barrier to protecting the right to technology worldwide.

The confluence of these factors has made it much more difficult to trigger strong protection of the right to technology. Given the legal inadequacies of both the UDHR and ICESCR, countries are not legally bound to protect the right to technology through their national constitutions or other relevant laws. These major human rights treaties also fail to lay out the minimum standards that countries must adopt to protect this human right domestically, and nor is there an international dispute resolution system capable of correcting a national government's failure to protect it.

3 Overemphasis on Intellectual Property Rights

Efforts to strengthen IP protection standards across the globe have eclipsed the invocation of the right to technology. Largely steered by developed countries, the international community has dedicated significant effort to applying IP protection mechanisms to distribute technological benefits through voluntary market transactions. Improvements in international relations after the Cold War generated more robust global trading and investment and cultural exchange. Hence, globalization has significantly increased cross-border flows of IP-intensive products and services, leading to calls for *harmonized* international IP protection standards. Meanwhile, breakthroughs in technology have given rise to demands for the global protection of inventions and creations through *stronger* IP protection standards.

Frustrated by the major problems with the IP treaties administered by the World Intellectual Property Organization (WIPO), the United States and European Union leveraged their political and economic power to mainstream the harmonization of IP laws through trade negotiations.[75] The Uruguay Round of multilateral trade negotiations,

---

[75] *See* DANIEL J. GERVAIS, THE TRIPS AGREEMENT: DRAFTING HISTORY AND ANALYSIS 12–13 (4th ed. 2012).

which took place between 1986 and 1993, culminated in the
Agreement on Trade-Related Aspects of Intellectual Property Rights
(TRIPS Agreement)[76] to be administered by the then newly created
WTO. The TRIPS Agreement increases international IP protection in
three ways. First, it sets more stringent substantive standards for IP
rights protection than those contained in WIPO-administered
treaties.[77] For example, it requires that member countries make patents
available for "all fields of technology,"[78] which is a minimum standard
absent from the Paris Convention for the Protection of Industrial
Property. Second, the TRIPS Agreement ushers in a host of procedural
standards for enforcing IP rights that are largely absent in WIPO-
administered treaties.[79] Third, it allows for the WTO's Dispute
Settlement Body to adjudicate a member state's alleged failure to
comply with its standards.[80]

However, the TRIPS Agreement does not deal with the legal challenges to IP protection posed by digital technology, the rise of the
Internet in particular. Therefore, WIPO, took the initiative to create
new treaties to address this legal vacuum.[81] In 1996, it concluded the
WIPO Copyright Treaty and Performances and Phonograms Treaty,
which introduced new standards for copyright protections in the digital
environment.

Intellectual property protection at the national and regional levels
was subsequently strengthened. Member states revised their national
laws to bring them into compliance with the TRIPS Agreement and
new WIPO treaties. Concurrently, in response to continuing technological progress, many developed countries strengthened their domestic IP protection standards, and some also sought to export those
standards via bilateral trade agreements. The United States and
European Union, for example, exported a host of new IP standards,

[76] Agreement on Trade-Related Agreements of Intellectual Property Rights art. 13, Apr. 15,
1994, Marrakesh Agreement Establishing the World Trade Organization, Annex 1C,
1869 U.N.T.S. 299 (1994) [hereinafter TRIPS Agreement].
[77] See J. H. Reichman, *Universal Minimum Standards of Intellectual Property Protection Under
the TRIPS Component of the WTO Agreement*, 29 INT'L LAW. 345, 347 (1995).
[78] TRIPS Agreement, art. 27.1.
[79] *See* TRIPS Agreement, arts. 41–63.
[80] *Id.* art. 64.
[81] *See* Ruth L. Okediji, *The Regulation of Creativity Under the WIPO Internet Treaties*, 77
FORDHAM L. REV. 2379, 2379 (2009).

including an extension of the duration of copyright protection by an additional twenty years,[82] that were adopted largely as a result of extensive lobbying by IP-intensive industries.[83]

As the international community focused on revamping the global IP system, the major IP treaties remained largely impervious to human rights concerns in general[84] and to implementation of the right to technology in particular. Without considering the equality issues that are central to the right to technology, the rapid expansion of IP protection has legally enabled technology developers, as IP owners, to distribute technological benefits as they wish through voluntary market transactions. Such developers enjoy the exclusive right to permit others to use their IP-protected technologies contingent upon royalties.[85] Hence, the extent to which members of the public can make use of a technological benefit often hinges upon how much they can pay the IP owner concerned.

For example, the Digital Millennium Copyright Act (DMCA) passed by the US Congress in 1998 dictates a strictly market-oriented approach to the dissemination of copyrighted works. The DMCA confers upon copyright holders a *de facto* right to restrict access to their works, making it difficult or even impossible for the public to make fair use of those works. Fair use presupposes that members of the public at large have free access to a work, which enables them to decide whether they should make fair use of it.[86] However, free access is not necessarily available. Technological measures deployed by copyright holders prevent users from accessing or using their works, and the DMCA furnishes penalties against circumvention of these digital fences. Unless members of the public pay royalties to copyright holders, they cannot access or use the latter's works.

---

[82] *See* James Thuo Gathii, *The Neo-Liberal Turn in Regional Trade Agreements*, 86 WASH. L. REV. 421, 466–67 (2011).

[83] *Id.* at 965.

[84] *See* Ruth L. Okediji, *Does Intellectual Property Need Human Rights?*, 51 N.Y.U. J. INT'L L. & POL. 1, 10 (2018) ("Historically, there was very little formal interaction between IP and human rights law, though this has changed dramatically as both fields expanded in scope.").

[85] *See* ROBERT P. MERGES, JUSTIFYING INTELLECTUAL PROPERTY, at xi (2011).

[86] *See* Jerome H. Reichman & Ruth L. Okediji, *When Copyright Law and Science Collide: Empowering Digitally Integrated Research Methods on a Global Scale*, 96 MINN. L. REV. 1362, 1362–480 (2012).

Intellectual property rights holders often have the final say on the price that non-owners have to pay to enjoy the benefits of technological progress in the marketplace.[87] Although certain European jurisdictions provide regulatory oversight on excessive pricing,[88] in many countries, including the United States, there is no bar to monopoly pricing or even excessive pricing in private transactions.[89] Accordingly, companies are free to price however they wish, even when they hold monopoly power. Drug patent holders, for example, are able to charge wildly discriminatory prices, as evidenced by the huge between-country variance in the prices of patented drugs.[90] Drugs with generic equivalents do not exhibit such extreme price discrepancies,[91] and can be much cheaper.[92] Moreover, pharmaceutical companies often limit supply of drugs to particular countries. This is because the low-priced drugs demanded in those markets could be resold in other markets at a higher price, hurting pharmaceutical companies' profits.[93]

D PROBLEMS WITH THE INDIVIDUAL RIGHTS APPROACH

Underlying the three aforementioned factors are deep-seated problems with the individual rights approach within the human rights regime. By focusing on the interests of individuals and corporate entities, this approach has resulted in a larger structural malfunction that prevents full actualization of the right to technology. It has severely weakened the ability of human rights enforcement mechanisms to protect that

[87] *See* Okediji, *Does Intellectual Property Need Human Rights?*, *supra* note 84, at 59 ("Public health technologies remain subject to the economic forces of market demand.").

[88] Organization for Economic Co-operation and Development [OECD], *Excessive Pricing in Pharmaceutical Markets – Note by the Netherlands*, ¶¶ 3–4 (Nov. 15, 2018), https://one .oecd.org/document/DAF/COMP/WD(2018)108/en/pdf.

[89] OECD, *Excessive Prices in Pharmaceutical Markets – Background Note by the Secretariat*, ¶ 11 (Oct. 3, 2018), https://one.oecd.org/document/DAF/COMP(2018)12/en/pdf.

[90] K. Bala and Kiran Sagoo, *Patents and Prices*, HAI NEWS, at 1–12 (April/May 2000).

[91] *Id.*

[92] Hannah Brennan et al., *A Prescription for Excessive Drug Pricing: Leveraging Government Patent Use for Health*, 18 YALE J. L. & TECH. 275, 285 (2016).

[93] Jean O. Lanjouw, *Patents, Price Controls and Access to New Drugs: How Policy Affects Global Market Entry* 3 (Ctr. for Glob. Dev., Working Paper No. 61, 2005), https://www .cgdev.org/sites/default/files/2679_file_WP61.pdf.

right while significantly strengthening the power of the IP rights regime to overshadow it.

Internationally recognized human rights are prevailingly regarded as individual rights.[94] By nature, individual rights are "bestowed upon persons primarily for the purpose of promoting their dignity and self-worth as individual human beings."[95] Personal property and privacy rights are typically individual rights. The law protects the individual's ability to choose what to do with things such as property and privacy in accordance with their own will, thereby preventing other individuals and governmental agencies from encroaching upon their individual rights.[96] Responding to the barbarous treatment of individuals during World War II, the drafting of the UDHR was overwhelmingly shaped by the idea of individual rights,[97] thereby cultivating the human rights "language of individual empowerment."[98] The Vienna Declaration and Program of Action adopted at the 1993 World Conference on Human Rights reaffirms the UDHR's individual rights approach to human rights protection by stating that "all human rights derive from the dignity and worth inherent in the human person, and . . . the human person is the central subject of human rights and fundamental freedoms."[99]

The individual rights approach is embedded in the culture of individualism that Western civilization has celebrated since the Enlightenment. Leading legal historian Professor Lawrence Friedman elaborates on the historical background to the approach as follows:

> [T]he human rights movement depends on a culture that is strongly individualistic. Law and society emphasize *individual* rights; and this corresponds with the way people feel about themselves – as unique individuals, with unique lives, destinies, strengths and weaknesses, desires and habits. Any account of modern culture,

---

[94] *See* Australian Human Rights Commission, *What Are Human Rights?* (2010), https://bit.ly /3m8m6QY ("The basic notion of human rights lies in people's recognition of the need to protect and affirm every other person's individual dignity.").

[95] Haochen Sun, *Fair Use as a Collective User Right*, 90 N. C. L. Rev. 125, 142 (2011).

[96] *See* Ronald Dworkin, Taking Rights Seriously xi (1977).

[97] *See* Michael Ignatieff, Human Rights as Politics and Idolatry 66 (2001).

[98] *Id.* at 57.

[99] World Conference on Human Rights, *Vienna Declaration and Programme of Action*, ¶ 2, U. N. Doc. A/CONF.157/23 (June 25, 1993).

moreover – of the culture in which the human rights movement, and individualism, flourish – must pay attention to certain leading aspects of modern history. These include the industrial revolution, the rise of capitalism, and that other revolution, the scientific and technological revolution.[100]

Professor Friedman's observation succinctly charts the economic and social background to the rise of human rights and the cultivation of individualism. The individualistic notion of human rights has been nurtured in part by the structural economic transformation brought about by capitalism, which celebrates individual interests in wealth accumulation through voluntary market transactions. Individualized human rights also cater to the formation of consumer societies in which individual choices made for personal welfare are regarded as the sovereignty of consumers.

The right to technology, to the extent that it has been recognized, has been treated as an individual right. According to Professor Samantha Besson, as currently conceived, "[t]he interest protected by the right to [technology] is individual, even if it pertains to a public or collective good."[101] Professor Besson therefore rejects the idea that under the *status quo* the right to technology "is held collectively as a group (*e.g.*, by the 'international community') or has to be exercised collectively, whether at the domestic or at the global level."[102]

The individual rights approach, however, has produced two negative consequences for the effectiveness of the human rights regime in general and the right to technology in particular. First, the approach weakens both owing to its inability to introduce any meaningful distributive justice agenda.[103] Although the Preamble to the UDHR refers to "recognition of the inherent dignity and of the equal and inalienable rights of all members of the human family," the UDHR and major

---

[100] Lawrence M. Friedman, The Human Rights Culture: A Study in History and Context 15 (2011).

[101] Samantha Besson, *Science Without Borders and the Boundaries of Human Rights: Who Owes the Human Right to Science?*, 4 Eur. J. Human Rts. 462, 478 (2015).

[102] *Id.*

[103] See Samuel Moyn, Not Enough: Human Rights in an Unequal World 2 (2018) ("The age of human rights has not been kind to full-fledged distributive justice, because it is also an age of the victory of the rich.").

human rights treaties bestow upon people only *symbolic*, not *substantive*, equality in the enjoyment of human rights.[104]

Take the right to health as an example. Symbolically, the UDHR grants everyone equal status to enjoyment of this human right,[105] as does the ICESCR.[106] Substantively, however, not everyone enjoys such status, as epitomized by the HIV epidemic. Wealthy people can purchase expensive, patent-protected HIV-related drugs, and others in the developed world can afford them with the aid of health insurance. However, vast numbers of poor people cannot afford these life-saving drugs despite possessing a human right to health. Patent protection has rendered them far too expensive for low-income HIV sufferers.[107] The World Health Organization has reported that an estimated 470,000 people in Africa died of HIV/AIDS in 2018 alone.[108] A lack of access to HIV medicines owing to their prohibitive cost was a major factor in this appalling number of deaths. In the battle between life and death, symbolic equality is literally meaningless.

It is exceedingly difficult to build any effective human rights enforcement mechanisms if the relevant international treaties celebrate only symbolic equality but contain no substantive distributive justice mandates. In normal circumstances, substantive equality deals with the interests of a group of people or all members of a society. For example, the "difference principle" proposed by John Rawls as one of the mandates for achieving social justice requires that resources be redistributed to "the least advantaged members of society."[109] A focus on the singular, personal interest supported by an individual right cannot

---

[104] *Id.* at 213 ("Human rights guarantee status equality but not distributive equality.").

[105] UDHR, art. 25(1) ("Everyone has the right to a standard of living adequate for the health and well-being of himself and of his family.").

[106] ICESCR, art. 12.

[107] *See* William W. Fisher & Talha Syed, *Global Justice in Healthcare: Developing Drugs for the Developing World*, 40 U.C. Davis L. Rev. 581, 646 (2006).

[108] World Health Organization, *Number of Deaths Due to HIV/AIDS*, www.who.int/gho/hiv/epidemic_status/deaths_text/en (last visited Nov. 28, 2019).

[109] This principle requires that "the higher expectations of those better situated are just if and only if they work as part of a scheme which improves the expectations of the least advantaged members of society." John Rawls, A Theory of Justice 65 (1999). Rawls also explained that "the intuitive idea is that the social order is not to establish and secure the more attractive prospects of those better off unless doing so is to the advantage of these less fortunate." *Id.*

generate the robust collective action necessary for substantive equality serving the interests of large groups of people or society as a whole.[110]

The individual rights approach lends support to demands for stronger IP protection, demands that have outweighed the collective interest in equal access to technological benefits that facilitate dynamic social innovation and political democracy. Given its emphasis on the right to property in particular, the individual rights approach affords the free market unwarranted weight in the distribution of technological benefits. Treated as an individual right, the right to technology cannot necessarily override the other individual rights that support IP protection. From this perspective, the individual right to technology does not provide legal or ethical grounds for a distributive justice agenda capable of reforming the IP system to grant equal access to technological benefits.[111]

Second, the success of the open access model calls into question the viability of the individualistic notion of the right to technology, which supports the IP-based, market-oriented distribution of technological benefits. For example, the free software movement and Creative Commons initiative demonstrate the dynamism of knowledge production and technological progress that are not reliant upon IP rights protection. The rise of the sharing economy, propelled by social media such as Wikipedia, YouTube, and Google Books, has promoted free access to knowledge and conferred tremendous technological benefits.

The open access model reveals the importance of distributing such benefits through channels that are not solely reliant upon IP rights. People need greater access to technological benefits to boost their engagement in cultural and political activities. Indeed, many scholars have noted these positive functions of digital technologies.[112] For

---

[110] *See, e.g.,* Richard McIntyre, *Globalism, Human Rights and the Problem of Individualism,* 3:1 HUM. RTS. & HUM. WELFARE (2003).

[111] Against this backdrop, the UN Special Rapporteur in the Field of Cultural Rights has stressed the urgent need to adjust the tension between IP and the public's enjoyment of the right to technology: "[IP] laws should place no limitations upon the right to [technology], unless the State can demonstrate that the limitation pursues a legitimate aim, is compatible with the nature of this right and is strictly necessary for the promotion of general welfare in a democratic society." *Copyright Policy and the Right to Science and Culture,* ¶ 98, *supra* note 47.

[112] *See, e.g.,* William W. Fisher III, *The Implications for Law of User Innovation,* 94 MINN. L. REV. 1417, 1460 (2010).

example, Jack Balkin has insightfully pointed out that "[t]he digital age provides a technological infrastructure that greatly expands the possibilities for individual participation in the growth and spread of culture and thus greatly expands the possibilities for the realization of a truly democratic culture."[113]

SUMMARY

The birth of the right to technology, as I have shown, reflected one of the most profound lessons that international leaders learned from World War II. Technology must be used in the public interest.

However, the right to technology does not fit well within the individual rights approach commonly applied to human rights law. Structurally, this approach protects human rights on the basis of personal interests without providing broader distributive justice for the collective interests of all humankind. Unable to disentangle itself from this conventional system, the right to technology has suffered from obscurity and a lack of definition, the ineffective human rights enforcement system, and the international community's overemphasis on IP protection.

---

[113] Jack M. Balkin, *Digital Speech and Democratic Culture: A Theory of Freedom of Expression for the Information Society*, 79 N.Y.U. L. REV. 1 (2004).

2   THE COLLECTIVE RIGHT
TO TECHNOLOGY

In July 2019, I hosted at the University of Hong Kong an international conference on technology law, which attracted around 120 attorneys and law students. Before I presented my paper on the right to technology, I asked the attendees whether they knew of the existence of a right to enjoy the benefits of scientific progress and its applications, a human right that is protected by both the Universal Declaration on Human Rights (UDHR) and the International Covenant on Economic, Social and Cultural Rights (ICESCR). Much to my surprise, no attendee raised their hand in affirmation. Their silence indicated to me that this human right is unknown even to those with a demonstrable interest in the subject area. This example is by no means an isolated case. In Chapter 1 of this book, I demonstrated that the right to technology is a forgotten human right.

How can we resurrect the right to technology? In this chapter, I propose that redefining the right to technology as a collective right would help to address the causes of its languishing under the existing international human rights regime. I consider how and why this right should be redefined as a collective right that entitles people to enjoy the benefits of technological progress and minimizes the harms such progress can cause. I argue that a collective right to technology would embrace distributive justice agendas by protecting larger societal interests in public freedom and dignity while safeguarding specific groups against the prejudicial use of technologies. I further explore how this collective right could be protected as a civil liberty by domestic courts, and apply this legal transformation to intellectual

property (IP) protection, which regulates the distribution of technological benefits more than any other area of law. I then consider how
the collective right to technology could be applied to interpret the
nature and scope of both copyright fair use and the IP Clause under
the US Constitution.

A THE IDEA OF COLLECTIVE RIGHTS

Individual rights protect personal interests in freedom and ward off
undesirable interference from the government and other persons.[1]
Collective rights, in contrast, empower people to become better members of their society or of the social groups to which they belong. By
shaping people's sense of social membership, collective rights promote
social interactions and improve social well-being by raising the quality
of life for the larger whole.[2] Therefore, the confluence of individual and
collective rights reflects the duality of human identity, viewing human
beings as both individual rights holders and societal members who hold
collective rights.

   While individual rights have long been entrenched in domestic and
international laws, there is only nascent recognition of and protection
for collective rights.[3] According to the interest theory of rights, personal interests – such as those concerning property, privacy, and bodily
integrity – give rise to individual rights, holding others under a duty to
respect those rights.[4]

   Grounded in the interest theory of rights are two conditions for
recognizing and protecting collective rights. First, the identification of

---

[1] *See* JEREMY WALDRON, *'NONSENSE UPON STILTS': BENTHAM, BURKE, AND MARX ON THE RIGHTS
OF MAN* 185 (1987) ("A right is always somebody's right, and we never attempt to secure
things as a matter of right unless there is some individual or individuals whose rights are in
question.").

[2] *See* Dwight Newman, *Collective Interests and Collective Rights*, 49 AM. J. JURIS. 127, 141
(2004) ("The collective interests of a particular collectivity ... are not unrelated to members' individual interests, for the collectivity's moral existence depends on its ability to
provide a collective interest that improves the lives of its individual members.");
JOSEPH RAZ, THE MORALITY OF FREEDOM 208 (1986).

[3] MIODRAG A. JOVANOVIC, COLLECTIVE RIGHTS: A LEGAL THEORY 1 (2012).

[4] RAZ, *supra* note 2, at 166.

collective interests constitutes a necessary condition for holding others responsible for respecting societal rights and group rights.[5] The existence of collective interests that are enjoyed by all members of a society or a given group of people supports the recognition and protection of collective rights. In the following discussion, I identify two kinds of collective interests, namely, *societal interests* and *group interests*, that undergird the protection of collective rights.[6] Second, *membership identities* that are jointly held constitute a sufficient condition for people to claim collective rights.[7] Individual rights are assigned to people who have the requisite personal agency.[8] Collective rights, in contrast, are assigned to people whose societal or group membership is legally and morally recognized.

1 Societal Rights

Following the above-discussed interest theory, the existence of societal interests in public freedom and dignity is a necessary condition for people to claim societal rights as the first type of collective rights. The freedom to take part in civic life in public spaces is essential to a well-functioning society.[9] People have a collective interest in such public freedom because the goods and institutions that form the public sphere

---

[5] *See id*, at 208 (arguing that a collective right "exists because an aspect of the interest of human beings justifies holding some persons(s) to be subject to a duty"); *see also* Dwight Newman, Community and Collective Rights: A Theoretical Framework for Rights Held by Groups 57 (2011); Leslie Green, *Two Views of Collective Rights*, 4 Canadian J.L. & Juris. 315, 320–21 (1991) (explaining why collective rights should be viewed as rights to collective interests).

[6] *See* Haochen Sun, *Fair Use as a Collective User Right*, 90 N.C. L. Rev. 125, 177–83 (2011) (suggesting that in the context of fair use, collective rights fall into two categories: identity-based group rights and society-based rights).

[7] According to Joseph Raz, the second and third conditions for recognizing a collective right are "the interests in question are the interests of individuals as members of a group in a public good and the right is a right to that public good because it serves their interest as members of the group" and "the interest of no single member of that group in that public good is sufficient by itself to justify holding another person to be subject to a duty." *See supra* note 2, at 208. In my opinion, both of these conditions set the "identity of membership" requirement for recognizing a collective right.

[8] Raz, *supra* note 2, at 208.

[9] *Id.* at 165 ("A well-functioning society has participatory goods because each individual's enjoyment of his environment depends upon how other individuals participate in various aspects of social life.").

shape the civic environment for all members of society.[10] For example, clean air is vital to human health and civic engagement in public spaces. Heavily polluted air harms human health, physically preventing citizens from participating in public activities. Public security also affects people's active interactions in public spaces. An unsafe social environment results in instability and disorder, prompting people to remain sheltered in private spaces such as their homes. A democratic election system serves as a public vehicle for citizens to have a say in the decision-making process governing society as a whole. An independent judiciary functions as a public institution to maintain justice by settling disputes. Rather than catering to individuals separately, these public goods and institutions provide collective protection for societal members' interests in their freedoms.[11]

Public goods and institutions also play a crucial role in maintaining the public dignity of all members of society. The protection of individual dignity is fundamental to the value of human life and to the value of a society.[12] It determines whether the society affords public goods and institutions that collectively protect the citizenry's sense of social membership and self-worth. A clean, safe, and ethical society makes people feel like respected members of that society, whereas a dirty, dangerous, and corrupt society degrades people's sense of membership. Heavily polluted air and poor public security impair the social environment that is supposed to sustain collective self-worth. Malfunctioning electoral and judicial systems can give way to economic and political manipulation that renders citizens vulnerable to inhumane coercion and suppression. The end result is distortion of the collective interest in upholding a society's public dignity.

At the same time, people's societal memberships are a sufficient condition for them to claim societal rights. The formation of societal memberships has both political and social dimensions. Societal membership is a *political* phenomenon, as the decision to recognize such

---

[10] *See, e.g.*, DANA VILLA, PUBLIC FREEDOM 26 (2008) ("Beyond the realization of our political liberty, the purpose of public freedom is to make concrete – to actualize – the 'active and constant surveillance over . . . [the people's] representatives.'").

[11] *Id.*

[12] The UDHR begins by recognizing that "the inherent dignity" of "all members of the human family is the foundation of freedom, justice and peace in the world." UDHR, pmbl.

membership operates via hierarchical government agencies. At the macro level, a country can be considered a large society, and citizenship of the country is a form of societal membership. Whether one becomes a citizen by birth or through immigration, a relevant governmental agency will normally issue the birth certificate or passport recognizing such citizenship. At the micro level, cities, districts, towns, and even villages can be considered smaller societies that exist in a given country. If an individual becomes a resident of one of these societies, the relevant government agency will normally issue him or her an identification card and document the residency. A major function of societal membership is that it allows people to engage in the political life of a society. It then follows that the realization of societal rights entails holding political dialogues with both governmental agencies and one's fellow members of society.

Societal memberships are also a *social* phenomenon because the societal interests undergirding them are indivisible and relational. As a member of a society, a person enjoys indivisible societal interests in public goods and institutions. The aim of maintaining the quality of such goods and institutions is to serve all members' interests rather than those of a single person or particular group of persons.[13] Therefore, it is not desirable to separate public goods and institutions into divisible, discrete parts, making each part available to only a single person or a particular group. Given their indivisible nature, the enjoyment of these goods by one member of a society does not exclude their enjoyment by other members of the society in public spaces.[14] Clean air is an example of a public good that serves the interests of all members of a society. A particular area of clean air in a public space cannot be designated to a particular person or group. Otherwise, it would defeat societal interests in the good by prioritizing individual interests. To put it differently, worsening air quality or a deterioration in other public goods, such as threats to public security, harm the interests of all members of society. However, the indivisible nature of societal interests does not prevent each member of a society from enjoying clear air and security within private spaces such as their own homes.

---

[13] RAZ, *supra* note 2, at 198 (arguing that a public good "is not subject to voluntary control by anyone").

[14] *Id.*

At the same time, the enjoyment of social memberships within a society is *relational*. Every member of a society is regarded as a stakeholder in the societal interests concerned and may therefore be called upon to protect those interests. For instance, to improve air quality, public security, and democratic institutions, every member of society is expected to make contributions by paying taxes, casting votes, or engaging in social discourse. Such positive relational protection is inextricably intertwined with the indivisible nature of societal interests because one person's contribution to improving public goods or institutions can confer benefits upon all members of society, and, conversely, a failure to contribute can cause harm to all members of society. In contrast, individual rights have different relational attributes that are protected in a negative sense. Individual rights entitle their holders to prevent infringing acts by others or to recover losses caused by infringing acts as a means of protecting the holders' own individual interests in a given subject matter, such as private property and privacy.[15]

The right to development is a typical collective right that has been recognized by the international community. Pursuant to the United Nations Declaration on the Right to Development, the right to development collectively entitles "all peoples ... to participate in, contribute to, and enjoy economic, social, cultural and political development, in which all human rights and fundamental freedoms can be fully realized."[16] It protects the collective interests of a society's members in public freedom and dignity. In *Democratic Republic of the Congo v. Burundi, Rwanda and Uganda*,[17] the African Commission of Human and Peoples' Rights ruled that the people of the Democratic Republic of the Congo collectively hold the right to development in relation to their natural resources. The joint military invasion of the country by Burundi, Uganda, and Rwanda, according to the commission, resulted in the mass killing of civilians and the occupation of a hydroelectric dam, thereby violating this collective right enjoyed by

---

[15] *Id.*
[16] *Id.*
[17] (2004) AHRLR 19 (ACHPR 2003).

the Congolese.[18] This ruling recognizes that people are citizens of the Democratic Republic of the Congo (societal membership) share societal interests in the natural resources that belong to them collectively. Such resources are crucial to their public freedom and dignity because they help to achieve the "economic, social and cultural development" of their country.[19]

According to the justificatory reasoning of collective rights I suggest above, the societal interests and societal membership of the citizens of the Democratic Republic of the Congo give rise to their right to develop the natural resources of that country. This right, therefore, holds state governments responsible for respecting the collective interests in the natural resources of the Democratic Republic of the Congo.[20]

2 Group Rights

Unlike societal rights, group rights do not serve the collective interests of all members of a society, but instead only those of a given social group within that society.[21] For example, the International Covenant on Civil and Political Rights guarantees the right of persons belonging to minority groups to enjoy their own culture. It states that "[i]n those States in which ethnic, religious or linguistic minorities exist, persons belonging to such minorities shall not be denied the right, in community with the other members of their group, to enjoy their own culture, to profess and practise their own religion, or to use their own language."[22]

Group rights are recognized as collective rights because of the existence of collective interests in forming and maintaining a social group[23] (the necessary condition) and the formation of a group

---

[18] *Id.* at para. 94–95.

[19] *Id.* at para. 95.

[20] *Id.* (stating "the general duty of states to individually or collectively ensure the exercise of the right to development").

[21] *See* Peter Jones, *Group Rights and Group Oppression,* 7 J. Pol. Phil. 353, 357 (1999) ("What unites and identifies a set of individuals as a group for right holding purposes is simply their possessing a shared interest of sufficient moment").

[22] International Covenant on Civil and Political Rights, Dec. 16, 1966, S. Exec. Rep. 102–23, 999 U.N.T.S. 171, art. 27.

[23] *See* Jones, *supra* note 21, at 354 (arguing that "group rights are often articulated as demands for group freedom"); Frank Hindriks, Group Freedom: A Social Mechanism

membership identity (the sufficient condition). Social groups can be formed on the basis of identities such as race, gender, age, national origin, sexual orientation, language, disability, and religious belief.

For instance, freedom of religion can be seen as a group right given that it protects the collective interests of believers as members of a religious group.[24] The development of any religious teaching/thought itself is the outgrowth of the collective efforts of all of those who believe in the religion rather than the exercise of religious freedom by individual believers. Countless religious masters, scholars, and believers have contributed to the teachings of the world's major religions.[25] Therefore, a collective interest exists in the development of a given religion and the exercise of religious freedom.[26] It is common for believers to manifest their religious beliefs through joint activities in churches, temples, or mosques.[27] Therefore, religious freedom entails believers' collective interest in associating freely with their fellow believers to form and enrich their religious communities or organizations.[28] There is also a collective interest in the development

---

Account, 47 PHIL. Soc. Sci 410, 411 (2017) (discussing "how group rights can be seen as legitimate demands for group freedom").

[24] *See, e.g.*, UK Human Rights Act 1998, ch. 42, § 13 (recognizing the collective aspect of religious freedom: "If a court's determination of any question arising under this Act might affect the exercise by a religious organisation (itself or its members collectively) of the Convention right to freedom of thought, conscience and religion, it must have particular regard to the importance of that right.").

[25] *See, e.g.*, JONATHAN Z. SMITH, IMAGINING RELIGION: FROM BABYLON TO JONESTOWN xi (1982) ("Religion is solely the creation of the scholar's study. It is created for the scholar's analytic purposes by his imaginative acts of comparison and generalization.") (emphasis omitted); Frederick Mark Gedicks, *Toward a Constitutional Jurisprudence of Religious Group Rights*, 1989 WIS. L. REV. 99, 105–06 (1989) (concluding that "constitutional recognition of a strong right of religious group autonomy in making membership decisions is necessary to preserve religious pluralism and the individual autonomy that is at the heart of liberalism.").

[26] W. COLE DURHAM, JR., *The Right to Autonomy in Religious Affairs: A Comparative View*, in *CHURCH AUTONOMY: A COMPARATIVE SURVEY* 1 (Gerhard Robbers ed., 2001) ("We often think of religious freedom as an individual right rooted in individual conscience, but in fact religion virtually always has a communal dimension, and religious freedom can be negated as effectively by coercing or interfering with a religious group as by coercing one of its individual members.").

[27] *See* CHARLES TAYLOR, VARIETIES OF RELIGION TODAY: WILLIAM JAMES REVISITED (2002) (discussing the inherently collective aspects of many religious practices).

[28] *See* Wisconsin v. Yoder, 406 U.S. 205, 216 (1972) ("The traditional way of life of the Amish is not merely a matter of personal preference, but one of deep religious conviction, shared by an organized group, and intimately related to daily living."); Ronald R. Garet,

of a religion, which is the outgrowth of the collective efforts of all of those who believe in the religion rather than the personal exercise of religious freedom by individual believers.[29]

Members of a social group hold a collective interest in warding off actions that prejudice the dignity of their group identities through discriminatory or unfair practices. The Declaration on the Rights of Indigenous Peoples[30] recognizes that indigenous people enjoy a bundle of collective rights as an ethnic group.[31] This bundle of group rights includes rights to protect the indigenous community's culture through practices, languages, education, media, and religion. These rights guarantee that the indigenous people in question can live in freedom, peace, and security as a distinct group of people and that they are not subjected to any act of genocide or other violence, including the forcible removal of the children of one group to another group.

The right of an indigenous community to protect its culture exemplifies the critical importance of collective interest protection for group identity.[32] Indigenous peoples around the world have throughout history developed technical and cultural creations, such as traditional medicine and folklore, for the subsistence and enrichment of their

Communality and Existence: The Rights of Groups, 56 S. CAL. L. REV. 1001, 1009 (1983) ("Courts have and can further extend a jurisprudence that promotes 'communality' or 'groupness' as among the key social goods.").

[29] *See, e.g.*, JONATHAN Z. SMITH, IMAGINING RELIGION: FROM BABYLON TO JONESTOWN xi (1982) ("Religion is solely the creation of the scholar's study. It is created for the scholar's analytic purposes by his imaginative acts of comparison and generalization.") (emphasis omitted).

[30] Declaration on the Rights of Indigenous Peoples, G.A. Res. 61/295, U.N. Doc. A/RES/61/295 (Sept. 13, 2007).

[31] United Nations Declaration on the Rights of Indigenous Peoples, Discussion Guide: Acknowledging Truths, Winter 2018 PPH Reading, www.unric.org/en/indigenous-people/27309-individual-vs-collective-rights (last visited Dec. 28, 2019) ("[F]or many indigenous peoples their identity as an individual is inseparably connected to the community to which that individual belongs. . . . [I]ndigenous peoples ask for protection of their collective rights as a group.").

[32] *See* William Fisher, *The Puzzle of Traditional Knowledge*, 67 DUKE L.J. 1511, 1511 (2018) ("In some settings, . . . group identity formation would be promoted by according indigenous groups more power to control or to benefit from uses of knowledge developed and sustained by their members."); Ruth L. Okediji, *A Tiered Approach to Rights in Traditional Knowledge*, 58 WASHBURN L.J. 271, 271 (2019) ("[Indigenous] groups have created institutions and systems distinctly associated with their lifestyles, producing an array of creative goods, processes, and systems of knowledge that serve to anchor group identity in established governance frameworks."); Madhavi Sunder, *The Invention of Traditional Knowledge*, 70 LAW & CONTEMP. PROBS. 97, 109 (2007).

own communities.[33] In the contemporary world, a major function of traditional knowledge is the preservation of a community's unique identity to maintain its members' dignity as an indigenous people. Wandjina spirit images, for example, are regarded as a form of traditional knowledge collectively created by Australia's aboriginal Worrorra people in honor of the Wandjina, their spiritual creators.[34] There has been criticism, however, that graffiti portraits and sculptural representations of the Wandjina distort them, causing the Worrorra to feel "offended and distressed"[35] about threats to their "traditions and beliefs."[36] Hence, Professor William Fisher cautions that "[c]ontroversies like [those surrounding] Wandjina Spirit Images make clear that traditional knowledge is sometimes central to the identities of indigenous groups and that unauthorized use of that knowledge by outsiders corrodes those identities."[37]

B THE COLLECTIVE RIGHT TO TECHNOLOGY

Drawing upon the theory of collective rights, I examine how and why the right to technology should be recognized and protected as a collective right. Technological benefits by nature serve the collective interest in societal or group freedom and dignity. The collective right to technology entitles people to enjoy the benefits of technological progress as members of a society or of a group within that society. At the same time, this right also entitles them to prevent technological

---

[33] *See* Fisher, *supra* note 32, at 1513 ("[T]raditional knowledge is defined as understanding or skill developed and preserved by the members of an indigenous group concerning either actual or potential socially beneficial uses of natural resources (such as plants, animals, or components thereof) or cultural practices (such as rituals, narratives, poems, images, designs, clothing, fabrics, music, or dances)."); Stephen R. Munzer & Kal Raustiala, *The Uneasy Case for Intellectual Property Rights in Traditional Knowledge*, 27 CARDOZO ARTS & ENT. L.J. 37, 38 (2009)("[Traditional knowledge] is the understanding or skill possessed by indigenous peoples pertaining to their culture and folklore, their technologies, and their use of native plants for medicinal purposes.").

[34] *See* Fisher, *supra* note 32, at 1526.

[35] *See* Fisher, *supra* note 32, at 1553.

[36] *Id.*

[37] *Id.*

progress from seriously jeopardizing their societal and group interests as members of a society or group. To realize legal entitlements in practice, the collective right to technology could be protected as two distinct rights: a societal right and a group right.

1 The Societal Right to Technology

The societal right to technology promotes the collective interest in public freedom derived from the enjoyment of technological progress. It protects society members' fair share of technological benefits in sectors ranging from public communication and health to transportation, all of which are crucial to the provision of the goods and institutions necessary to take part in civic life in public spaces.

Internet-related technologies epitomize collective interests in public communication derived from technological progress.[38] In *Reno v. American Civil Liberties Union*,[39] the US Supreme Court noted that the Internet as a whole serves as a "vast democratic forum[]."[40] The court further explained how users can enjoy the freedom facilitated by the Internet as a public forum to take part in civic life through communicative actions.[41] In *Packingham v. North Carolina*,[42] the Supreme Court further considered the Internet's role in safeguarding public freedom, making two important points. First, the court suggested that the Internet is as important a venue for free speech as public streets and

---

[38] *See* Ruth L. Okediji, *Does Intellectual Property Need Human Rights?*, 51 N.Y.U. J. INT'L L. & POL. 1, 36 (2018) (arguing that there is a human rights "obligation to facilitate access to technologies that are indispensable to civic and economic engagement, such as the internet.").

[39] Reno v. American Civil Liberties Union, 521 U.S. 844 (1997).

[40] *Id.* at 868.

[41] Regarding this point, the court explained as follows.

> [T]he Internet ... provides relatively unlimited, low-cost capacity for communication of all kinds. Th[e] dynamic, multifaceted category of communication includes not only traditional print and news services, but also audio, video, and still images, as well as interactive, real-time dialogue. Through the use of chat rooms, any person with a phone line can become a town crier with a voice that resonates farther than it could from any soapbox. Through the use of Web pages, mail exploders, and newsgroups, the same individual can become a pamphleteer.

> *Id.* at 870.

[42] 137 S. Ct. 1730 (2017).

parks, the traditional public forums that merit the full spectrum of free speech protection.[43] Second, the court demonstrated that social media, as a pervasive part of the Internet, has become a vehicle for socially beneficial communicative activities:

> Social media offers "relatively unlimited, low-cost capacity for communication of all kinds." On Facebook, for example, users can debate religion and politics with their friends and neighbors or share vacation photos. On LinkedIn, users can look for work, advertise for employees, or review tips on entrepreneurship. And on Twitter, users can petition their elected representatives and otherwise engage with them in a direct manner. Indeed, Governors in all 50 States and almost every Member of Congress have set up accounts for this purpose. In short, social media users employ these websites to engage in a wide array of protected First Amendment activity on topics "as diverse as human thought."[44]

This opinion highlights the significant role that social media technologies play in promoting citizens' public freedom of communicative action.[45] They have enabled many more people than ever before to express their views and exchange information publicly. They have also opened up new avenues for the dissemination of views and the attainment of information, thereby increasing the diversity of communicative action in the public sphere.

At the same time, the societal right to technology also confers a right to prevent technologies from being used to harm the collective interest in public dignity. Take human genome editing as an example. The technology of heritable human genome editing has matured to the extent that it has clinical application in human reproduction. However, worldwide

---

[43] *See id.* at 1735 ("While in the past there may have been difficulty in identifying the most important places (in a spatial sense) for the exchange of views, today the answer is clear. It is cyberspace – the 'vast democratic forums of the Internet' in general, and social media in particular.") (quoting Reno v. American Civil Liberties Union, 521 U.S. 844, 868 (1997)).

[44] *Id.* at 1735–36 (quoting Reno v. American Civil Liberties Union, 521 U.S. 844, 870 (1997)).

[45] Lawrence Byard Solum, *Freedom of Communicative Action: A Theory of the First Amendment Freedom of Speech*, 83 Nw. U.L. Rev. 54, 106 (1989) ("Any society that wants to enable rational agreement through public discourse must provide for a right to free speech which allows all citizens the right to participate in communication on equal terms without the fear of compulsion.").

public concern was sparked when a Chinese scientist announced the birth of genome-edited twin girls in November 2018.[46] Human genome editing for eugenic purposes could serve to degrade the dignity of society by causing disrespect for differences among individuals and by worsening inequality by widening the gap between those with access to human genome editing and those without.[47] According to the International Bioethics Committee, "interventions on the human genome should be admitted only for preventive, diagnostic or therapeutic reasons and without enacting modifications for descendants," as "[t]he alternative would be to jeopardize the inherent and therefore equal dignity of all human beings and renew eugenics, disguised as the fulfilment of the wish for a better, *improved* life."[48]

2 The Group Right to Technology

The group right to technology protects the collective interest in group freedom by allowing group members to take advantage of technological benefits.[49] Take access to HIV medicines as an example. Patent protection of such medicines has rendered them too expensive for low-income HIV sufferers.[50] The World Health Organization reported that, in 2018 alone, an estimated 470,000 people in Africa died of HIV/AIDS.[51] A lack of access to HIV medicines, owing to their prohibitive cost, was a major factor in this appalling number of deaths. It is thus imperative that low-income people infected with HIV be viewed as a group who have a collective interest in HIV-related pharmaceutical

---

[46] David Cyranoski & Heidi Ledford, *Genome-Edited Baby Claim Provokes International Outcry*, NATURE (Nov. 26, 2018), www.nature.com/articles/d41586-018-07545-0.

[47] Seppe Segers & Heidi Mertes, *Does Human Genome Editing Reinforce or Violate Human Dignity?*, 34 BIOETHICS 1, 5–6 (2019).

[48] UN Int'l Bioethics Committee, *Report of the IBC on Updating Its Reflection on the Human Genome and Human Rights*, at 26, U.N. DOC. SHS/YES/IBC-22/15/2 REV.2 (2015), https://unesdoc.unesco.org/ark:/48223/pf0000233258.

[49] *See* GEORGE W. RAINBOLT, THE CONCEPT OF RIGHTS 206 (Franciso Laporta et al. eds., 2006) ("Many group rights seem to be rights to participatory goods."); Denise Réaume, *Individuals, Groups, and Rights to Public Goods*, 38 U. TORONTO L.J. 1, 1 (1988) (arguing that "any rights to participatory goods must be held by groups rather than individuals").

[50] *See* William W. Fisher & Talha Syed, *Global Justice in Healthcare: Developing Drugs for the Developing World*, 40 U.C. DAVIS L. REV. 581, 646 (2006).

[51] WORLD HEALTH ORGANIZATION, *Number of Deaths Due to HIV/AIDS*, www.who.int/gho/hiv/epidemic_status/deaths_text/en (last visited Nov. 28, 2019).

technologies. Otherwise, the deterioration in group members' health will degrade their ability to take part in civic life and ultimately deprive them of the freedom to live. In such circumstances, it does not make sense to focus on the harm to HIV-infected persons that causes each to suffer individually. The group rights approach instead recognizes a collective interest in HIV medicines and related pharmaceutical technologies, and thus lends stronger moral support to an institutional resolution to the HIV-related public health crisis.

The group right to technology also entitles group members to prevent prejudice to the dignity of the groups to which they belong. Many new technological developments pose serious threats of prejudice that ultimately risk degrading the dignity of all members of the group in question. For example, the use of algorithms in facial recognition technology has been found to introduce systematic bias in classifying race-based information.[52] Current facial recognition systems misidentify dark-skinned people at a much higher rate than light-skinned people because the systems are often trained on predominantly white faces, leading to many false positives.[53] For instance, Google Photos has misclassified black people as gorillas,[54] and Amazon Rekognition falsely identified many Congressmen of color as crime suspects.[55] Similarly, a black man was barred from operating as an Uber driver because the facial recognition software on the Uber app did not recognize him.[56] If such deleterious effects are not kept at bay,

[52] Ali Breland, How White Engineers Built Racist Code – and Why It's Dangerous for Black People, GUARDIAN (Dec. 4, 2017); Fabio Bacchini & Ludovica Lorusso, *Race, Again: How Face Recognition Technology Reinforces Racial Discrimination*, 17 J. INFO., COMM. & ETHICS IN SOC'Y. 321 (2019).

[53] Tom Simonite, *The Best Algorithms Struggle to Recognize Black Faces Equally*, WIRED (July 22, 2019), https://bit.ly/3B1z3Cq; *see also* ANDREW GUTHRIE FERGUSON, THE RISE OF BIG DATA POLICING: SURVEILLANCE, RACE, AND THE FUTURE OF LAW ENFORCEMENT 92–95 (2017).

[54] Maggie Zhang, *Google Photos Tags Two African-Americans As Gorillas Through Facial Recognition Software*, FORBES (July 1, 2015); Tom Simonite, *When It Comes to Gorillas, Google Photos Remains Blind*, WIRED (Jan. 11, 2018).

[55] Natasha Singer, *Amazon's Facial Recognition Wrongly Identifies 28 Lawmakers, A.C.L.U. Says*, N.Y. TIMES (July 26, 2018); Jacob Snow, *Amazon's Face Recognition Falsely Matched 28 Members of Congress with Mugshots*, ACLU (July 26, 2018); Sasha Ingber, *Facial Recognition Software Wrongly Identifies 28 Lawmakers As Crime Suspects*, NPR (July 26, 2018).

[56] Olivia Rudgard, *Uber Faces Racism Claim Over Facial Recognition Software*, TELEGRAPH (Apr. 23, 2019).

facial recognition technology may profoundly harm group-based interests in racial equality.

3 Convergence of the Collective Right to Technology with Domestic Law

Treating the human right to technology as a collective right makes possible in theory and in practice its transformation into a civil liberty that the judiciary can protect.[57] The societal and group interests in technological benefits identified in Section 2 align with and support those of civil rights that are protected by domestic courts, from freedom of information to racial equality.[58] If the collective right to technology were protected as a civil liberty, then the public would be afforded recourse to domestic courts to protect the collective interest in enjoying the benefits of technological progress.

The transformation of the collective right to technology into a domestic civil liberty would serve three major functions. First, it would allow courts to rely on the social justice mandate of the collective rights approach to recognize and protect the collective right to technology. Courts could decide that awaiting a lengthy legislative process to dispense any given benefit of the right could result in injustice and irreparable harm to the citizenry's collective interests. With respect to the protection of rights that are not expressly enumerated by law, the US Supreme Court has forcefully stated that

> [t]he nature of injustice is that we may not always see it in our own times. The generations that wrote and ratified the Bill of Rights and the Fourteenth Amendment did not presume to know the extent of freedom in all of its dimensions, and so they entrusted to future generations a charter protecting the right of all persons to enjoy

---

[57] *See* Okediji, *Does Intellectual Property Need Human Rights?*, *supra* note 38, at 49 ("Beyond the multilateral treaty platform, national and regional courts in developed countries rely heavily on human rights ideals when addressing IP disputes."). For a discussion of how to transform human rights into civil rights domestically, see BETH A. SIMMONS, MOBILIZING FOR HUMAN RIGHTS: INTERNATIONAL LAW IN DOMESTIC POLITICS 159–201 (2009).

[58] Dominique Harrison, *Civil Rights Violations in the Face of Technological Change*, ASPEN INSTITUTE (Apr. 22, 2019), https://bit.ly/3B3Em46 ("Civil rights by definition are sets of guaranteed privileges that include equal treatment, equal opportunity, and the ability to be free from discrimination.").

liberty as we learn its meaning. When new insight reveals discord between the Constitution's central protections and a received legal stricture, a claim to liberty must be addressed [by courts].[59]

This statement presents the case for judicial intervention if the legislature fails to protect liberties. Justice empowers domestic courts to protect liberties when statutes provide no protection.[60] So too does international law. As the UN Committee on Economic, Social and Cultural Rights has stated, "[a]t minimum, the national and local judiciaries of States parties must consider international human rights laws such as the [ICESCR] an interpretative aid to domestic law and ensure that domestic law is interpreted and applied in a manner consistent with the provisions of international human rights instruments ratified by the State."[61] Thus, to promote justice, domestic courts in states that have signed the ICESCR may draw on the relevant ICESCR provisions to interpret whether their domestic laws already provide a legal basis for protecting civil liberties such as the right to technology.[62]

Second, treating the collective right to technology as a civil liberty would encourage citizens to take legal action to defend their interest in enjoying the benefits of technological progress. They would not need to await legislative action enacting the right statutorily, but rather could invoke it when seeking legal protection from the courts when their

---

[59] Obergefell v. Hodges 135 S. Ct. 2584, 2598 (2015).

[60] Nat'l Mut. Ins. Co. v. Tidewater Transfer Co., 337 U.S. 582, 646 (1949) (Frankfurter, J., dissenting) ("Great concepts like ... 'liberty' ... were purposely left to gather meaning from experience. For they relate to the whole domain of social and economic fact, and the statesmen who founded this Nation knew too well that only a stagnant society remains unchanged.").

[61] The UN Committee on Economic, Social and Cultural Rights, Fact Sheet No.16 (Rev.1), ¶ 5 www.ohchr.org/Documents/Publications/FactSheet16rev.1en.pdf.

[62] See, e.g., KATHARINE G. YOUNG, CONSTITUTING ECONOMIC AND SOCIAL RIGHTS 133 (2012) ("In enforcing the duty to respect, protect, or promote economic and social rights – indeed, in being a duty-holder themselves – courts may be called upon to decide on the nature of such rights, their scope, and the obligations that flow from them."); DEPARTMENT OF JUSTICE OF THE HKSAR, APPLICATION OF THE INTERNATIONAL COVENANT ON ECONOMIC, SOCIAL AND CULTURAL RIGHTS IN HONG KONG 10, www.doj.gov.hk/eng/public/basiclaw/basic17_3.pdf ("Although the ICESCR has not been directly incorporated into domestic law, the [Government of the Hong Kong Special Administrative Region] has an international obligation to respect, protect and fulfil the rights recognized in the Covenant. Our courts may use the ICESCR provisions ... as an aid in interpreting local laws and relevant provisions of the Basic Law.").

interests are unduly harmed. As von Jhering has aptly suggested, rights
"suppose a continual readiness" by persons "to assert [them] and
defend [them]."[63] The more often that citizens assert their right to
technology, the more often the courts will deal with disputes involving
that civil liberty, thus allowing them to properly delineate its contours.
Therefore, treating the right to technology as a civil liberty would
gradually address its obscure nature and scope and place people in
a better position to assert the right more wisely in the future. These
positive developments would gradually create a dynamic legal culture
that promotes the sharing and enjoyment of the benefits of technological progress.

Third, a collective right to technology would also encourage
governments to protect that right as a positive liberty, which
would require them to take such proactive measures as providing
people with the resources necessary to exercise the right. Scholars
from scientific and engineering disciplines hope that in fulfilling
their responsibility to protect the right to technology, governments
will make it a priority to "[i]ncrease funding for scientific infrastructure and research, [p]rovide adequate science education to the
general public, [p]romote a positive view of science and scientists
among the public, [e]nsure open access to scientific information,
[and p]romote and protect academic freedom."[64]

Equipped with the right to technology, citizens could critically
examine whether their government has fulfilled its responsibilities in
this regard, and then decide whether they should launch lawsuits or
take part in civic action such as media campaigns and public shaming
to call the government to account for its failures. In 2001, the Supreme
Court of Venezuela (Bolivarian Republic of) ruled that the Venezuelan
Institute for Social Security violated its obligations to protect the right
to technology because it failed to ensure a regular and consistent supply
of medicines for HIV-positive patients.[65]

---

[63] RUDOLF VON JHERING, THE STRUGGLE FOR LAW 1 (1915).

[64] See J. M. Wyndham et al., Giving Meaning to the Right to Science: A Global and
Multidisciplinary Approach 16 (report prepared under the auspices of the AAAS
Scientific Responsibility, Human Rights and Law Program and the AAAS Science and
Human Rights Coalition, 2017).

[65] See Manisuli Ssenyonjo, ECONOMIC, SOCIAL AND CULTURAL RIGHTS IN INTERNATIONAL LAW
639–40 (2016).

C APPLYING THE COLLECTIVE RIGHTS APPROACH

To protect the collective right to technology as a civil liberty, I suggest that the judicial application of IP laws presents an opportunity to determine whether judicial protection should be extended to the right to technology. When adjudicating IP lawsuits involving the distribution of technological benefits, courts can attempt to interpret the nature and scope of the relevant IP principles and rules to determine whether they can provide the legal basis for protecting the right to technology. In this context, a court may first decide whether an IP lawsuit directly affects the equitable distribution of technological benefits and is thus inextricably linked with enjoyment of the right to technology. If so, it may further redefine the limitations on IP rights, such as copyright fair use, on the basis of a collective user right to technological benefits.

In this section, I consider how courts could apply the right to technology to deal with cases involving the invocation of limitations on IP rights such as fair use and the interpretation of the IP Clause in the US Constitution. Drawing on judicial rulings on the Google Books Library Project (Google Library), I first discuss how courts could recognize and protect the right to technology through their interpretation of existing limitations on IP rights. I also consider how courts can address potential conflicts between protection of this collective right and of individual IP rights. I then propose that courts could also rely upon the right to technology to reinterpret the nature and scope of the IP Clause in the US Constitution.

1 Identifying Technological Benefits

The emergence of scanning and data-processing technologies, together with the invention of the Internet, has paved the way for digital libraries that offer unprecedented access to a vast body of knowledge, undoubtedly facilitating engagement in educational and free speech activities.[66] Technically, digital libraries allow users to read, borrow, search, copy,

---

[66] MAURIZIO BORGHI & STAVROULA KARAPAPA, COPYRIGHT AND MASS DIGITIZATION 10 (2013).

paste, highlight, and comment in ways that traditional libraries cannot.[67] In the age of big data and artificial intelligence, digital libraries appear more desirable than ever,[68] promoting speedy information searches and knowledge-sharing for a diverse array of human activities and ambitions.

Amid copyright disputes on the legality of digital libraries, academics and policymakers have considered how digital libraries can promote the rights to education[69] and freedom of expression.[70] Easier access to books undoubtedly facilitates the dissemination of knowledge to individual citizens to allow them to engage in educational and free speech activities. However, copyright disputes over digital libraries are, to a large extent, legal cases dealing with how to share the benefits of advances in scanning and data-mining technologies. The resulting judicial rulings, as demonstrated by those concerning Google Library, determine to what extent the benefits of digital libraries using those technologies can be distributed in the public interest.

Hailed as "the most significant humanities project of our time,"[71] Google Library has scanned over twenty million books, accounting for approximately one-seventh of all books published since the invention of the printing press.[72] In 2005, the Authors Guild challenged the legality of Google Library before the Southern District Court of New York, alleging that Google had committed copyright infringement by scanning copyrighted books and displaying them publicly without the permission of the copyright owners.[73] Subsequent rulings

---

[67] *See* Karen Calhoun, Exploring Digital Libraries: Foundations, Practice, Prospects 18 (2014).

[68] *See* Jian Wu et al., *CiteSeerX: AI in a Digital Library Search Engine, in* Proceedings of the Twenty-Sixth Annual Conference on Innovative Applications of Artificial Intelligence (2014); Catherine Nicole Coleman, *Artificial Intelligence and the Library of the Future, Revisited,* Stanford Libraries (Nov. 3, 2017), https://stanford.io/3FcEvET.

[69] *See* Susan Perry & Claudia Roda, Human Rights and Digital Technology: Digital Tightrope 163–64 (2017).

[70] *See* Molly Land, *Toward an International Law of the Internet,* 54 Harv. Int'l L.J. 393, 420 (2013).

[71] James Somers, *Torching the Modern-Day Library of Alexandria,* Atlantic (Apr. 20, 2017); Tim Wu, *What Ever Happened to Google Books?,* New Yorker (Sept. 11, 2015).

[72] Jon Orwant, *Ngram Viewer 2.0,* Google Research Blog (Oct. 18, 2012), https://research .googleblog.com/2012/10/ngram-viewer-20.html.

[73] Paul Aiken, *Authors Guild Sues Google, Citing "Massive Copyright Infringement",* Authors Guild (Sept. 20, 2005), https://bit.ly/3mfVCgD (asserting that Google's "unauthorized scanning and copying of books through its Google Library program is a 'plain and brazen

by the US courts have examined the technological benefits that Google Library offers to the public. In *Authors Guild, Inc. v. Google, Inc.*,[74] the District Court took pains to examine the digital technologies that Google Library applies and their potential public benefits:

> In scanning books for its Library Project, including in-copyright books, Google uses optical character recognition technology to generate machine-readable text, compiling a digital copy of each book. Google analyzes each scan and creates an overall index of all scanned books. The index links each word or phrase appearing in each book with all of the locations in all of the books in which that word or phrase is found. The index allows a search for a particular word or phrase to return a result that includes the most relevant books in which the word or phrase is found. Because the full texts of books are digitized, a user can search the full text of all the books in the Google Books corpus.[75]

This discussion captures the three major digital technologies that Google Books employs: optical character recognition, data mining, and data searching.[76] It also considers how they benefit the public by creating new ways of disseminating information and knowledge. Building upon the above findings of the District Court, the Court of Appeals for the Second Circuit compared the Google Books Library Project with the HathiTrust Digital Library and considered the extent to which the former makes use of more advanced digital technologies. For example, the Second Court pointed out that both libraries offer search functions to users, but Google Books' search function is more technologically advanced because it displays snippet views of specific content relevant to search words.[77]

---

violation of copyright law'" because "[i]t's not up to Google or anyone other than the authors, the rightful owners of these copyrights, to decide whether and how their works will be copied").

[74] Authors Guild, Inc. v. Google Inc., 954 F. Supp. 2d 282, 286 (S.D.N.Y. 2013).

[75] *Id.* at 286 (citations omitted).

[76] *Id.* at 286–87.

[77] Authors Guild, Inc. v. Google, Inc., 804 F.3d 202, 217 (2nd Cir. 2015) ("HathiTrust did not 'display to the user any text from the underlying copyrighted work,' ... whereas Google Books provides the searcher with snippets containing the word that is the subject of the search.").

2 Protecting the Right to Technology through the Fair Use Doctrine

Upon identifying the centrality of technological benefits to an IP case, courts could further consider how limitations on IP rights such as the copyright fair use doctrine can be invoked to protect the right to technology. Typically, a conventional "fair use" dispute is concerned with whether a particular user, namely, the defendant, is legally allowed to use a particular work belonging to the plaintiff.[78] For example, in *Shepard Fairey v. Associated Press*,[79] the central legal issue was whether or not the creator of the 2008 "Hope" poster had made fair use of a portrait of President Obama.[80]

By contrast, IP disputes dealing with the right to technology such as the Google Library cases interrogate whether the provision of new technologies for accessing and using copyrighted works should be privileged as fair use. In other words, they grapple with the question of whether the fair use doctrine should legalize the public benefits of new digital technologies in providing new technological means of accessing and using copyrighted works.[81] Notably, the public can still access the information and knowledge contained in books that are captured in Google Library by purchasing them or visiting other libraries that house them. With the relevant digital technologies, Google Library simply makes such access easier and cross-referencing content more convenient.

Both the District Court and Second Circuit ruled that Google's application of digital technologies to books constitutes "fair use" under Section 107 of the US Copyright Act.[82] Fair use is a limitation on copyright, allowing the public to use a copyrighted work without

---

[78] *See* Sun, *Fair Use as a Collective User Right*, *supra* note 6, at 146.

[79] No. 09-01123 (S.D.N.Y. 2010).

[80] *See generally* JULIE COHEN, CONFIGURING THE NETWORKED SELF: LAW, CODE, AND THE PLAY OF EVERYDAY PRACTICE 80–106 (2012); William W. Fisher III et al., *Reflections on the Hope Poster Case*, 25 HARV. J.L. & TECH. 243, 256–57 (2012); William Landes, *Copyright, Borrowed Images, and Appropriation Art: An Economic Approach*, 9 GEO. MASON L. REV. 1, 2 (2000).

[81] *See* Edward Lee, *Technological Fair Use*, 83 S. CAL. L. REV. 797, 798 (2010) (arguing that "technological fair uses" deal with "the legality of new technologies that can have a profound impact on innovation and the growth of the U.S. economy, as well as on people's daily lives").

[82] 17 U.S.C. § 107 (2019).

obtaining permission from, or paying royalties to, the rights holder.[83] The Google Library rulings provide two important lessons on how the fair use doctrine could be applied to protect the collective right to technology.

First, courts could invoke the doctrine to determine whether the benefits of new technologies for disseminating copyrighted works should be legally distributed in the public interest. The District Court and Second Circuit relied upon the fair use concept of "transformative" use to determine whether Google had applied new technologies to scan and display works in the public interest. By adding a "new expression, meaning, or message"[84] or function[85] to an original work, transformative use communicates a new work or the original to the public with benefits that the copyright holder of the original work did not intend to offer.[86] Transformative uses are permitted by US copyright law because they ultimately "enrich public knowledge."[87] The immediate beneficiary of a transformative use is the party who uses a work for a transformative purpose, as Google Library does. By making transformative use of copyrighted books, Google received the immediate benefits from the creation of the library. Nevertheless, the ultimate beneficiaries of the transformative use are members of the public. When assessing the search function afforded by Google Library, the Second Circuit pointed out the public benefits that accrued from Google's transformative use:

> As with HathiTrust (and iParadigms), the purpose of Google's copying of the original copyrighted books is to make available significant information about those books, permitting a searcher to identify those that contain a word or term of interest, as well as those that do not include reference to it. In addition, through the Ngrams tool, Google allows readers to learn the frequency of usage of selected words in the aggregate corpus of published books in

---

[83] *Id.*

[84] Campbell v. Acuff-Rose Music, Inc., 510 U.S. 569, 579 (1994).

[85] Kelly v. Arriba Soft Corp., 336 F.3d 811, 819 (9th Cir. 2003).

[86] Authors' Guild, Inc. v. Google Inc., 804 F.3d 202 (2015) ("[T]ransformative uses tend to favor a fair use finding because a transformative use is one that communicates something new and different from the original or expands its utility, thus serving copyright's overall objective of contributing to public knowledge").

[87] *Id.* at 214 (quoting Campbell v. Acuff-Rose Music, Inc., 510 U.S. 569, 591 (1994)).

different historical periods. We have no doubt that the purpose of this copying is the sort of transformative purpose described in *Campbell* as strongly favoring satisfaction of the first factor.[88]

Thus, the purpose of Google's reproduction of copyrighted books, according to the Second Circuit, was to add an information search function to those books, a function that the books' copyright holders had not offered. The search function ultimately benefits readers, who are members of the public, enabling them to efficiently locate particular information contained within a book, as well as information on the frequency of particular word usage.

The snippet view function of Google Books also helped the Second Circuit to find that Google had developed a transformative use for the original copyrighted material. This is because snippet view "adds importantly to the highly transformative purpose of identifying books of interest to the searcher."[89] The Second Circuit shows that the ultimate beneficiaries of the snippet view function are members of the public in their capacity as information searchers. That function thus serves the public interest in evaluating the content surrounding searched words, providing users with a better understanding of search results extracted from a vast pool of information.

Second, the other lesson to be gleaned from the Google Library rulings is that courts can redefine fair use as a collective right to technology enjoyed by users of copyrighted works. Conventionally, most US courts have treated fair use as an affirmative defense against allegations of copyright infringement.[90] Such a fixed characterization of fair use has encouraged legislators and judges to balance the individual interests of each owner and user of a copyrighted work, leading to a wide range of harms to the public interest in the free flow of information and knowledge.[91]

---

[88] *Id.* at 217.

[89] *Id.* at 218.

[90] *See* Pamela Samuelson, *Unbundling Fair Uses*, 77 FORDHAM L. REV. 2537, 2539 (2009) ("Fair use has been invoked as a defense to claims of copyright infringement in a wide array of cases over the past thirty years."); *See generally* Sun, *Fair Use as a Collective User Right, supra* note 6, at 134–42 (examining how fair use has been treated as an affirmative defense judicially).

[91] *See* Sun, *Fair Use as a Collective User Right, supra* note 6, at 151–63.

In several isolated cases, the US courts have redefined fair use as a right for users under US copyright law. In *Suntrust Bank v. Houghton Mifflin Co.*, for example, the US Court of Appeals for the Eleventh Circuit rejected the characterization of fair use as an affirmative defense, positing that it "should be considered an affirmative *right*."[92] The US Court of Appeals for the Second Circuit also made an attempt to redefine fair use as a right in *NXIVM Corp. v. Ross Institute* by relying on the Copyright Clause of the US Constitution.[93]

Other cases support the redefinition of fair use as a user right. In *CCH Canadian Ltd. v. Law Soc'y of Upper Canada*,[94] for example, the Supreme Court of Canada ruled that the fair dealing doctrine under the Canadian Copyright Act should be redefined as "a user's right."[95] To achieve balanced protection of the rights of both the copyright holder and user, fair dealing "must not be interpreted restrictively."[96] Later, in *Soc'y of Composers, Authors and Music Publishers of Canada v. Bell Canada*,[97] the Canadian Supreme Court reiterated its liberal understanding of fair dealing, stating that "users' rights are an essential part of furthering the public interest objectives of the [Canadian] Copyright Act."[98]

None of these courts, however, has determined the nature of a user's right. Should it be protected as the constitutional right to free speech under the US Constitution? Or as the right to education under other relevant US law? The courts have also failed to elaborate

[92] SunTrust Bank v. Houghton Mifflin Co., 268 F.3d 1257, 1260 n.3 (11th Cir. 2001) (internal citations omitted). In this footnote, the court cited a footnote in Bateman v. Mnemonics, Inc., which proposed fair use as a right: "Although the traditional approach is to view 'fair use' as an affirmative defense, this writer, speaking only for himself, is of the opinion that it is better viewed as a right granted by the Copyright Act of 1976." 79 F.3d 1532, 1542 n.22 (11th Cir. 1996).

[93] 364 F.3d 471, 485 (2d Cir. 2004) (Jacobs, J., concurring) ("Fair use is not a doctrine that exists by sufferance, or that is earned by good works and clean morals; it is a right – codified in § 107 and recognized since shortly after the Statute of Anne – that is "necessary to fulfill copyright's very purpose, [t]o promote the Progress of science and the useful arts.").

[94] [2004] 1 S.C.R. 399, ¶ 48 (Can.).

[95] *Id.*

[96] *Id.*

[97] [2012] S.C.R 326, ¶ 11 (Can.).

[98] *Id.* ¶ 27.

on how the user right concept should be invoked in fair use or fair dealing cases.

Nevertheless, as the Google Library rulings demonstrate, courts can redefine fair use as a collective user right to technology in cases that involve the use of copyrighted works to distribute technological benefits. In this sense, fair use is a civil liberty that allows the public to collectively enjoy the benefits of new technologies by enhancing access to and the use of copyrighted works.

First, in the Google Library cases, the courts examined users' group and collective interests in improved access to knowledge with the aid of digital technologies. Pointing out that the collective interests in Google Library "are many,"[99] the District Court specifically identified five uses of the library that serve the public interest: providing "a new and efficient way for readers and researchers to find books";[100] promoting "a type of research referred to as 'data mining' or 'text mining'";[101] expanding "access to books";[102] preserving old books, including out-of-print ones;[103] and "helping readers and researchers identify books."[104] The court also explained how these collective interests can be enjoyed by different groups of users, such as librarians, researchers, students,[105] teachers, and blind people.[106]

Second, the courts also identified how Google's digital technologies protect societal interests. After duly applying the four-factor test for fair use, the District Court noted that the protection of larger societal interests by Google's digital technologies can dictate the outcome of fair use analysis: "Google Books provides significant *public benefits*. It advances the progress of the arts and sciences . . . . It preserves books, in particular out-of-print and old books that have been forgotten in the bowels of libraries, and it gives them new life. . . . . Indeed, *all society benefits*."[107]

---

[99] Authors Guild, Inc. v. Google, Inc., 954 F. Supp. 2d 282, 287 (S.D.N.Y. 2013).
[100] *Id.*
[101] *Id.*
[102] *Id.* at 288.
[103] *Id.*
[104] *Id.*
[105] *Id.* at 287 (citations omitted).
[106] Authors Guild, 954 F. Supp. 2d, at 293.
[107] *Id.*

Similarly, the Second Circuit concluded that the case in question should first be decided by careful scrutiny of the four fair use factors and then by the application of societal interest considerations:

> [C]onsidering the four fair use factors in light of the goals of copyright, we conclude that Google's making of a complete digital copy of Plaintiffs' works for the purpose of providing the public with its search and snippet view functions (at least as snippet view is presently designed) is a fair use and does not infringe Plaintiffs' copyrights in their books.[108]

Both opinions aggregated the benefits provided by Google's digital technologies as societal interests.[109] In short, they found that Google's advances in digital technologies render its digital library an ideal vehicle for the enhanced sharing of knowledge.[110]

Hence, the Google Library rulings demonstrate that by redefining the nature of fair use as a civil liberty to exercise the collective right to technology, courts could resolve similar cases about the distribution of technological benefits associated with copyrighted works. They could also apply this collective rights approach to further redefine other limitations on IP rights, such as the "experimental use" defense and "exhaustion of rights" doctrine.

In the Google Library rulings, the courts identified and protected public interests as group interests and societal interests. In following these analytical tactics, the courts could determine whether any group of people or all members of a society have benefited from unauthorized uses of copyrighted works or patents under a related limitation on IP rights.[111] Subsequently, they could consider whether those collective

---

[108] Authors Guild, 804 F.3d at 225.

[109] *See* Douglas Lichtman, *Google Book Search in the Gridlock Economy*, 53 ARIZ. L. REV. 131, 142 (2011); Hannibal Travis, *Building Universal Digital Libraries: An Agenda for Copyright Reform*, 33 PEPP. L. REV. 761, 765–66 (2006).

[110] *See* Pamela Samuelson, *The Google Book Settlement as Copyright Reform*, 2011 WIS. L. REV. 479, 562 (2011) (emphasizing that "the accumulated knowledge of human-kind contained in millions of books from major research library collections can be made widely available to future generations through digitally networked environments.").

[111] *See, e.g.*, Haochen Sun, *Copyright Law as an Engine of Public Interest Protection*, 16 NW. J. TECH. & INTELL. PROP. 123, 171 (2019) (arguing that courts can protect the public interest proactively).

interests merit protection by applying factor-based analysis, such as a consideration of the four fair use factors.

3 Potential Conflicts between Collective Rights and Individual Rights

Collective rights have been accused of unduly jeopardizing individual rights. Similarly, the criticism could also be made that applying the right to technology to IP disputes could easily infringe upon individual interests in IP rights. Were that to occur, the argument goes, IP rights holders would end up sacrificing too much financially and the policy balance struck by IP law would be completely upended. For example, the US Supreme Court has cautioned the following. "Any copyright infringer may claim to benefit the public by increasing public access to the copyrighted work. But . . . we see no warrant for judicially imposing, a 'compulsory license' permitting unfettered access."[112]

The single-minded prioritization of collective interests would render IP as an individual right meaningless. It would deprive IP rights holders of their economic interests in circulating their creations in the marketplace, ultimately deterring them from creating and disseminating new works,[113] which would in turn impair collective interests. With respect to patent policy, Professor Rochelle Dreyfuss has emphasized that the right to technology "must not be interpreted in a manner that hinders the motivation or capacity to invent discoveries that society will eventually desperately need, or interfere with the establishment of industries that will, in the long run, promote social welfare."[114]

In response to these valid concerns, I argue that application of the collective right to technology would actually continue to require courts to seriously consider IP rights holders' individual interests in merchandizing their creations in the marketplace. They would still need to remain vigilant in safeguarding these individuals' economic interests.

---

[112] Harper & Row, Publishers, Inc. v. Nation Enterprises, 471 U.S. 539, 569 (1985).

[113] *See* Authors Guild, Inc. v. HathiTrust, 755 F.3d at 95 ("A fair use must not excessively damage the market for the original by providing the public with a substitute for that original work.").

[114] Rochelle Cooper Dreyfuss, *Patents and Human Rights: The Paradox Re-Examined* 65, *in* INTELLECTUAL PROPERTY AND ACCESS TO SCIENCE AND CULTURE: CONFLICT OR CONVERGENCE? 65 (Christophe Geiger ed., 2016).

Although the collective right to technology situates the overall fair use analysis within the context of the public interest at large, it still requires courts to follow the traditional judicial practice of applying fair use factors in a holistic and balanced manner.[115] The fourth factor under the fair use doctrine mandates that courts consider "the effect of the use upon the potential market for or value of the copyrighted work."[116] When weighing the fair use factors, especially the first factor, which examines "the purpose and character of the use"[117] in the public interest, courts should take full account of the fourth factor, guarding against uses that would cause substantial economic harm to the copyright holder concerned.

The collective right to technology by no means empowers the first fair use factor to override the other factors. Instead, the right still upholds the fourth fair use factor to guard against a substantively harmful disruption of the IP rights holder's market by maintaining the fourth factor on an equal footing with other fair use factors. With these built-in safeguards, the application of the right to technology could serve as a vehicle for courts to achieve the proper application of all four fair use factors by permitting them to serve as checks on one another.

4 Interpreting the IP Clause

Courts should also rely on the collective right to technology when they re-interpret the nature and scope of the IP Clause of the US Constitution, which empowers Congress "[t]o promote the Progress of Science and useful Arts, by securing for limited Times to Authors and Inventors the exclusive Right to their respective Writings and Discoveries."[118] This

---

[115] Cambridge Univ. Press v. Patton, 769 F.3d 1232, 1283 (11th Cir. 2014) (ruling that Section 107 requires "a holistic analysis which carefully balance[s] the four factors"); Peter Letterese & Assocs., Inc. v. World Inst. of Scientology Enters., 533 F.3d 1287, 1308 (11th Cir. 2008) ("The fair use doctrine is an 'equitable rule of reason'; neither the examples of possible fair uses nor the four statutory factors are to be considered exclusive.") (quoting Stewart v. Abend, 495 U.S. 207, 236–37 (1990)).

[116] 17 U.S.C. § 107 (2019).

[117] Id.

[118] U.S. CONST. art. I, § 8, cl. 8.

clause defines the objective of the legislative power of Congress and prescribes means to achieve that objective in several ways. First, the wording of the clause shows that it is intended to promote technological progress and knowledge growth.[119] It is commonly understood that "Science" is not confined to scientific inquiry but encompasses all knowledge and that "useful Arts" does not refer to artistic endeavors, but rather to fields related to technology or the technological arts.[120]

Second, the IP Clause capitalizes on the legal protection of copyrights and patents as a means to promote technological progress and knowledge growth. Under the clause, Congress's enactment of copyright and patent laws functions to financially incentivize authors and inventors to create new works and inventions and to further make them available to the public in the marketplace. While authors and inventors receive monetary rewards for doing so, the public benefits from the new knowledge embodied in works and technological solutions presented by inventions.[121]

Orthodoxically, the US courts interpret the nature and scope of the IP Clause in light of utilitarianism-based policy, under which IP rights protection serves government economic policy by optimizing technological progress and knowledge growth. The more new inventions and works created, the better the promotion of technological progress and knowledge growth. Central to the realization of this policy goal is the

---

[119] *See* Barton Beebe, Bleistein, *The Problem of Aesthetic Progress, and the Making of American Copyright Law*, 117 COLUM. L. REV. 319, 341 (2017) (arguing that in "the late eighteenth century, the realms of 'Science and useful Arts' had developed well-accepted, positive, and seemingly objective standards of judgment, standards that Congress and courts could rely on to limit the reach of monopoly rights to those 'Writings' and 'Discoveries' the creation of which did indeed promote scientific and technological progress").

[120] *See* Bilski v. Kappos, 561 U.S. 593, 634 (2010) (ruling that "the term 'useful arts' was widely understood to encompass the fields that we would now describe as relating to technology or 'technological arts'").

[121] *See* Sony Corp. of Am. v. Universal City Studios, Inc., 464 U.S. 417, 429 (1984). "The monopoly privileges that Congress may authorize are neither unlimited nor primarily designed to provide a special private benefit. Rather, the limited grant is a means by which an important public purpose may be achieved. It is intended to motivate the creative activity of authors and inventors by the provision of a special reward, and to allow the public access to the products of their genius after the limited period of exclusive control has expired."

incentive to increase the creation of inventions and works. As the Supreme Court has elaborated:

> [t]he patent laws promote [technological] progress by offering a right of exclusion for a limited period as an incentive to inventors to risk the often enormous costs in terms of time, research, and development. The productive effort thereby fostered will have a positive effect on society through the introduction of new products and processes of manufacture into the economy, and the emanations by way of increased employment and better lives for our citizens. In return for the right of exclusion – this "reward for inventions," – the patent laws impose upon the inventor a requirement of disclosure.[122]

The court has also used the same utilitarian logic to justify copyright protection.[123] These opinions show that the "incentive" thesis and cost-and-benefit analysis are two major components of utilitarian theory. First, IP protection promotes technological progress for society because it provides the requisite incentives to create new inventions and works. While the initial process of creation can be arduous and costly, copying is easy and cheap. This stark contrast means that copiers can easily free ride on creators' efforts. Creators can lose their competitiveness in the marketplace gradually or even overnight if copyists can distribute cheaper copies. This vulnerability to free-riding activities can deter risk-averse creators from investing in innovation and creativity. By contrast, IP protection gives creators a set of exclusive rights to use their creations, with copiers penalized if they use copyrighted materials without the IP rights owners' consent.[124] Hence, IP protection provides an incentive in the form of assurance to creators that their efforts will be protected against unauthorized uses and that they can recoup their investments through commercial exploitation of their creations.[125]

---

[122] Kewanee Oil Co. v. Bicron Corp., 416 U.S. 470, 480 (1974).

[123] Sony Corp. of America v. Universal City Studios, Inc., 464 U.S. 417, 429 (1984).

[124] However, copiers will not be penalized if the unauthorized uses of IP fall within the scope of limitations on IP rights. For example, fair use as a limitation on copyright allows the public to make limited uses of copyrighted works without their owners' consent.

[125] See, e.g., WILLIAM M. LANDES & RICHARD A. POSNER, THE ECONOMIC STRUCTURE OF INTELLECTUAL PROPERTY LAW 40 (2003) ("In the absence of copyright protection the market price of a book or other expressive work will eventually be bid down to the marginal cost of copying, with the result that the work may not be produced in the first place because the author and publisher may not be able to recover their costs of creating it."); Stanley M. Besen & Leo J. Raskind, An Introduction to the Law and Economics of

Second, utilitarianism applies cost-and-benefit analysis to make sure that the benefits of technological progress accrued from IP protection far exceed the costs of maintaining such a legal system. By focusing on the "access versus incentive" trade-off,[126] cost-and-benefit analysis requires close scrutiny of the costs that IP protection may incur and then caps them way below the benefits potentially generated.[127] This analysis normally leads to the assertion that "the more extensive copyright protection is, the greater the incentive to create intellectual property."[128]

However, a major problem with utilitarianism lies in its mishandling of distributive justice. While it dictates maximizing the utilities of a policy based on its social outcome, it fails to take into account the fair distribution of utilities among members of a society. Utilitarianism abstracts wealth as a utility, with the result that it makes no difference if one individual enjoys many more utilities than most others. The main concern is that the general sum of all utilities is maximized. A social policy that results in a larger number of utilities, say a one-billion-dollar growth in wealth, for the rich, but a smaller loss of utilities, say one-million-dollars in wealth, for the poor, can still pass utilitarianism's scrutiny even if it damages the poor because all that matters is maximizing the sum of utilities, regardless of the profound injustice caused. John Rawls has criticized utilitarianism for causing injustice as follows.

[T]here is no reason in principle why the greater gains of some should not compensate for the lesser losses of others; or more importantly, why the violation of the liberty of a few might not be made right by the greater good shared by many ... No doubt the strictness of common sense precepts of justice has a certain usefulness in limiting men's propensities to injustice and to socially injurious actions, but the utilitarian believes that to affirm this strictness as a first principle of morals is a mistake.[129]

Intellectual Property, J. ECON. PERSPECTIVES, at 5 (1991) (stating that producers will innovate only if they receive an appropriate return).

[126] LANDES & POSNER, *supra* note 125, at 20.

[127] Glynn S. Lunney, Jr., *Reexamining Copyright's Incentives-Access Paradigm*, 49 VAND. L. REV. 483, 499–554 (1996) (exploring the premises of the "incentive/access paradigm").

[128] William M. Landes & Richard A. Posner, *Indefinitely Renewable Copyright*, 70 U. CHI. L. REV. 471, 474 (2003).

[129] JOHN RAWLS, A THEORY OF JUSTICE 23 (rev. ed. 1999).

This criticism also applies to the IP Clause, which fails to tackle the relationship between social justice and technological progress properly. Based upon utilitarianism, the clause is silent on how the benefits of technological progress should be equitably distributed among members of the public. A proper IP protection system undoubtedly facilitates the constitutional objective of promoting technological progress.[130] However, there are a host of policy concerns about how the benefits accrued from technological progress, as promoted by new inventions and works, should be distributed among the public, who are non-IP owners. Should IP rights owners primarily control the distribution of technological benefits through voluntary transactions, and would such an arrangement bring about injustices in access to such benefits? If so, what is the role of the government in channeling the equitable distribution of technological benefits in the marketplace? Moreover, does the unfair distribution of technological benefits ultimately deter technological progress?

The principles of justice proposed by Rawls reveal the roots of the IP Clause's neglect of distributive justice. Rawls argues that injustices can be tolerated only to the extent that the difference principle and equal opportunity principle are met. The equal opportunity principle dictates that "offices and positions [are] open to all under conditions of fair equality of opportunity."[131] By applying legal standards equally to everyone who might become an author or inventor, with legal protection then afforded their works or inventions, copyright and patent laws that emanate from the IP Clause satisfy the equal opportunity principle.[132]

However, the IP Clause runs counter to the difference principle, which requires that certain injustices caused by an institution be excused on the condition that the institution distributes resources to "the greatest benefit of the least advantaged."[133] This principle is

---

[130] *See* Beebe, *supra* note 119, at 333, 337, 345.

[131] RAWLS, *supra* note, 129 at 266.

[132] *See* Justin Hughes & Robert P. Merges, *Copyright and Distributive Justice*, 92 NOTRE DAME L. REV. 513, 552 (2017) (arguing that the US copyright system is in line with the equal opportunity principle).

[133] RAWLS, *supra* note 129, at 266. Rawls further explains that "[t]he intuitive idea is that the social order is not to establish and secure the more attractive prospects of those better off unless doing so is to the advantage of those less fortunate." *Id.* at 65.

intended to achieve distributive justice in "property-owning democracy."[134] As noted above, being built upon utilitarianism, the IP Clause is meant only to maximize technological progress through the increased production of works and inventions. It does not deal with how the benefits accrued from technological progress should be distributed among members of the public. Hence, it does not require the distribution of such benefits to the least advantaged according to the difference principle. The public, including the least advantaged, need to obtain IP rights owners' authorization – primarily through voluntary market transactions – to enjoy the technological benefits of inventions and works.[135] Such a market-based rights protection system may well encourage the increased production of inventions and works as the IP Clause intends, thereby further privileging the ability of those who are financially able to afford those products to benefit from the relevant technological progress.[136] The IP Clause does not mandate any distributive justice measures to allow those who are the least advantaged, financially, politically, and/or culturally, to gain necessary benefits from inventions and works before their IP protection expires.

In *Golan v. Holder*,[137] the constitutionality of the Uruguay Round Agreements Act (URAA) was challenged for automatically restoring copyright protection to all works of foreign origin that were not yet in the public domain in their source countries but were in the public domain in the United States for specified reasons. That restoration of copyright protection actually "carries distributive consequences that have disadvantaged certain groups of content users."[138] In his dissenting opinion, Justice Breyer criticized the URAA's copyright restoration

---

[134] *Id.* at 67.

[135] *See* ROBERT P. MERGES, JUSTIFYING INTELLECTUAL PROPERTY 5 (2011)(contending that "the most important core principle" of property rights over intangible assets such as copyright is this: "[I]t assigns to individual people control over individual assets. It creates a one-to-one mapping between owners and assets.").

[136] *See, e.g.*, JAMES BOYLE, THE PUBLIC DOMAIN: ENCLOSING THE COMMONS OF THE MIND 18 (2008)("Copyright law is supposed to give us a self-regulating cultural policy in which the right to exclude others from one's original expression fuels a vibrant public sphere indirectly driven by popular demand."); Molly Shaffer Van Houweling, *Distributive Values in Copyright*, 83 TEX. L. REV. 1535, 1537 (2005)("Copyright law generally addresses the relationship between creative expression and money in terms of maximizing total creativity.").

[137] 565 U.S. 302 (2012).

[138] Haochen Sun, *Copyright and Responsibility*, 4 HARV. J. SPORTS & ENT. L. 263, 297 (2013).

from the distributive justice perspective, stating that "[i]f a school orchestra or other nonprofit organization cannot afford the new charges [caused by copyright restoration] ... [t]hey will have to do without."[139] Thus, he accused the URAA's copyright restoration of "aggravat[ing] the already serious problem of cultural education in the United States."[140]

A collective right to technology would serve as a check on the legislative power granted Congress by the IP Clause. It would require Congress to scrutinize distributive justice when legislative proposals to expand IP rights are placed on the agenda. Accordingly, legislators would have to rigorously examine the extent to which a proposed expansion of rights protection would allow the public, particularly various groups of the least advantaged, to enjoy the technological benefits accruing from the subsequently stronger IP rights protection. Moreover, legislators would be required to proactively consider ways in which limitations should be placed on IP rights so as to adequately protect the fundamental right to technology.

SUMMARY

Humanity's future depends in large part on the promotion of distributive justice in the enjoyment of technological benefits. [141] Hence, the right to technology should become a centerpiece of the global human rights regime.

As this chapter has demonstrated, redefining the right to technology as a collective right would pave the way for its transformation into a civil liberty, triggering citizens' active recourse to the adjudication of justice. The continued combination of civic engagement and judicial protection of this civil liberty would inform its nature and scope

---

[139] *Golan*, 565 U.S. at 354 (Breyer, J., dissenting).

[140] *Id.*

[141] Professor Ruth Okediji has urged a more robust agenda for reforming the current human rights system based on the notion of distributive justice. Okediji, *Does Intellectual Property Need Human Rights?*, *supra* note 38, at 10 (arguing that "the current narrow construction of the IP/human rights interface provides reprieve from the grander, more contested, distributive justice-oriented vision of human progress and flourishing embodied in the economic, social, and cultural rights").

consistent with rapidly developing technological conditions in society. However, the right to technology does not have to upend the IP protection system that distributes technological benefits through voluntary market transactions. Rather, it allows for a limited exception to this market-oriented system by empowering courts to protect the public's equal enjoyment of technological benefits when necessary.[142]

The collective right to technology is crucial to enhancing human rights protection in years to come because it can usher in a more socially dynamic distribution of technological benefits. This will be one of the most significant distributive justice agendas in the contemporary world, especially given the role of technology in protecting many other human rights, including those to health, food, education, and free speech. With the collective right to technology in everyone's hands, we will be in a much better position to harness technology in the full service of humanity.

---

[142] *See* Kal Raustiala, *Density and Conflict in International Intellectual Property Law*, 40 U.C. Davis L. Rev. 1021, 1038 (2007) ("Given the pernicious effects of overly robust IP protection on many individuals and societies around the world, the combination of IP and human rights may produce many beneficial effects.").

3 THE FUNDAMENTAL RIGHT
TO TECHNOLOGY

The multiple rounds of COVID-19-related lockdowns in 2020 and beyond have required around 50 million American students to rely on the Internet to receive their education.[1] However, 9.7 million of them have no reliable internet access in their homes.[2] Some schools resorted to installing Wi-Fi networks in their parking lots that were made accessible to students.[3] Moreover, the impact on their schooling is not the only impact exerted on young people by a lack of reliable internet access. It has also meant a lack of access to Netflix, TikTok, YouTube, and other forms of social media entertainment that have become important outlets for coping with boredom, loneliness, and even despair during the pandemic. Worse still, because virtually all health information about COVID-19 is online, a lack of internet access can be a matter of life or death.

In 2010, the US Federal Communications Commission (FCC) published a National Broadband Plan in which it committed to ensuring that all Americans would have access to broadband internet by 2020.[4] In 2015, President Obama proclaimed that the Internet was "no longer a luxury" for the American people.[5] Yet the reality is that as of

[1] Enjoli Francis, *Organizations Help Kids Bridge Digital Schooling Divide by Providing Internet Learning Tools*, ABC News (Sept. 22, 2020).

[2] *Interactive Map: America's Unconnected Students*, DIGITAL BRIDGE K-12 https://digitalbrid gek12.org/toolkit/assess-need/connectivity-map (last visited Dec. 6, 2020).

[3] Cecilia Kang, *Parking Lots Have Become a Digital Lifeline*, N.Y. TIMES (May 5, 2020).

[4] *See* FED. COMMC'NS COMM'N, CONNECTING AMERICA: THE NATIONAL BROADBAND PLAN 135–136 (2010).

[5] Presidential Memorandum, THE WHITE HOUSE, *Expanding Broadband Deployment and Adoption by Addressing Regulatory Barriers and Encouraging Investment and Training* (Mar. 23, 2015).

February 2020, 42 million Americans were still not able to purchase broadband internet access.[6] Globally, the digital divide is even worse. In 2019, nearly half the world's population had no access to broadband internet.[7]

How can we address the worsening inequality in internet access? In this chapter, I put forward a thought experiment, proposing that it is time to recognize the fundamental right to technology of which internet access is a vital part. Recognizing that right, I argue, would create a constitutional mandate entitling everyone to the benefits of progress in fundamental technologies such as the Internet, thereby paving the way for their fair distribution and beneficial use. I propose another means of resurrecting the right to technology in domestic law.

Following an overview of fundamental rights protected under the US Constitution, I first discuss how the US Supreme Court has developed a liberal approach to identifying fundamental rights not enumerated in the Constitution. I then apply this liberal approach to consider why the right to technology should be deemed an unenumerated fundamental right, and further how that new right can be applied to promote the equal distribution of technological benefits. In particular, I will discuss how this right can more effectively tackle problems associated with digital divide.

A THE LIBERAL APPROACH TO FUNDAMENTAL RIGHTS PROTECTION

1 Constitutional Status of Unenumerated Fundamental Rights

Under the US Constitution, some liberties are so important that they can be deemed fundamental rights.[8] The Constitution guards against any encroachment upon such rights unless the government provides

---

[6] John Busby, Julia Tanberk, & BroadbandNow Team, *FCC Reports Broadband Unavailable to 21.3 Million Americans, BroadbandNow Study Indicates 42 Million Do Not Have Access*, BROADBANDNOW RESEARCH (Feb. 3, 2020), https://bit.ly/2YhfB68.

[7] UNESCO, *New Report on Global Broadband Access Underscores Urgent Need To Reach the Half of the World Still Unconnected* (Sept. 23, 2019), https://bit.ly/3l9zCVk.

[8] *See* ERWIN CHEMERINSKY, CONSTITUTIONAL LAW: PRINCIPLES AND POLICIES 812 (4th ed. 2011).

compelling reasons for doing so.[9] The first ten Amendments of the Constitution, known as the Bill of Rights, enumerate certain fundamental rights, ranging from freedom of expression and religion, the right to keep and bear arms, and freedom from unreasonable searches and seizures to the right to property.[10]

The Constitution also allows courts to recognize unenumerated fundamental rights as liberties protected by the Due Process Clause of the Fourteenth Amendment.[11] The clause prescribes that no state shall "deprive any person of life, liberty, or property, without due process of law."[12] To follow this constitutional mandate, courts circumspectly analyze whether an unenumerated right constitutes a liberty deserving due process protection as a fundamental constitutional right. For example, nothing in the text of the Constitution expressly protects marriage as a fundamental right. Yet, the US Supreme Court has ventured to interpret marriage as a liberty that merits due process protection, thereby identifying and protecting it as an unenumerated fundamental right.[13] In *Loving v. Virginia*,[14] the Supreme Court struck down a statute that prohibited interracial marriage, declaring that "[t]he freedom to marry has long been recognized as one of the vital personal rights essential to the orderly pursuit of happiness by free men."[15] Because the statute in question prejudiced freedom of marriage – "one of the 'basic civil rights of man,' fundamental to our every existence and survival"[16] – it "surely ... deprive[d] all the State's citizens of liberty without due process of law."[17]

The Supreme Court has embraced the identification and protection of unenumerated fundamental rights as two of its core

---

[9] *See* Regents of the Univ. of Cal. v. Bakke, 438 U.S. 265, 357 (1978) ("[A] government practice or statute which restricts 'fundamental rights' ... is to be subjected to 'strict scrutiny' and can be justified only if it furthers a compelling government purpose and, even then, only if no less restrictive alternative is available.").

[10] U.S. CONST. amends. I, II, IV, V.

[11] *See* Griswold v. Connecticut, 381 U.S. 479, 486 (1965) (Goldberg, J., concurring) ("[T]he concept of liberty protects those personal rights that are fundamental, and is not confined to the specific terms of the Bill of Rights.").

[12] U.S. CONST. amend. XIV, § 1.

[13] *Griswold*, 381 U.S. at 495 (Goldberg, J., concurring).

[14] 388 U.S. 1 (1967).

[15] *Id.* at 12.

[16] *Id.*

[17] *Id.*

duties.[18] Over the course of a century of adjudication, rights so identified and protected in addition to the right to marriage[19] include the right to interstate travel[20] and the right to parent one's children,[21] among others. The way in which the Supreme Court identifies fundamental rights "has not been reduced to any formula."[22] Rather, it has stated that it is necessary to vigilantly identify and justify individual interests that are so fundamental that the government must afford them adequate protection.[23] This recognition process follows broad constitutional principles.[24]

2 Protecting Unenumerated Fundamental Rights

Through a series of watershed cases, the Supreme Court has developed and harnessed a liberal approach to interpreting the nature and scope of liberties protected by the Due Process Clause as unenumerated fundamental rights. This approach dynamically improves the separation of powers by shedding new light on the role of the judiciary in protecting fundamental rights. It also revitalizes constitutional commitments to promote interests that are of the utmost value to individuals and society as a whole. There are three major components in the liberal approach to identifying unenumerated fundamental rights.

The first is a dynamic interpretation of the nature and scope of liberty protected by the Due Process Clause, which empowers courts to identify unenumerated fundamental rights. Starting with its *Meyer v. Nebraska*[25] decision in 1923, the Supreme Court has attempted to provide a sweeping definition of liberty under the Due Process Clause.[26] Drawing on its previous rulings on the clause, the court stated in *Meyer* that liberty

---

[18] Obergefell v. Hodges, 135 S. Ct. 2584, 2598 (2015); Washington v. Glucksberg, 521 U.S. 702, 759, 772 (1997) (Souter, J., concurring).
[19] *Loving*, 388 U.S. at 12.
[20] Saenz v. Roe, 526 U.S. 489, 501 (1999).
[21] Troxel v. Granville, 530 U.S. 57, 66 (2000).
[22] Poe v. Ullman, 367 U.S. 497, 542 (1961) (Harlan, J., dissenting).
[23] *Obergefell*, 135 S. Ct. at 2598.
[24] *Id.*
[25] 262 U.S. 390 (1923).
[26] *Id.* at 399.

denotes not merely freedom from bodily restraint but also the right of the individual to contract, to engage in any of the common occupations of life, to acquire useful knowledge, to marry, establish a home and bring up children, to worship God according to the dictates of his own conscience, and generally to enjoy those privileges long recognized at common law as essential to the orderly pursuit of happiness by free men.[27]

Liberty, according to this statement, has two dimensions. First, it protects bodily integrity, shielding individuals against harm caused to their bodies.[28] Second, liberty allows individuals to choose actions that are essential to their achievement of happiness in orderly societies.[29] Despite providing such a broad-based definition, the court took a common law approach to protecting liberties so long as they were recognized as privileges.[30] It did not, however, expressly elevate them to fundamental rights directly pursuant to the Due Process Clause.[31]

Justice Harlan's dissenting opinion in *Poe v. Ullman*[32] in 1961 marks a critical turning point in the Supreme Court's jurisprudence of fundamental rights protection:[33]

> [T]he full scope of the liberty guaranteed by the Due Process Clause cannot be found in or limited by the precise terms of the specific guarantees elsewhere provided in the Constitution. This "liberty" is not a series of isolated points pricked out in terms of the taking of property; the freedom of speech, press, and religion; the right to keep and bear arms; the freedom from unreasonable searches and seizures; and so on. It is a rational continuum which, broadly speaking, includes a freedom from all substantial arbitrary impositions and purposeless restraints.[34]

---

[27] *Id.*

[28] Judge Cardozo argued that "[e]very human being of adult years and sound mind has a right to determine what shall be done with his own body" in relation to his medical needs. Schloendorff v. Soc'y of N.Y. Hosp., 105 N.E. 92, 93 (N.Y. 1914).

[29] *See Meyer*, 262 U.S. at 401, 403.

[30] *Id.* at 400.

[31] *See* Laurence H. Tribe, Lawrence v. Texas: The "Fundamental Right" That Dare Not Speak Its Name, 117 Harv. L. Rev. 1893, 1934 (2004).

[32] 367 U.S. 497, 522 (1961) (Harlan, J., dissenting).

[33] *See, e.g.*, Moore v. City of East Cleveland, 431 U.S. 494, 544–45 (1977) (White, J., dissenting) ("[N]o one was more sensitive than Mr. Justice Harlan to any suggestion that his approach to the Due Process Clause would lead to judges 'roaming at large in the constitutional field.'").

[34] *Poe*, 367 U.S. at 543 (Harlan, J., dissenting).

This opinion asserts a broad and dynamic understanding of the nature and scope of the liberty protected by the Due Process Clause. It forthrightly affirms that the constitutional protection afforded by the clause stretches to fundamental rights not specifically identified by the Constitution.[35] It does so because liberty, according to Justice Harlan, is a broad-based concept not confined to the rights itemized by the Constitution.[36] Instead, it is a "rational continuum" that confers upon courts the judicial power to recognize new fundamental rights.

Relying on this robust understanding of liberty, the Supreme Court revolutionized constitutional rights protection by elevating privacy and abortion to the status of unenumerated fundamental rights.[37] In *Roe v. Wade*,[38] while acknowledging that the Constitution is silent on the right to privacy, the court held that privacy should be deemed a liberty under the Due Process Clause and therefore protected as a fundamental right.[39] It further founded women's fundamental right to abortion upon the right to privacy, ruling that the latter "is broad enough to encompass a woman's decision whether or not to terminate her pregnancy."[40] In other words, the right to abortion entitles women to make decisions for their privacy interests. Without protection of that right, women could suffer severe physical and psychological harm.[41]

[35] *Id.*

[36] *Id.* at 544, 549–52.

[37] John Hart Ely, *The Wages of Crying Wolf: A Comment on* Roe v. Wade, 82 YALE L.J. 920 (1973) ("The right to privacy, though not explicitly mentioned in the Constitution, is protected by the Due Process Clause of the Fourteenth Amendment.").

[38] 410 U.S. 113 (1973).

[39] *Id.* at 152–53 ("[O]nly personal rights that can be deemed 'fundamental' or 'implicit in the concept of ordered liberty,' are included in this guarantee of personal privacy . . . This right of privacy . . . [is] founded in the Fourteenth Amendment's concept of personal liberty and restrictions upon state action.") (citation omitted).

[40] *Id.* at 153.

[41] *Id.*

The detriment that the State would impose upon the pregnant woman by denying this choice altogether is apparent. Specific and direct harm medically diagnosable even in early pregnancy may be involved. Maternity, or additional offspring, may force upon the woman a distressful life and future. Psychological harm may be imminent. Mental and physical health may be taxed by child care. There is also the distress, for all concerned, associated with the unwanted child, and there is the problem of bringing a child into a family already unable, psychologically and otherwise, to care for it. In other cases, as in this one, the additional difficulties and continuing stigma of unwed motherhood may be involved. All these are factors the woman and her responsible physician necessarily will consider in consultation.

Second, by applying the liberal approach, the Supreme Court posits that *reasoned judgment* must be applied in determining what personal interests of utmost value to individuals amount to unenumerated fundamental rights. This reasoned judgment standard can be traced back to Justice Harlan's dissenting opinion in *Poe v. Ullman*,[42] where he stated that the liberty protected by the Due Process Clause "recognizes, what a reasonable and sensitive judgment must, that certain interests require particularly careful scrutiny of the state needs asserted to justify their abridgment."[43] Later, in *Planned Parenthood of Southeastern Pennsylvania v. Casey*,[44] the Supreme Court spelled out how reasoned judgment should be applied to determine whether an unenumerated right can be recognized as a liberty that merits due process protection.[45] This interpretive process, as the court pointed out, is intended to "define the liberty of all" rather than enforce judges' "moral code."[46] Guided by this caveat, the court explicated its reasoning in defining the nature of the liberty that triggers fundamental rights protection:

> [Matters] involving the most intimate and personal choices a person may make in a lifetime, choices central to personal dignity and autonomy, are central to the liberty protected by the Fourteenth Amendment. At the heart of liberty is the right to define one's own concept of existence, of meaning, of the universe, and of the mystery of human life. Beliefs about these matters could not define the attributes of personhood were they formed under compulsion of the State.[47]

Following this choice-oriented conception of liberty, the court considered various reasons why the prohibition of abortion severely harms women's dignity and autonomy in controlling and enjoying their

[42] 367 U.S. 497 (1961).
[43] *Id.* at 543 (Harlan, J., dissenting); *see also* Washington v. Glucksberg, 521 U.S. 702, 769 (1997) (Souter, J., concurring) ("The *Poe* dissent ... reminds us that the process of substantive review [is] by reasoned judgment.").
[44] 505 U.S. 833 (1992).
[45] *Id.* at 834 ("[T]he adjudication of substantive due process claims may require this Court to exercise its reasoned judgment in determining the boundaries between the individual's liberty and the demands of organized society.").
[46] *Id.* at 850.
[47] *Id.* at 851.

lives.[48] Given that decisions on abortion are so fundamental to women's interests, abortion must be protected as a fundamental right allowing women to choose the personal and social life that they wish to live.[49]

Later, in *Lawrence v. Texas*,[50] the Supreme Court also applied the reasoned judgment standard to justify homosexuals' fundamental right to consensual sodomy.[51] Liberty, according to the court, protects personal freedom in two dimensions. Physically, it shields the boundaries of private spaces, preventing unwarranted interferences by the government.[52] Mentally, it affords individuals the autonomy to choose what they wish to do.[53] Relying upon *Casey*'s choice-oriented characterization of liberty,[54] the court invalidated the anti-sodomy law of Texas on the ground that it prevented homosexuals from enjoying the same autonomy to engage in intimate acts as heterosexuals.[55]

The Supreme Court recently reaffirmed this jurisprudence on the recognition of fundamental rights when it tackled same-sex marriage. In *Obergefell v. Hodges*,[56] the court took pains to identify the right to marriage as of fundamental importance to all, stating that "[c]hoices about marriage shape an individual's destiny ... [B]ecause 'it fulfils yearnings for security, safe haven, and connection that express our common humanity, civil marriage is an esteemed institution, and the

---

[48] *Id.* at 852.

[49] *Id.* ("The destiny of the woman must be shaped to a large extent on her own conception of her spiritual imperatives and her place in society.").

[50] 539 U.S. 558 (2003).

[51] *Id.* at 564–65, 574, 578–79.

[52] *Lawrence*, 539 U.S. at 567, 578.

[53] *Id.* at 562

> Liberty protects the person from unwarranted government intrusions into a dwelling or other private places. In our tradition the State is not omnipresent in the home. And there are other spheres of our lives and existence, outside the home, where the State should not be a dominant presence. Freedom extends beyond spatial bounds. Liberty presumes an autonomy of self that includes freedom of thought, belief, expression, and certain intimate conduct. The instant case involves liberty of the person both in its spatial and in its more transcendent dimensions.

[54] *Id.* at 573–74.

[55] *Id.* at 574 ("Persons in a homosexual relationship may seek autonomy for these purposes, just as heterosexual persons do. The decision in *Bowers* would deny them this right.").

[56] 135 S. Ct. 2584 (2015).

decision whether and whom to marry is among life's momentous acts of self-definition.'"[57]

Third, the Supreme Court has also reinforced the justification for the constitutional protection of unenumerated fundamental rights on the basis of *societal interests*. If a constitutional right is central to achieving larger interests in maintaining a free and ordered society, it can be recognized as a fundamental right. According to Justice Harlan's dissenting opinion in *Poe v. Ullman*,[58] the identification and protection of fundamental rights through the Due Process Clause must be weighed against "the demands of organized society."[59] He indicated that fundamental rights should be rooted in societal interests, without which they would weaken in symbolic and practical value.[60] Similarly, the majority opinion in *Obergefell v. Hodges*[61] treats societal interest as another justification for marriage as a fundamental right. Citing Tocqueville's view[62] and the Supreme Court's *Maynard v. Hill*[63] ruling, the court in *Obergefell* states that "marriage is a keystone of our social order."[64] It further discusses ways in which marriage as a public institution maintains the legal and social order by allocating benefits and responsibilities to married couples.[65] Relying on the social justification posited by *Obergefell*, the US District Court for the District of Oregon recently rendered

---

[57] *Id.* at 2599 (quoting *Goodridge v. Department of Public Health*, 798 N.E.2d 941, 955 (Mass. 2003)).

[58] 367 U.S. 497, 522 (1961) (Harlan, J., dissenting).

[59] *Poe*, 367 U.S. at 542 (Harlan, J., dissenting) ("The best that can be said is that through the course of this Court's decisions it has represented the balance which our Nation, built upon postulates of respect for the liberty of the individual, has struck between that liberty and the demands of organized society.").

[60] *Id.*

[61] 135 S. Ct. 2584 (2015).

[62] *Obergefell*, 135 S. Ct., at 2601 ("[W]hen the American retires from the turmoil of public life to the bosom of his family, he finds in it the image of order and of peace. . . . [H]e afterwards carries [that image] with him into public affairs.") (citing ALEXIS DE TOCQUEVILLE, 1 DEMOCRACY IN AMERICA 304 (Phillips Bradley ed., Henry Reeve transl., Vintage Books ed. 1990) (1945)).

[63] 125 U.S. 190, 211, 213 (1888) (holding that marriage is "the foundation of the family and of society, without which there would be neither civilization nor progress" and also stating that marriage is "a great public institution, giving character to our whole civil polity").

[64] *Obergefell*, 135 S. Ct. at 2601.

[65] *Id.* ("[J]ust as a couple vows to support each other, so does society pledge to support the couple, offering symbolic recognition and material benefits to protect and nourish the union. . . . The States have contributed to the fundamental character of the marriage right by placing that institution at the center of so many facets of the legal and social order.").

a pathbreaking decision on environmental protection.[66] The court identified "the right to a climate system capable of sustaining human life" as
a fundamental right under the Due Process Clause because of the right's
fundamental role in maintaining a free and ordered society.[67]

With these three interpretive methods, the liberal approach defies
the originalist approach. The latter asserts that any fundamental right
must be "deeply rooted in this Nation's history and tradition,"[68] rendering the meaning of "liberty" fixed and static under the Due Process
Clause. Based on the originalist approach, protection of abortion as an
unenumerated fundamental right for women was rejected,[69] as was
homosexuals' right to privately engage in consensual sodomy.[70]

The liberal approach, however, has removed the legal stigma from
both abortion and consensual sodomy. Compared with the originalist
approach, it has proved better at promoting personal and public freedoms
through its robust interpretation of the scope of liberty protected as
a fundamental right under the Due Process Clause. The liberal approach
views "liberty," as protected by the clause, as a dynamic concept capable
of encompassing new fundamental rights, provided that their intrinsic
worth in ensuring basic individual freedoms and promoting social interests can be established through reasoned judgment.

Such a robust interpretation of the scope of fundamental rights is
a crucial step toward a conception of the Constitution as a supreme law
capable of adapting itself in response to new necessities in the United
States.[71] As Justice Frankfurter has observed of the Constitution, "[g]reat

---

[66] *See* Juliana v. United States, 217 F. Supp. 3d 1224, 1250 (D. Or. 2016).

[67] *Id.*

[68] Washington v. Glucksberg, 521 U.S. 702, 703 (1997) (quoting Moore v. East Cleveland, 431 U.S. 494 (plurality opinion)).

[69] Roe v. Wade, 410 U.S. 113, 174 (1973) ("The fact that a majority of the States reflecting, after all the majority sentiment in those States, have had restrictions on abortions for at least a century is a strong indication, it seems to me, that the asserted right to an abortion is not 'so rooted in the traditions and conscience of our people as to be ranked as fundamental.'") (Rehnquist, J., dissenting) (quoting Snyder v. Massachusetts, 291 U.S. 97, 105 (1934)).

[70] Bowers v. Hardwick, 478 U.S. 186, 192–94 (1986) (refusing to "extend a fundamental right to homosexuals to engage in acts of consensual sodomy" because "[p]roscriptions against sodomy have 'ancient roots'" and concluding that "to claim that a right to engage in such conduct is 'deeply rooted in this Nation's history and tradition' or 'implicit in the concept of ordered liberty' is, at best, facetious").

[71] *See, e.g.,* DAVID A. STRAUSS, THE LIVING CONSTITUTION 1 (2010) ("A 'living constitution' is one that evolves, changes over time, and adapts to new circumstances, without being formally amended.").

concepts like ... 'liberty' ... were purposely left to gather meaning from experience. For they relate to the whole domain of social and economic fact, and the statesmen who founded this Nation knew too well that only a stagnant society remains unchanged."[72]

B RECOGNIZING THE RIGHT TO INTERNET ACCESS

Can the US courts apply the liberal approach to recognize an unenum- erated fundamental right to technology under the Due Process Clause? In this part of the chapter, I first use the Internet as a case study to wrestle with this question. I show that internet access is fundamentally important to protect individual liberty and promote social interests. I then argue for recognition of a new fundamental right to technology that ensures equal access to the Internet and other benefits of techno- logical progress.

1 The Internet as a Fundamental Technology

Due to rapid developments in hardware and software that allow us to disseminate and receive critical information, the Internet has become a fundamental communications technology. Internet access plays an essential role in promoting liberties ranging from free speech and media freedom to education, as demonstrated by a wealth of scholarly research.[73] Seminal judicial rulings have upheld the importance of the Internet for freedom of expression. In *Reno v. American Civil Liberties Union*,[74] the US Supreme Court explained how the Internet revolutionized ways in which freedom of expression is promoted:

> [The Internet] provides relatively unlimited, low-cost capacity for communication of all kinds ... Th[e] dynamic, multifaceted

---

[72] Nat'l Mut. Ins. Co. v. Tidewater Transfer Co., 337 U.S. 582, 646 (1949) (Frankfurter, J., dissenting).

[73] *See generally*, YOCHAI BENKLER, THE WEALTH OF NETWORKS: HOW SOCIAL PRODUCTION TRANSFORMS MARKETS AND FREEDOM 7–16 (2006); CHRISTOPHER YOO, THE DYNAMIC INTERNET: HOW TECHNOLOGY, USERS, AND BUSINESSES ARE TRANSFORMING THE NETWORK 1 (2012).

[74] Reno v. ACLU, 521 U.S. 844, 844 (1997).

category of communication includes not only traditional print and news services, but also audio, video, and still images, as well as interactive, real-time dialogue. Through the use of chat rooms, any person with a phone line can become a town crier with a voice that resonates farther than it could from any soapbox. Through the use of Web pages, mail exploders, and newsgroups, the same individual can become a pamphleteer.[75]

Apart from its speech-enhancing functions, courts and researchers have ascertained that the Internet also promotes liberty more broadly through our daily participation in modern society.[76] The Internet is a source of information and knowledge and makes services provided by public and private institutions more accessible.[77] In so doing, it is a daily utility that "transform[s] nearly every aspect of our lives, from profound actions like choosing a leader, building a career, and falling in love to more quotidian ones like hailing a cab and watching a movie."[78]

Another important role of the Internet is in creating digital public spaces that are vital to societal interests. As former Secretary of State Hillary Clinton famously stated, internet freedom is as fundamental as free speech itself because the Internet is the twenty-first century town square.[79] Journalists involved in Occupy Wall Street collectively issued a statement emphasizing that "[a]ccess to open communications platforms is critical for the human species evolution and survival."[80] Judicial rulings have concurred with these views. In *Packingham v. North Carolina*, the Supreme Court pointed out that the Internet is as important as public streets and parks, traditional public forums that merit the full spectrum of free speech protection.[81] Further, the rise of

---

[75] *Id.* at 870.

[76] Carpenter v. United States, 138 S. Ct. 2206, 2210 (2018) (holding that Internet access through cell or smart phones "is indispensable to participation in modern society").

[77] United States v. Eaglin, 913 F.3d 88, 98 (2d Cir. 2019) ("[A]ccess to the Internet is essential to ... everyday life, as it provides avenues for seeking employment, banking, accessing government resources, reading about current events, and educating oneself.").

[78] U.S. Telecom Ass'n v. FCC, 825 F.3d 674, 698 (D.C. Cir. 2016).

[79] Hillary Rodham Clinton, U.S. Sec'y of State, Internet Rights and Wrongs: Choices & Challenges in a Networked World, Remarks at The George Washington University (Feb. 15, 2011), *available at* https://bit.ly/3BglEGy.

[80] Mera Szendro Bok, *What Does Occupy Wall Street Have to Do with Internet Freedom and Media Reform? Everything!*, MEDIA JUSTICE (Oct. 26, 2011), https://bit.ly/3uGNR70.

[81] Packingham v. North Carolina, 137 S. Ct. 1730, 1735 (2017) ("While in the past there may have been difficulty in identifying the most important places (in a spatial sense) for

social media outlets as dynamic new additions to the Internet makes it a vehicle for socially beneficial communicative activities ranging from debating and sharing photos on Facebook to seeking jobs and advertising for professionals on LinkedIn.[82] Accordingly, courts have ruled that online search engines benefit society by improving public access to information.[83]

2 The Internet and COVID-19

The COVID-19 pandemic has reinforced the Internet's fundamental role in promoting individual and societal well-being. According to a recent Pew Research Center survey, 53 percent of US adults said the Internet was essential during the pandemic.[84] A study of mobile device data showed that in February 2020, before the effects of the virus had begun to be felt in the United States, individuals from high-income areas with full access to the Internet were more likely to leave their homes, but following state social distancing directives in March, individuals from low-income areas with limited access to the Internet became more likely to leave their homes.[85] Furthermore, the study found the same result in areas of high and low internet penetration, noting the correlation between income and internet access.[86] More people from low-income areas have breached social distancing guidelines during the pandemic, partly because they are unable to take advantage of the important functions provided by the Internet and are forced to leave their homes to work or meet friends.[87]

the exchange of views, today the answer is clear. It is cyberspace – the 'vast democratic forums of the Internet' in general, and social media in particular." (citation omitted) (citing Reno v. ACLU, 521 U.S. 844, 868 (1997)).

[82] *Id.* at 1735–36 (citations omitted) (quoting *Reno*, 521 U.S. at 870).

[83] Perfect 10, Inc. v. Amazon.com, Inc., 508 F.3d 1146, 1165 (9th Cir. 2007) (Ruling that "a search engine provides social benefit by incorporating an original work into a new work, namely, an electronic reference tool").

[84] Emily A. Vogels, Andrew Perrin, Lee Raine, & Monica Anderson, *53% of Americans Say the Internet Has Been Essential During the COVID-19 Outbreak*, PEW RES. CTR. (Apr. 30, 2020), https://pewrsr.ch/3FmeFhO.

[85] Lesley Chiou & Catherine Tucker, *Social Distancing, Internet Access and Inequality*, 7–8 (Nat'l. Bureau of Econ. Rsch., Working Paper No. 26982, 2020), https://www.nber.org /papers/w26982.

[86] *Id.*

[87] *Id.*

Given these inequities, the pandemic has underscored the fundamental importance of the Internet in four ways. First, it has demonstrated that the Internet is essential to modern education. Although many students have long been disadvantaged by not having access to the Internet at home, the pandemic exposed the severity of this often-overlooked hardship. In one study, 21 percent of surveyed parents claimed that their children would be unable to complete their schoolwork due to a lack of home internet access, 22 percent that their children had to leave the house to access public Wi-Fi networks to for their schoolwork, and a further 29 percent that their children would have to do their schoolwork on a cell phone.[88]

Second, internet access has been essential for adults to be able to work from home in keeping with social distancing guidelines. Companies and individuals alike have used the pandemic as an opportunity to experiment with a working-from-home model that may become the norm in an increasingly digital world.[89] The pandemic has increased demand for digital services that facilitate remote working, most dramatically for apps such as Zoom and WebEx.[90] However, the move toward remote working creates serious problems for those without a stable internet connection. Worse, the digital divide has left some with no means of working while social distancing guidelines are in place, putting their livelihoods at risk.[91]

Third, the Internet has performed an important service throughout the pandemic in providing entertainment. One study suggested that since the outbreak, as many as 38 percent of American consumers have tried out a new digital media subscription; more than two-thirds of that group say they will continue their subscription after the pandemic has passed.[92]

---

[88] *See* Vogels et al., *supra* note 84.

[89] Shelly Banjo, Livia Yap, Colum Murphy & Vinicy Chan, *Coronavirus Forces World's Largest Work-From-Home Experiment*, BLOOMBERG (Feb. 2, 2020, 4:00 PM), https://bloom .bg/3oAPwu6.

[90] Ella Koeze & Nathaniel Popper, *The Virus Changed the Way We Internet*, N.Y. TIMES (Apr. 7, 2020), https://nyti.ms/3mureyS (finding that Zoom rose from around 2 million daily uses on February 29th to well above 6 million in March and Google Classroom rose from a similar level to around 5 million and Microsoft Teams rose by around 1 million daily sessions).

[91] *See, e.g.*, Ephrat Livni, *The Coronavirus Crisis Proves the Internet Should Be a Public Utility*, QUARTZ (Mar. 26, 2020), https://bit.ly/2YjUlxb.

[92] Don Reisinger, *Coronavirus Is Conditioning New Entertainment Habits That May Not Change Post-Pandemic*, FORBES (June 23, 2020, 12:10 AM), https://bit.ly/3ozIhSR.

The Internet has also facilitated personal connections during periods of increased isolation. For instance, people have livestreamed religious services, weddings, and funerals that they were unable to attend physically,[93] and individuals have created popular online pop quizzes and book clubs.[94] These new forms of socialization have also given a huge boost to relatively obscure video chatting apps such as Duo and Houseparty.[95] However, the online setting of these resources means those without internet access are at greater risk of feeling cut off from family members, friends, and society in general.[96]

Finally, the Internet has provided important access to essential information, supplies, and services throughout the pandemic. It remains an important source of information about the virus itself and in some cases the primary means available for contacting a doctor.[97] People also rely on the Internet to ensure access to justice. At certain times in 2020, the vast majority of federal and state courts in the United States were conducting virtual court proceedings via the Internet.[98] The Supreme Court recently conducted a virtual hearing for the very first time.[99]

3 Global Recognition

The fundamental importance of internet access is attracting growing global recognition and support. For example, several major surveys have indicated overwhelming public support for protection of the right to such access. A 2009–10 BBC World Service poll found that almost four in five people worldwide regard internet access as a fundamental

---

[93] Eleanor Sarpong, *Covid-19 Shows Why Internet Access Is a Basic Right. We Must Get Everyone Connected.*, ALL. FOR AFFORDABLE INTERNET (Apr. 15, 2020), https://bit.ly/3aa2uq0.

[94] Cristina Criddle, *Coronavirus: Ways to Stay Social Online While in Self-Isolation*, BBC NEWS (Mar. 20, 2020), www.bbc.com/news/technology-51966087.

[95] *See* Koeze & Popper, *supra* note 90.

[96] *See* Amanda Holpuch, *US's Digital Divide "is Going to Kill People" as Covid-19 Exposes Inequalities*, GUARDIAN (Apr. 13, 2020).

[97] *See id.*

[98] *See* Janna Adelstein, *Courts Continue to Adapt to Covid-19*, BRENNAN CTR. FOR JUST. (Sept. 10, 2020), https://bit.ly/3DeUS21.

[99] *See Covid-19 Forces Courts to Hold Proceedings Online*, THE ECONOMIST (June 14, 2020), https://econ.st/3DcmLrn.

right.[100] Similarly, a 2012 survey of more than 10,000 internet users from twenty countries found that "[e]ighty-three percent of respondents agreed or agreed strongly that internet access should be considered a basic human right."[101]

Recognizing the importance of internet access, the United Nations (UN) has called for a global movement to fully integrate it into human rights considerations.[102] In a 2011 report, Frank La Rue – the former Special Rapporteur on the Promotion and Protection of the Right to Freedom of Opinion and Expression – underscored the fact that the Internet not only enables individuals to exercise their human rights, but also promotes the progress of society as a whole.[103] Subsequently, the UN Human Rights Council adopted a resolution in 2016 emphasizing "the importance of applying a comprehensive human rights-based approach when providing and expanding access to the Internet."[104] Media coverage of these developments suggested that the UN recognized internet access as a human right.[105] Based upon these UN efforts, scholars have argued for a liberal reading of Article Nineteen of the International Covenant on Civil and Political Rights as the legal basis for recognizing and protecting internet access as a human right.[106]

The European Court of Human Rights has also safeguarded internet access through the right to freedom of expression, as prescribed by Article Ten of the European Convention on Human Rights. In *Cengiz and Others v. Turkey*, the court ruled that the Turkish government's

---

[100] *Internet Access is "a Fundamental Right"*, BBC NEWS. (Mar. 8, 2010), http://news.bbc.co.uk/2/hi/technology/8548190.stm.

[101] Press Release, Internet Soc'y, Global Internet User Survey Reveals Attitudes, Usage, and Behavior (Nov. 20, 2012), https://bit.ly/2YiXIJN.

[102] UN Human Rights Council, *The Promotion, Protection and Enjoyment of Human Rights on the Internet*, U.N. Doc. A/HRC/32/L.20 (June 27, 2016), https://undocs.org/A/HRC/32/L.20.

[103] Special Rapporteur on the Promotion and Protection of the Right to Freedom of Opinion and Expression, Human Rights Council, U.N. Doc. A/HRC/17/27, at 1 (May 16, 2011) (by Frank La Rue).

[104] Human Rights Council Res. 32/13, U.N. Doc. A/HRC/RES/32/13, at 2 (July 18, 2016).

[105] David Kravets, *UN Report Declares Internet Access a Human Right*, WIRED (June 3, 2011, 2:47 PM), www.wired.com/2011/06/internet-a-human-right; Nicholas Jackson, *United Nations Declares Internet Access a Basic Human Right*, THE ATLANTIC (June 3, 2011), https://bit.ly/3uJVNo5.

[106] *See, e.g.*, Molly Land, *Toward an International Law of the Internet*, 54 HARV. INT'L L.J. 393, 394 (2013) ("Article 19's guarantee of a right to the technologies of connection also fills a critical gap in human rights law.").

blocking of YouTube violated the right to freedom of expression.[107] In particular, the court highlighted the role of the Internet as speech-enhancing technology that promotes participation in political and social discourse and facilitates the creation of user-generated content.[108]

Indian courts have also recognized internet access as a fundamental right. In September 2019, the Kerala High Court held that the right to internet access should be protected as a fundamental right because it is related to the right to education as well as the right to privacy under the Constitution of India.[109] In January 2020, the Indian Supreme Court concurred with that opinion, ruling that "the freedom of speech and expression and the freedom to practice any profession or carry on any trade, business or occupation over the medium of [I]nternet enjoys constitutional protection."[110] Similarly, courts in Costa Rica and France have recognized internet access as a fundamental right.[111]

C RECOGNIZING THE FUNDAMENTAL RIGHT TO TECHNOLOGY

1 The Critical Importance of Technology

Like the Internet, many other technologies play a vital role in safe-guarding individual liberties and improving societal well-being. Advances in medical technology, for example, have led to lower infant mortality rates, cures for diseases, and many more improvements in health. More and more household and personal home healthcare apparatuses are being rolled out in the market, reducing repeat admissions to hospitals. Similarly, advances in biological technology have improved the quantity and quality of food. The invention of environmentally friendly technologies has equipped us with tools to better

---

[107] Cengiz v. Turkey, Apps. Nos. 48226/10 & 14027/11, Eur. Ct. H.R. (2015).

[108] *Id.* para. 49, 52.

[109] Shirin R.K. v. State of Kerala, WP(C). NO. 19716 OF 2019(L), 20 High Court of Kerala (Sept. 19, 2019), https://bit.ly/3izz2P3.

[110] Bhasin v. Union of India No. 1031/2019, Supreme Court of India 127 (Jan. 10, 2020), https://bit.ly/3B9uIx0.

[111] Liu Huawen & Yan Yuting, *Interpretation of the Concept of the Right to Internet Access from the Perspective of International Law*, 15 J. Hum. Rts. 140, 147 (2016).

protect the water, air, and land essential to our survival. Various renewable energy-generating devices, such as solar panels and wind turbines, have been developed to provide alternatives to traditional fossil fuels and combat climate change.

Technology also plays an essential role in promoting the quality of life. In contemporary society, new technologies such as smartphones and tablets make it much easier for people to locate and obtain information on various aspects of their lives, helping them to make better-informed decisions. These technologies also provide an easy means of connecting with one another as well as better access to a variety of entertainment content.

From the societal standpoint, technology plays a vital role in economic development, for example, through creating new tools and methods of production that improve efficiency and productivity. Technology also shapes cultural development, changing our work and lifestyles dramatically. The motorcar has given people opportunities to express their individualism and to enjoy geographical freedom, while the combustion engine that powers cars, ferries, trains, and airplanes has reduced traveling time and distance.[112] Particularly influential has been the rise of mass and social media. The invention of cameras and projectors in the late nineteenth and early twentieth centuries and the formation of major studios such as MGM and Paramount in the 1920s produced a thriving US film industry. Radio then television flourished, and both remain accessible sources of information and entertainment. Social media has enabled unprecedentedly wide access to information and means of expression.

2 The Nature and Scope of the New Right

Because the Internet is not the only technology that plays a vital role in promoting individual liberties and societal well-being, the Due Process Clause should be extended to a broader fundamental right to technology. This contention aligns with several surveys demonstrating the importance of technologies. For example, in a recent survey the Pew

---

[112] GARY CROSS & RICK SZOSTAK, *Technology and American Society: A History* 272 (2d ed. 2005).

Research Center asked Americans what had contributed to the greatest improvement in their lives in the past five decades.[113] Respondents gave technology greater credit than both the expansion of civil rights and economic improvement.[114] They also predicted that technology would be the most important force for improvements in their lives in the next five decades.[115] Another recent study by the Charles Koch Institute produced similar results, showing that more than an absolute majority of Americans believe that technology has made their lives better and expect technology to continue improving the quality of life of their children.[116]

The new fundamental right to technology has two major functions. First, it entitles everyone to the benefits of *fundamental technologies*, creating a positive rights mandate that ensures their equal distribution. Fundamental technologies, such as electricity, transportation, telephony, and the Internet, sustain lives.[117] They also enhance quality of life, enabling the pursuit of economic, political, and cultural freedoms.[118] With respect to societal interests, these technologies are essential to increasing productivity and efficiency in the provision of goods and services and to promoting the quality of communications and healthcare systems.

Second, the fundamental right to technology can also be applied to protect people from seriously harmful uses of technologies. From this perspective, it creates a negative right that prohibits governments, companies, and individuals from utilizing technology in a manner that may jeopardize the maintenance of a democratic political system, improvement of the environment, the enhancement of innovation capacity, and the

---

[113] Mark Strauss, *Four-in-Ten Americans Credit Technology with Improving Life Most in the Past 50 Years*, PEW RES. CTR. (Oct. 12, 2017), https://pewrsr.ch/2YjU78G.

[114] *Id.*

[115] *Id.*

[116] Press Release, Ipsos Public Affairs, GET Creative/USA Today Network, Charles Koch Institute – Technology Survey (Mar. 1, 2019).

[117] *See* Rochelle Cooper Dreyfuss, Patents and Human Rights: The Paradox Re-Examined, in INTELLECTUAL PROPERTY AND ACCESS TO SCIENCE AND CULTURE: CONVERGENCE OR CONFLICT? 65, 65 (Christophe Geiger ed., 2016) (arguing that the right to technology "extends only to basic technologies, such as medicines, transportation, telephones, and computers – as opposed to Ferraris, smartphones, high-definition televisions, Roombas or Fitbits").

[118] *See, e.g.*, RONALD C. TOBEY, TECHNOLOGY AS FREEDOM 3 (1997).

achievement of food security, among other societal interests. For example, when a government utilizes digital technologies to unduly filter or even shut down the Internet, it undermines or denies completely both the individual's freedom of information and the Internet's power to promote socially beneficial exchanges of information.[119]

The positive right to technology differs from the negative right to technology in two ways. First, it requires the government to take proactive measures to distribute the benefits of fundamental technologies equally among citizens. Private parties, including technology companies that are holders of intellectual property, are encouraged to partake in this distribution process. The negative right to technology, in contrast, prohibits any party, be it a governmental agency or a technology company, from using any technology to unduly cause serious harm to individual and societal interests.

Second, while the negative right to technology guards against using any technology in a harmful fashion, the positive right to technology requires the government to promote distribution of the benefits of fundamental technologies alone. It does not apply to *derivative technologies* that embody improvements to fundamental technologies and offer extra benefits. For example, one could assert that to protect the fundamental right to technology, a local government should provide public transportation and telecommunication services. Both transportation and phones are fundamental technologies consisting of basic techniques for making various vehicles and phones. However, one cannot rely upon the fundamental right to technology to assert that Mercedes Benz buses should be utilized for public transportation or that the local government should provide every resident with an iPhone. Both the Mercedes Benz bus and iPhone are derivative technologies developed from fundamental transportation and communication technologies.

3 Objections to the New Right to Technology

Despite the potential benefits of a new right to technology, there have been vehement objections to recognizing internet access as a legal right.

---

[119] *See* JONATHAN ZITTRAIN, THE FUTURE OF THE INTERNET AND HOW TO STOP IT 8–9, 117–18 (2008).

Were these objections to be accepted, then a legal right to the benefits of other fundamental technologies could also be denied. Vinton Cerf, who is considered one of the "fathers of the Internet" for co-designing a set of protocols used for data transmission over computer networks,[120] is a leading dissenting voice. For example, he has argued that

> technology is an enabler of rights, not a right itself. There is a high bar for something to be considered a human right. Loosely put, it must be among the things we as humans need in order to lead healthy, meaningful lives, like freedom from torture or freedom of conscience. It is a mistake to place any particular technology in this exalted category, since over time we will end up valuing the wrong things. For example, at one time if you didn't have a horse it was hard to make a living. But the important right in that case was the right to make a living, not the right to a horse.[121]

Human rights, in Cerf's view, are synonymous with the ends of human life, such as freedom of expression and freedom from torture.[122] The Internet merely facilitates these ends by providing access to and disseminating information with unprecedented ease.[123] Therefore, it is not desirable to protect the Internet, a technological tool, as a human right. This line of reasoning can be extended to other technologies as well. Relying upon the views of Cerf and others, governments have rejected the idea that internet access should be protected as a fundamental right.[124]

In my opinion, Cerf misunderstands the relationship between human rights and technology in three ways. First, human rights

---

[120] *Internet Hall of Fame Pioneer: Vint Cerf*, INTERNET HALL OF FAME, www .internethalloffame.org/inductees/vint-cerf (last visited on Dec. 6, 2020).

[121] Vinton G. Cerf, *Internet Access Is Not a Human Right*, N.Y. TIMES (Jan. 4, 2012), https:// nyti.ms/3abaqYi.

[122] *Id.* ("The best way to characterize human rights is to identify the outcomes that we are trying to ensure. These include critical freedoms like freedom of speech and freedom of access to information.").

[123] *Id.* ("The Internet has introduced an enormously accessible and egalitarian platform for creating, sharing and obtaining information on a global scale. As a result, we have new ways to allow people to exercise their human and civil rights.").

[124] *See, e.g.*, Azaan Javaid, *Access to Internet Is Not a Fundamental Right but an Enabler of Rights, J&K Govt Tells SC*, THE PRINT (Apr. 29, 2020), https://bit.ly/2Yw5jzo ("The [Jammu and Kashmir] government submitted that the internet was an 'enabler of rights and not a right in itself', and that 'the present 2G speed of internet does enable one to create, access, utilise and share information and knowledge'.").

themselves serve freedom, justice, and peace, and these are the greater ends of human life and society. The Universal Declaration of Human Rights (UDHR) makes this clear, stating that "recognition of the inherent dignity and of the equal and inalienable rights of all members of the human family is the foundation of *freedom, justice* and *peace* in the world."[125] The right to freedom of expression and to freedom from torture, as protected by the UDHR, facilitate the attainment of those goals. So does the right to technology. When the UDHR was created in 1948, its framers decided to protect technology as a human right because the enjoyment of the benefits of technology is of intrinsic worth to the goals of freedom, justice, and peace. Today, the COVID-19 pandemic has proved the practical value of the framers' decision. The Internet plays an indispensable role in promoting freedom and justice for people who suffer from a lack of access to in-person education and entertainment during the pandemic. If we were to protect the right to technology to eliminate the digital divide, then those people would be able to enjoy the benefits of technological progress in the form of the Internet.

Second, the human rights system recognizes and protects rights to resources that are crucially important to human flourishing. These basic resources, such as private property, food, water, and housing, enable individuals to sustain themselves and prosper in their private spaces and communities.[126] By the same token, fundamental technologies such as the Internet are crucial resources for human flourishing, as this section demonstrates, and the benefits of such technologies are therefore worthy of human rights protection. This is exactly why the UDHR has since its inception embraced the right to technology as a human right. Moreover, resource-based human rights are supportive or enabling. For example, realization of the rights to property, food, and water sustain the capability to exercise one's right to freedom of expression.

Third, beyond a narrow right to internet access, a broader right to technology is needed to protect a wide range of technological benefits. Returning to Cerf's analogy, there is no need to recognize "the right to

---

[125] UDHR, pmbl (emphasis added).
[126] *See, e.g.*, UDHR, arts. 17 (protecting the right to property), 25 (protecting the right to food).

a horse" over the right to make a living. However, there is a need to protect the right to property, which entitles one to own the horse that one utilizes to make a living, as well as other personal belongings. The same logic applies to internet access. There is no legal right that merely protects one's access to the Internet. However, internet access can be protected by the right to technology. As the property right protects many types of things, this broader right protects not only internet access but also the benefits of other fundamental technologies.

D PROTECTING THE FUNDAMENTAL RIGHT TO TECHNOLOGY

In this section, I consider how the fundamental right to technology can be protected to promote the equal distribution of technological benefits and to prevent harmful uses of technologies. I use internet access as a vantage point to illustrate the legal and policy implications of this right. I argue that recognizing and protecting the fundamental right to technology would help to bridge the digital chasm in the United States in three ways. First, it would require the government to proactively protect the right by expanding access to the Internet. Second, it would empower courts to conduct judicial reviews of the validity of relevant governmental decisions in the public interest.

1 Proactive Protection by the Government

If recognized, the fundamental right to technology would create two advantages in stimulating government action to ensure a fair distribution of benefits accruing from the Internet. First, it would motivate the government to embrace universal and affordable access to the Internet as an ultimate policy objective and to make every effort to protect internet access as a technological benefit that every individual is entitled to enjoy.[127] Internet access can no longer be regarded as a daily utility

---

[127] *See, e.g.*, Anne Peacock, Human Rights and the Digital Divide 17–18 (2019) (discussing how the recognition of a human right to access the Internet functions to impose obligations on governments to bridge the digital divide).

for some and an unaffordable luxury for others. As discussed through-out this chapter, the COVID-19 pandemic has revealed the urgency of protecting the right to technology. In the post-pandemic era, it will play an even more important role in promoting individual and societal well-being.[128] For instance, as more companies allow their employees to work remotely online, internet access will become a precondition for this major shift in the employment sector.[129]

Rather than a piecemeal approach that temporarily aids certain groups in dire need of internet access, the US government should adopt a comprehensive and systematic strategy. To this end, it should set up a commission comprising experts from various stakeholder sectors to examine why internet access remains inequitable and why the government has failed to tackle the issue competently. Based upon this thorough investigation, the commission should make recom-mendations on the crucial steps that the government should follow in order to achieve universal and affordable internet access nationwide.

To address the poverty-related aspects of the digital chasm, the commission should suggest ways for the government to ensure that all public spaces, including schools and libraries, are equipped with high-speed Wi-Fi. It should also consider whether it would be more desirable for the government to provide financial subsidies directly to low-income families to connect their homes to broadband internet or provide subsidies to telecommunications companies to provide broad-band internet connections at affordable rates. With respect to the digital divide attributable to geographical isolation, the commission should develop new plans to overcome the misguided actions taken by the government in the past. For example, some state laws forbid local governments from building municipally owned broadband networks.[130]

---

[128] Tom Wheeler, *5 Steps to Get the Internet to All Americans: COVID-19 and the Importance of Universal Broadband*, BROOKINGS (May 27, 2020) ("Our reliance on the internet during coronavirus has recast how we will behave after the crisis has passed. The big lesson is that we have incorporated the internet as a critical part of our personal and professional lives.").

[129] Rob McLean, *These Companies Plan to Make Working from Home the New Normal. As in Forever*, CNN BUSINESS (June 25, 2020); Christine Ro, *Why the Future of Work Might be "Hybrid"*, BBC (Aug. 30, 2020), https://bbc.in/3BfLzhR.

[130] *See* Ronald Klain, *Inequality and the Internet*, DEMOCRACY J. (Summer 2015), https://democracyjournal.org/magazine/37/inequality-and-the-internet.

Second, the fundamental right to technology, if recognized, would compel the government to make dynamic decisions about expanding internet access to keep pace with evolving technological circumstances, such as the transition to 5G networks. It would require the government to remain responsive and adjust its decisions to guarantee individuals' continued enjoyment of a technologically advanced internet. For instance, the public could capitalize on this fundamental right by urging the FCC to alter its 2015 definition of "broadband" as services that deliver 25 Mbps downstream and 3 Mbps upstream.[131] In 2015, these were indeed the speeds necessary to allow video streaming.[132] However, rapid technological developments have rendered the FCC's broadband definition obsolete and problematic.[133] Current fiber-optic networks, for example, can reach speeds as fast as 10,000 Mbps.[134] Relying on the FCC's outdated broadband definition, the major internet service providers (ISPs) have chosen not to upgrade fiber-optic networks in the United States so as to retain their very lucrative business.[135] Meanwhile, consumer demand for the technological benefits of faster internet speeds has increased dramatically. The COVID-19 pandemic has also strengthened families' need for enhanced internet capacity because it has necessitated that they have multiple devices connected simultaneously for such activities as online learning, working, entertainment, and telehealth.[136]

[131] *See* Wheeler, *supra* note 128 ("While technology and time have moved on ... the FCC's broadband definition has not."). Mbps, shorthand for "Megabits Per Second," is used to measure data transfer speeds of high bandwidth connections, such as the Ethernet and cable modems.

[132] *See* Wheeler, *supra* note 128.

[133] Ernesto Falcon, *The American Federal Definition of Broadband Is Both Useless and Harmful*, ELECTRONIC FRONTIER FOUNDATION (Jul. 17, 2020) ("In fact, the 25/3 metric is downright slow by today's standards and needs, and is practically near obsolescence.").

[134] *See A Complete Guide to Fiber Optic Internet*, OTELCO, www.otelco.com/resources/a-guide-to-fiber-optic-internet/ (last visited Dec. 6, 2020).

[135] Ernesto Falcon, *The House Has a Universal Fiber Broadband Plan We Should Get Behind*, ELECTRONIC FRONTIER FOUNDATION (June 24, 2020) ("The big ISPs, which fail to deliver universal access but enjoy comfortable monopolies and charge you prices at 200% to 300% above competitive rates, will resist this effort. Even when it is profitable to deliver fiber, the national ISPs have chosen not to do it in exchange for short-term profits.").

[136] *See* Wheeler, *supra* note 128 ("While technology and time have moved on – and COVID-19 has added to the importance of supporting multiple online devices in homes – the FCC's broadband definition has not. This decision affects the quality of service that rural Americans receive from a subsidized network provider."); Jed Pressgrove, *Does the Federal Broadband Definition Reflect Real-World Need?*, GOVERNMENT TECHNOLOGY (June 24, 2020) ("Freddoso said the 3 Mbps upload part of the definition seems

2 Enhanced Judicial Protection

The fundamental right to technology would also empower courts to conduct judicial reviews of governmental decisions that unduly impede access to the Internet. To date, courts have relied on the First Amendment to decide whether governmental decisions that restrict access to the Internet infringe the right to free speech.[137] Under the fundamental right to technology, courts would have a new legal basis for protecting people's legitimate interests in accessing the Internet when the First Amendment is not applicable.

Preserving network neutrality is an issue urgently in need of sensible judicial review. As one of the core principles underpinning a free and open internet, network neutrality requires ISPs to treat all content equally without discrimination.[138] It thereby treats the Internet as a public utility that should not be manipulated by private companies at the expense of the public interest. Without this principle, an ISP can legally discriminate against content or applications by refusing to transmit them or by slowing down the speed at which they are transmitted. Despite its importance, the FCC terminated the network neutrality principle in 2017, primarily because it inhibited market-driven innovation of digital technology.[139] Although the House of Representatives passed the 2019 Save the Internet Act to rescind the FCC's decision, the Senate blocked its further consideration, and President Trump proclaimed that he would veto it.[140]

By triggering the strict scrutiny test, the fundamental right to technology would serve as a new legal basis for courts to review the validity of government decisions such as the FCC's repeal of network neutrality. Pursuant to the jurisprudence of US constitutional law, courts should apply the strict scrutiny test to weigh whether there is a compelling interest for any governmental encroachment upon a fundamental right

especially behind the times, now that households are more likely to have multiple instances of two-way communication occurring at the same time.").
[137] *See, e.g.*, Packingham, 137 S. Ct. at 1730 (ruling that the government's prevention of convicted criminals from using the Internet infringes their free speech right).
[138] *See* Tim Wu, *Network Neutrality, Broadband Discrimination*, 2 J. TELECOMM. & HIGH TECH. L. 141, 167–68 (2003).
[139] *See* Restoring Internet Freedom, 33 FCC Rcd. 311 (2017) (declaratory ruling).
[140] Ella Nilsen, *Why the Senate Is Blocking a New Net Neutrality Bill, a Year After Trying to Save It*, VOX (Apr. 10, 2019, 12:00 PM), https://bit.ly/3ozl9nD.

and whether the government has adopted a narrowly tailored measure to achieve the compelling interest.[141] With regard to network neutrality, a court would first require the FCC to supply a compelling reason for repealing the principle. The need to reinstate a free market for digital technology innovation may not be sufficiently compelling because network neutrality is not intended to restrict telecommunications companies' freedom to research boosting internet speed and data transmission capacity. Rather, it requires such companies only to transmit all data without favor or disfavor. Also, it may prove exceedingly difficult for the FCC to demonstrate the necessity of overriding the need to maintain an open and free internet by giving telecommunications companies the absolute freedom to decide what content they wish to transmit.

The fundamental right to technology would also empower the courts to review whether the FCC's decision constitutes the least restrictive means of achieving its policy objective so as not to run afoul of the second requirement of the strict scrutiny test. A court may point out that, to encourage innovation in digital technology, the FCC could have adopted measures such as providing telecommunications companies with funds to stimulate their internet research and liaise with the Patent and Trademark Office to capitalize on stronger patent protection of internet innovations as a stimulus to innovative activities. Given these alternative avenues, the FCC's repeal of network neutrality is likely not the least restrictive means of achieving its policy objective and therefore contravenes the second requirement of the strict scrutiny test.

To summarize, this new fundamental right, if recognized, would directly empower courts to apply a strict scrutiny test in order to stop the government from unduly affecting people's ability to enjoy technological benefits. It also has the potential to prevent the government from making decisions that may run counter to the new right, given that such decisions would need to meet the higher judicial review standards of the strict scrutiny test.

---

[141] *See* Regents of the Univ. of Cal. v. Bakke, 438 U.S. 265, 357 (1978) ("[A] government practice or statute which restricts 'fundamental rights' ... is to be subjected to 'strict scrutiny' and can be justified only if it furthers a compelling government purpose and, even then, only if no less restrictive alternative is available.") (Brennan, White, Marshall, and Blackmun, JJ., concurring in the judgment in part and dissenting in part).

SUMMARY

The COVID-19 pandemic has triggered unprecedented use of the Internet, which has attracted media attention and scrutiny to the long-existing digital chasm that disadvantages too many people. Protection of a fundamental right to technology, as I have demonstrated, has the power to pave the way for legal and public policy reforms that are badly needed to better distribute the benefits of the Internet and other fundamental technologies to all Americans for generations to come. This thought experiment is made in the hope that if the United States, a jurisdiction with a constitution lacking protection of economic, social, and cultural rights, could venture to recognize and adopt the fundamental right to technology, it would encourage other jurisdictions to do the same, paving the way for global protection of this right.

Dynamic protection of the right to technology, as discussed in Chapters 1, 2 and 3, sheds new light on the nature and scope of public interests implicated in the development and application of technology as well as effective means of protecting those interests. First, technology-related public interests encompass the following three dimensions:

• societal interests in public freedom and dignity held by all members of a society in relation to the enjoyment of benefits of technological progress;
• group interests in collective freedom and dignity held by all members of a group of people in relation to the enjoyment of benefits of technological progress; and
• private interests in individual freedom and dignity in relation to the enjoyment of benefits of technological progress that are so fundamental that they merit constitutional protection.

Second, technology-related public interests may give rise to three levels of legal rights: a human right protected by international treaties, a collective right protected by domestic courts as a civil liberty, and a fundamental right protected by constitutions. From this perspective, governments must proactively examine their obligations to protect the right to technology under international human rights treaties and domestic civil rights and constitutional laws. Courts would play an important role in ensuring that governments protect this right adequately by serving as a venue where members of the public can actively assert their interests.

Third, it is vital to drive a social process of deliberating the nature and scope of technology-related public interests and means of effectively protecting them. The right to technology cannot be simply stated as a human right, a civil liberty, or a constitutional right on paper. Instead, we should set in motion an active process of deliberation, social learning, and rights assertion to transform ways in which technology-related public interests are promoted regionally, nationally, and globally. From this perspective, the thought experiment elevating the right to technology to a fundamental right activates a constitutional process where more dynamic protection of technology-related public interests is sought.

4   THE IRRESPONSIBILITY OF TECHNOLOGY COMPANIES

The responsibilities that technology companies have assumed are completely inadequate compared to the powers they have gained. Facebook is a prime example. It achieved unparalleled success among technology companies, attracting 2.3 billion users in just fifteen years following its inception in 2004.[1] It has also abused the trust of those users,[2] secretly selling private user data to Cambridge Analytica in the biggest privacy scandal in social network history, and allowing its platform to become a vehicle for the fake news that likely swayed the 2016 presidential election in the United States. A judge has even gone so far as to describe Facebook as "a tool for evil" in a judicial ruling.[3] Whistleblowers and journalistic investigation support this allegation, providing hard evidence that Facebook has prioritized profit over the well-being of its users and society.[4]

---

[1] Meira Gebel, *In 15 Years Facebook Has Amassed 2.3 Billion Users – More Than Followers of Christianity*, Bus. Insider (Feb. 4, 2019).

[2] *See* Roger McNamee, Zucked: Waking Up to the Facebook Catastrophe 2 (2019) ("Facebook . . . [has] taken advantage of our trust, using sophisticated techniques to prey on the weakest aspects of human psychology, to gather and exploit private data, and to craft business models that do not protect users from harm.").

[3] *Facebook is a "Tool for Evil", Says Judge as Mother Trolled Over Fake Claims She Tried to Kill a Baby Is Found Dead*, Telegraph (Feb. 7, 2017,), https://bit.ly/3izReIl.

[4] Bobby Allyn, *Here Are 4 Key Points from the Facebook Whistleblower's Testimony on Capitol Hill*, NPR (October 5, 2021), https://n.pr/3pydqoz ("[Facebook whistleblower Frances Haugen] said Facebook harms children, sows division and undermines democracy in pursuit of breakneck growth and 'astronomical profits.'"); *The Facebook Files*, Wall St. J. (Updated Oct. 1, 2021), https://on.wsj.com/3Gi4avL ("Facebook Inc. knows, in acute detail, that its platforms are riddled with flaws that cause harm, often in ways only the company fully understands.").

With great power, it is often said, comes great responsibility.[5] Leading technology companies, however, have reaped phenomenal profits with impunity, demonstrating no commitment to a conception of corporate responsibility that is anywhere near commensurate with the nature and extent of their ever-expanding powers. The public has invested their trust and support in Facebook and other technology companies, which have largely ignored their attendant responsibilities in return. Instead, they have created a "black box society"[6] and new forms of oppression, and a sector in which privacy breaches have become routine.

In this chapter, I argue that both shareholder value theory and US legal reforms in the past twenty years or so have encouraged technology companies to neglect their fundamental responsibilities. Guided by shareholder value theory, those reforms have failed to correct the asymmetry between technology companies' rights and their responsibilities. Major statutes have been enacted to minimize the legal liabilities of technology companies with respect to online infringing acts, privacy protection, and the payment of taxes. Although these statutes have undeniably promoted innovation, they have also had the unintended effect of breeding irresponsibility among technology companies.

A THEORETICAL SUPPORT FOR MINIMIZING RESPONSIBILITIES

For decades, shareholder value theory catalyzed the minimization of technology companies' responsibilities, leading the world to fully support the maximization of their wealth growth to encourage innovation. This theory was initially influential in shaping the development of corporate responsibilities to society.[7] Its main champion was Nobel

---

[5] *See* Kimble v. Marvel Entm't, LLC, 135 S. Ct. 2401, 2415 (2015) (citing S. Lee & S. Ditko, *Spider-Man*, AMAZING FANTASY, Aug. 1962, at 13 ("[I]n this world, with great power there must also come – great responsibility.")).

[6] FRANK PASQUALE, THE BLACK BOX SOCIETY: THE SECRET ALGORITHMS THAT CONTROL MONEY AND INFORMATION 191 (2015).

[7] *See* Domènec Melé, *Corporate Social Responsibility Theories*, in THE OXFORD HANDBOOK OF CORPORATE SOCIAL RESPONSIBILITY 47, 56 (Andrew Crane et al. eds., 2008).

Laureate in Economics Milton Friedman, who stated the following in his book *Capitalism and Freedom*.

> The view has been gaining widespread acceptance that corporate officials and labor leaders have a "social responsibility" that goes beyond serving the interest of their stockholders or their members. This view shows a fundamental misconception of the character and nature of a free economy. In such an economy, there is one and only one social responsibility of business – to use its resources and engage in activities designed to increase its profits so long as it stays within the rules of the game, which is to say, engages in open and free competition, without deception or fraud.[8]

In Friedman's view, a company's only social responsibility is to make as much profit as possible for its shareholders. To this end, the directors of a company, who serve as agents managing the company for shareholders as principals, should make decisions designed to maximize shareholders' interests.[9] Therefore, corporate directors' sole responsibility is to serve shareholders' interests, not societal interests at large.[10]

Shareholder value theory categorically denies that companies should be legally required to take any social responsibility whatsoever.[11] In Friedman's eyes, companies are, by nature, profit-maximizing institutions.[12] As long as they pursue profit-driven agendas legally, the law must not impose any social responsibilities upon them.[13] Social responsibility initiatives, if imposed, would directly prevent corporate directors from wholeheartedly serving shareholders' interests, thereby indirectly undermining the bedrock of a free economy.[14]

---

[8] MILTON FRIEDMAN, CAPITALISM AND FREEDOM 133 (1962).

[9] Milton Friedman, *The Social Responsibility of Business Is to Increase its Profits*, N.Y. TIMES, Sept. 13, 1970, § 6, at 33.

[10] *Id.*

[11] José Salazar & Bryan W. Husted, *Principals and Agents: Further Thoughts on the Friedmanite Critique of Corporate Social Responsibility* 137, 150, *in* THE OXFORD HANDBOOK OF CORPORATE SOCIAL RESPONSIBILITY (Andrew Crane et al. eds., 2008).

[12] FRIEDMAN, *supra* note 8, at 33.

[13] *Id.* at 33 ("[T]here is one and only one social responsibility of business – to use its resources and engage in activities designed to increase its profits so long as it stays within the rules of the game, which is to say, engages in open and free competition, without deception or fraud.").

[14] *Id.* at 135.

Shareholder value theory has fundamentally shaped the exclusion of social responsibilities in corporate law and effectively defied corporate social responsibility initiatives. Based upon the theory, US corporate law treats companies as profit-maximizing institutions and therefore imposes no social responsibilities upon them.[15] The fiduciary duty doctrine epitomizes the law's espousal of shareholder value theory.[16] Company directors are charged with certain fiduciary duties to the shareholders of the company,[17] primarily duties of care and loyalty. The duty of care requires that "prior to making a business decision," directors inform themselves "of all material information reasonably available to them."[18] Rather than simply accept the information presented to them, directors must assess it with a "critical eye" in order to protect the interests of the corporation and its shareholders.[19] The duty of loyalty requires that, in serving as corporate fiduciaries, the directors and officers of a company make all decisions in good faith and in the best interest of their shareholders.[20] This duty elevates "stockholder welfare as the only end" of corporate decisions, thereby allowing the consideration of "other interests" only if they are "rationally related to stockholder welfare."[21]

Due to the dominance of shareholder value theory in policymaking, campaigns to advance corporate social responsibility have produced only limited effects. Scholars have put forward ethical responsibility and corporate citizenship theories to justify corporate social responsibility, lending strong support to the creation of corporate social responsibility initiatives such as the United Nations Norms on the Responsibilities of

---

[15] In my opinion, paying corporate tax should be seen as a compulsory legal duty under tax law rather than a social responsibility.

[16] *See, e.g.*, Thomas A. Smith, *The Efficient Norm for Corporate Law: A Neotraditional Interpretation of Fiduciary Duty*, 98 MICH. L. REV. 214, 214 (1999); Gregory S. Crespi, *Rethinking Corporate Fiduciary Duties: The Inefficiency of the Shareholder Primacy Norm*, 55 SMU L. REV. 141, 141 (2002).

[17] *See, e.g.*, Francis v. United Jersey Bank, 432 A.2d 814, 824 (N.J. 1981); Revlon, Inc. v. MacAndrews & Forbes Holdings, Inc., 506 A.2d 173, 179 (Del. 1986).

[18] Aronson v. Lewis, 473 A.2d 805, 812 (Del. 1984).

[19] Smith v. Van Gorkem, 488 A.2d 858, 872 (Del. 1985).

[20] According to the Delaware Supreme Court, "[c]orporate officers and directors are not permitted to use their position of trust and confidence to further their private interests." Guth v. Loft, 5 A.2d 503, 510 (Del. 1939).

[21] Frederick Hsu Living Tr. v. ODN Holding Corp., No. 12108, 2017 WL 1437308, at *17 (Del. Ch. Apr. 24, 2017).

Transnational Corporations and Other Business Enterprises with Regard to Human Rights. However, only a tiny proportion of the world's major corporations has signed up to such initiatives.

Many scholars and policymakers have tended to focus on particular issues such as environmental protection[22] rather than comprehensively examining the relationship between corporate social responsibility and technology companies. In fact, in the past twenty years or so, the major technology companies have been largely immune from scrutiny over whether they should have strong social responsibilities imposed upon them. Many scholars and policymakers have forcefully argued that technology companies – in particular online intermediaries – should bear as few responsibilities as possible. Otherwise, they would be financially overburdened, with innovation ultimately stifled, resulting in grave financial losses. Following this line of reasoning, the US Congress has adopted laws minimizing the responsibilities of online intermediaries. [23]

The upshot of all this is that the market cares too much about the economic value of technology companies. Those who invest in those companies are primarily interested in whether the companies will eventually go public and how much their stock value will soar if they do. The media has become a cheerleader, following and reporting on technology companies' stock market successes.[24] As technology companies' wealth has skyrocketed, they have become immune to ethical scrutiny of their responsibilities.[25]

B LEGAL SUPPORT FOR MINIMIZING RESPONSIBILITIES

Swayed by shareholder value theory, the US Congress has enacted major statutes that minimize the legal liability of technology companies

---

[22] See Alwyn Lim & Kiyoteru Tsutsui, *The Social Regulation of the Economy in the Global Context*, in CORPORATE SOCIAL RESPONSIBILITY IN A GLOBALIZING WORLD 8–9 (Kiyoteru Tsutsui & Alwyn Lim eds., 2015).

[23] See Anupam Chander, *How Law Made Silicon Valley*, 63 EMORY L.J. 639, 645 (2014) (summarizing these policy arguments).

[24] See Ryan Chittum, *The Press and the Tech Bubble*, COLUM. JOURNALISM REV. (Apr. 9, 2014), https://bit.ly/3Ds392n.

[25] A notable exception is the recent media discussion about Uber's IPO. See, e.g., Farhad Manjoo, *The Uber I.P.O. Is a Moral Stain on Silicon Valley*, N.Y. TIMES (May 1, 2019).

with respect to online infringing acts, privacy protection, and the payment of taxes. These statutes were adopted largely on the assumption that technology companies in the start-up stage had little financial capacity and that minimizing their responsibilities would incentivize the development of innovative services and products. However, they have had the unintended consequence of breeding a mentality of irresponsibility in the technology sector.

1 Exempting Internet Service Providers from Liability

In the 1990s, reforms of intermediary platforms' legal liabilities contributed tremendously to the rapid growth of technology companies. Under the Clinton administration, laws and regulations that hindered electronic commerce were reviewed, and in some cases eliminated, to respond to the needs of a new era of digital technology.

The first stage of legal reforms dealt with the extent to which internet service providers should be shielded from civil liability for online infringing acts. Congress enacted the Communications Decency Act (CDA) in 1996 as a legal tool to provide internet service providers with immunity from platform users' illegal activities, such as spreading defamatory information and provoking racial discrimination.[26] Before 1996, judicial rulings had exposed internet service providers to high risks, holding them accountable for illegal activities occurring on their platforms. In *Stratton Oakmont, Inc. v. Prodigy Services Co.*,[27] for example, an investment firm sued Prodigy, an internet service provider, for defamation based on statements posted by a user on Prodigy's online bulletin boards. Prodigy was held liable as the publisher of the defamatory statements posted by the user because it exercised editorial control over content posted on its online bulletin boards.[28]

In enacting § 230 of the CDA, Congress was responding to concerns over the *Stratton Oakmont* ruling. Section 230 provides that internet service providers should not be treated as publishers of

---

[26] Telecommunications Act of 1996, Pub. L. No. 104-104, §§ 501–61, 110 Stat. 56, 133–43 (codified as amended in scattered sections of 18 and 47 U.S.C.).

[27] 1995 WL 323710 (N.Y. Sup. Ct. 1995).

[28] *Id.* at *7.

material that they did not develop,[29] thereby generally protecting them from liability for user-generated content. The courts have interpreted § 230 broadly. Notably, they have determined that the provision excludes internet service providers from distributor liability in addition to publisher liability, despite offline distributors facing strict liability if they have knowledge of wrongdoing but fail to act.[30] Some commentators have defended § 230, celebrating the size that the online marketplace of ideas has achieved, and noting that that marketplace makes the Internet unsuitable for the rules applied to quantifiable offline publications.[31] However, others have argued that the protection provided has also stimulated the illicit digital economy, distorting the original intention of the CDA as a whole.[32] Rather than ensuring decency, § 230 has meant that the CDA has, for example, enabled online platforms such as Craigslist, Backpage, and many others to host and benefit from the sex-trafficking industry with impunity.[33]

Given that § 230 does not deal with intellectual property claims,[34] the second stage of legal reforms determined the extent to which internet service providers should be exempted from copyright liabilities arising from online infringing acts. Their online platforms allow users to reproduce and disseminate copyrighted works with unprecedented ease. Accordingly, it was determined that the strong possibility of users frequently infringing copyrights exposed internet service providers to contributory or vicarious liabilities to a dire and unmanageable extent. In this context, the Digital Millennium Copyright Act (DMCA) was enacted in 1998 to establish a safe harbor for internet service providers, shielding them from liability for their users' infringements of copyright.[35]

The DMCA has contributed positively to the legitimacy and survival of internet service providers. One of its primary legislative objectives was to preserve "strong incentives for service providers and copyright

---

[29] 47 U.S.C. § 230(c)(1) (2018).

[30] *See* Chander, *supra* note 23, at 652.

[31] *See* William H. Freivogel, *Does the Communications Decency Act Foster Indecency?*, 16 Comm. L. & Pol'y 17, 45 (2011).

[32] *See* Mary Graw Leary, *The Indecency and Injustice of Section 230 of the Communications Decency Act*, 41 Harv. J. L. & Pub. Pol'y 553, 554, 572 (2011).

[33] *Id.* at 572.

[34] 47 U.S.C. § 230(e)(2) (2018).

[35] Digital Millennium Copyright Act, Pub. L. No. 105-304, §§ 201–03, 112 Stat. 2860, 2877–86 (1998).

owners to cooperate to detect and deal with copyright infringements that take place in the digital networked environment."[36] Such cooperation operates as a notice-and-take-down system, whereby copyright owners have the right to order internet service providers to remove copyrighted works, and in return the providers are immunized from copyright infringement liabilities.[37] However, many have questioned whether the regime assigns sufficient responsibility to internet platforms. For instance, as take-down action becomes necessary only once an internet service provider has obtained knowledge of an infringement, it has been suggested that the DMCA has created strong disincentives for the proper monitoring of online content. [38]

2 Weakening Personal Data Protection

The current privacy protection regime in the United States is focused on stimulating technological innovation. Not only is there a lack of strong privacy regulations and laws, but the existing regulations/laws appear to accommodate the interests of technology companies.

The US privacy protection regime has been accused of being generally less robust than its EU counterpart,[39] a situation that stems in part from the weak status of information privacy in the US Constitution. In terms of privacy protection, the constitution only guards against intrusion by the government, thereby playing little role in governing breaches of privacy by private actors.[40] As a result, the free flow of information through private transactions has been given priority over the right to privacy. Further, the constitution does not protect privacy as a fundamental right. Rather, the right to privacy is accepted as merely implied in the Fourth, Fifth, and Fourteenth Amendments.[41]

---

[36] H.R. REP. No. 105-796, at 72 (1998) (Conf. Rep.).

[37] 17 U.S.C. §§ 512(b)(E), (c)(C), (d)(3) (2018).

[38] *See* Danny Freidmann, *Sinking the Safe-Harbor with the Legal Certainty of Strict Liability in Sight*, 9 J. INTELL. PROP. L. & PRACT. 148, 149 (2014).

[39] *See, e.g.*, Shawn Marie Boyne, *Data Protection in the United States*, 66 AM. J. COMP. L. 299, 299 n.3 (2018); Svetlana Yakovleva, *Privacy Protection(ism): The Latest Wave of Trade Constraints on Regulatory Autonomy*, 74 U. MIAMI L. REV. 416, 473–81 (2020).

[40] Paul M. Schwartz & Karl-Nikolaus Peifer, *Transatlantic Data Privacy Law*, 106 GEO. L.J. 115, 155 (2017).

[41] U.S. CONST. amends. IV, V, XIV.

The United States also lacks a single, coherent, and comprehensive federal law that regulates the collection and use of personal data. Instead, it has chosen to implement federal data protection laws that are sector-specific (e.g., financial institutions, healthcare entities, and communications common carriers) and type of information-specific (e.g., children's information on the Internet), complemented by state laws, administrative regulations, and industry-specific self-regulatory guidelines.[42] This piecemeal, sectoral approach to personal data protection leaves large areas, including the collection of personal data, unregulated in the age of big data and artificial intelligence.[43] The absence of federal law has prompted states to begin developing their own privacy regulations. Most notably, California's Consumer Privacy Act, which came into effect in January 2020, introduces measures akin to the EU's General Data Protection Regulation for the state's forty million residents and the technology companies of Silicon Valley.[44] These measures include a requirement of notice prior to the collection of personal information and an opportunity for consumers to opt out of the sale of their personal information and to request knowledge of or the deletion of information that a business has collected.[45] However, technology companies have responded by lobbying for a weaker federal privacy law, which, if successful, would roll back some of the stronger state protections and limit future state-based reforms.[46]

The current mishmash of federal, state, and industry regulations creates overlapping and contradictory protections. The inadequacy of such an approach becomes especially clear when regulations prove to be ineffective. For example, online platforms avoided the increased data collection responsibility arising from the Children's Online Privacy Protection Act of 1998 by banning those under the age of

---

[42] Boyne, *supra* note 39, at 299.

[43] *See* Daniel J. Solove & Woodrow Hartzog, *The FTC and the New Common Law of Privacy*, 114 COLUM. L. REV. 583, 587 (2014); Avner Levin & Mary Jo Nicholson, *Privacy Law in the United States, the EU and Canada: The Allure of the Middle Ground*, 2 U. OTTAWA L. & TECH. J. 357, 361–67 (2005).

[44] Zach Whittaker, *Silicon Valley is Terrified of California's Privacy Law. Good.*, TECHCRUNCH (Sep. 20, 2019), https://tcrn.ch/3Bdn4BW.

[45] California Consumer Privacy Act §§ 999.305(a)(1), 999.306(a)(1), 999.312 (2018).

[46] The Editorial Board, *Why Is America So Far Behind Europe on Digital Privacy?*, N.Y. TIMES (Jun. 8, 2019), https://nyti.ms/2YkSqsb.

thirteen, prompting millions of American children to simply lie about their age.[47] The time and effort spent developing a specific framework to protect the online privacy of children certainly appears wasted when one considers that as many as 7.5 million under-thirteens had Facebook accounts in 2011.[48] Furthermore, these data privacy laws are largely based on the principles of both tort law and contract law, which can result in conflicting interpretations and applications.[49] While contract principles might require companies to provide notice, choice, and access to any transfer of personal information, under tort law the focus is instead on whether the company has met the industry standard duty of care.[50]

The absence of a designated central data protection authority has also contributed to the weak protection of personal data in the United States.[51] The Federal Trade Commission (FTC) has essentially assumed responsibility for consumer protection, which covers the online protection of personal data.[52] However, the FTC can provide only limited protection owing to inherent problems in the Federal Trade Commission Act (FTCA).[53] Section 45(a) of the FTCA is seen as restrictive, as it enables users to sue only in cases where an internet service provider has committed "unfair or deceptive acts or practices in or affecting commerce."[54] What that effectively means, as Professor Anupam Chander notes, is that "as long as the services do not promise more privacy than they actually deliver, online companies in the United States have a free hand with information."[55]

[47] Chander, *supra* note 23, at 666.
[48] *7.5 Million Facebook Users are Under 13: Study*, INDEPENDENT (May 11, 2011), https://bit.ly/3izRlUh.
[49] Carolyn Hoang, *In the Middle: Creating a Middle Road Between US and EU Data Protection Policies*, 32 J. NAT'L ASS'N ADMIN. L. JUDICIARY 810, 843 (2012).
[50] *Id.*
[51] Steven Chabinsky & F. Paul Pittman, *USA: Data Protection 2019*, ICLG (Mar. 7, 2019), https://bit.ly/3AiuMsV.
[52] *See generally Bureau of Consumer Protection*, FED. TRADE COMMISSION, https://bit.ly/3oBYZkv (last visited Jan. 18, 2020) (explaining that "[t]he FTC's Bureau of Consumer Protection stops unfair, deceptive and fraudulent business practices by collecting complaints and conducting investigations, suing companies and people that break the law, developing rules to maintain a fair marketplace, and educating consumers and businesses about their rights and responsibilities").
[53] Federal Trade Commission Act, 15 U.S.C. §§ 41–58 (2018).
[54] *Id.* at § 45(a)(1).
[55] Chander, *supra* note 23, at 667.

3 Providing Tax Deduction Incentives

Legal reforms have also pushed for the provision of tax incentives to technology companies. In 1998, the US Congress enacted the Internet Tax Freedom Act (ITFA)[56] to promote the growth and development of the Internet and nurture its commercial, educational, and informational potential when it was still in its commercial infancy.[57] The ITFA prevented state and local governments from taxing internet access or imposing multiple or discriminatory taxes on electronic commerce. As a result, exposure and support for what are now billion-dollar internet companies, such as Google, were not compromised.

The US government has also supported technology firms' business research and development (R&D) through direct R&D funding, as well as tax incentives. At the federal level, firms are allowed an unlimited expense allowance for qualified research spending[58] and, most importantly, a research and experimentation tax credit that provides a non-refundable income tax credit for qualified R&D expenditures.[59] The latter was established in 1981 with the aim of incentivizing technological innovation in response to the decline in R&D expenditures.[60] The 2017 tax reform increased the tax value of the R&D tax credit indirectly and encouraged corporations to relocate their R&D activities to the United States.[61] The maximum assistance available to large corporations by way of the R&D tax credit is 15.8 percent of qualified research expenditure.[62]

---

[56] Internet Tax Freedom Act, Pub. L. No. 105-277, 112 Stat. 2681 (1998).

[57] Grant Gross, *US House Approves Permanent Ban on Internet Access Taxes*, PC WORLD (July 15, 2014, 12:03 PM), https://bit.ly/2YpBIaQ.

[58] 26 U.S.C. § 174 (2012).

[59] Economic Recovery Tax Act of 1981, Pub. L. No. 97-34, § 221, 95 Stat. 172, 241–47.

[60] STAFF OF JOINT COMM. ON TAXATION, 97TH CONG., GENERAL EXPLANATION OF THE ECONOMIC RECOVERY TAX ACT OF 1981 119–20 (Comm. Print 1981)

In the case of research and development activities conducted by business, company-financed and Federal expenditures over the 12-year period 1968–79 remained at a fairly stable level in real terms, fluctuating between $19 and $22.8 billion in constant dollars. Relative to real gross national product, such expenditures for company research declined from 2.01 percent in 1968 to 1.58 percent in 1975, essentially remaining at that level since then.

[61] ERNST & YOUNG, R&D INCENTIVES CONTINUE TO DRAW GOVERNMENT FAVOR: REFLECTIONS FROM EY'S THE OUTLOOK FOR GLOBAL TAX POLICY IN 2018 9 (2018), https://go.ey.com/3a9lYv1.

[62] DELOITTE, SURVEY OF GLOBAL INVESTMENT AND INNOVATION INCENTIVES 269 (2018), https://bit.ly/2Ywm2Tc.

Major technology companies have benefited tremendously from the tax incentive regime. For instance, Tesla received a $1.25 billion tax break over a twenty-year period for building a battery factory in Nevada, and Apple received a $214 million tax break for setting up a data center in Iowa.[63] Tax incentives like these are of great importance to technology companies, especially during their start-up period. For many start-up technology companies, finding and keeping the right technically skilled workers can be a challenge, and their revenues may be low while their costs soar.[64] Tax incentives can therefore help them to stabilize their workforce.[65] However, several major companies have continued to benefit from such tax breaks or sought ways to avoid paying tax despite achieving significant revenues. For instance, Facebook has faced significant criticism in the UK for directing its profits through Ireland and the Cayman Islands, paying only £28 million in UK tax in 2019 despite a record £1.6 billion in UK revenue.[66]

4 Breeding a Mentality of Irresponsibility

Although the lax regulatory system introduced by the statutes discussed above has undoubtedly promoted innovation, it has also created an environment in which technology companies have been able to act irresponsibly. Without users' knowledge or consent, these companies have disclosed personal data to third parties and/or used private data for targeted advertising.

Beyond the Cambridge Analytica scandal, Facebook has misused private data in a considerable number of incidents. In 2011, Facebook

---

[63] Ron Miller, *Amazon Isn't the Only Tech Company Getting Tax Breaks*, TECHCRUNCH (Aug. 25, 2018, 9:00 AM), https://tcrn.ch/3BqATNa.

[64] Lynda Finan, *Government Investment in Technology: How Governments Use Tax Regimes to Attract R&D Activity*, DLA PIPER (Jan. 17, 2018), https://bit.ly/3iv5pOL.

[65] *Id.* Tax incentives allow high-tech firms to focus on R&D, which leads to innovation, and, in a highly competitive field like technology, innovation is crucial for business survival. The UK has set out objectives such as a $2.3 billion investment in R&D in 2021 and 2022 in order to secure itself a position as the most innovative nation by 2030. *Id.* These UK objectives demonstrate both the importance of R&D and the tremendous value of tax incentives for technology firms.

[66] Mark Sweney, *Facebook Paid Just £28m Tax After Record £1.6bn Revenues in UK*, GUARDIAN (Oct. 11, 2019), https://bit.ly/3mlUAzA.

agreed to settle FTC charges alleging that it had made false and misleading material statements to its users relating to user privacy[67] by assuring them that their information on Facebook would be kept private, and then, without users' knowledge or consent, repeatedly allowing that information to be shared and made public.[68] It was reported that Facebook had harvested the e-mail contacts of 1.5 million users without their knowledge or consent since May 2016, asking new users for e-mail passwords and then importing the contacts without users' permission.[69] Facebook was also found to have stored the data of non-Facebook users, who were not even allowed to provide consent or accept the company's privacy agreement.[70] In 2019, Facebook was further criticized after an investigation found that it was receiving data from external apps, including sensitive information on individuals' menstruation cycles, body weight, and blood pressure.[71]

Platforms such as Facebook have also taken inadequate care with the information they receive from users. For example, in 2019 it was revealed that Facebook had stored the passwords of hundreds of millions of users as plaintext on its internal platform.[72] Although

---

[67] *Facebook Settles FTC Charges That It Deceived Consumers by Failing to Keep Privacy Promises*, FED. TRADE COMMISSION (Nov. 29, 2011), https://bit.ly/3DiP4ET.

[68] *Id.* The settlement agreement, which became final in 2012, prohibited Facebook from misrepresenting the extent to which it maintains users' data privacy and security and required the firm to seek express consent from users before sharing information beyond their privacy settings. Facebook, Inc., 0923184 F.T.C. No. C-4365, at 3–4 (2012); *see also FTC Approves Final Settlement with Facebook*, FED. TRADE COMMISSION (Aug. 10, 2012), https://bit.ly/3BeqxQL.

[69] Rob Price, *Facebook Says it "Unintentionally Uploaded" 1.5 Million People's Email Contacts Without Their Consent*, BUS. INSIDER (Apr. 17, 2019, 8:07 PM), https://bit.ly/3BeqvbB.

[70] Russell Brandom, *Shadow Profiles are the Biggest Flaw in Facebook's Privacy Defence*, THE VERGE (Apr. 11, 2018), https://bit.ly/3l8piNb.

The most concrete example of a shadow profile comes from Facebook's People You May Know service . . . Even if you've never signed up for Facebook, you've appeared in the contacts lists of people who did. When users connect their email account or texting data with Facebook, countless non-users are swept up. Instead of discarding their information, Facebook keeps non-user data attached to . . . a reliable bank of information held in reserve so that, if you ever do sign up for Facebook, the company will know exactly who to recommend as friends.

[71] Sam Schechner & Mark Secada, *You Give Apps Sensitive Personal Information. Then They Tell Facebook*, WALL ST. J. (Feb. 22, 2019), https://on.wsj.com/3owLsuN.

[72] Lily Hay Newman, *Facebook Stored Millions of Passwords in Plaintext – Change Yours Now*, WIRED (Mar. 21, 2019), www.wired.com/story/facebook-passwords-plaintext-change-yours.

Facebook claimed that the information had not been internally abused or externally accessed, such sensitive data had undoubtedly been exposed to security breach risks. Similarly, owing to a software glitch, Google inadvertently exposed the names, e-mail addresses, ages, and other personal details of 52.5 million Google+ users to third-party developers between 2015 and March 2018,[73] causing Google to accelerate its plan to shut down Google+.[74] However, it was reported that Google intentionally opted not to disclose the incident as early as it could have done, in part because it was worried that the incident would trigger "immediate regulatory interest" and lead to reputational damage.[75]

Moreover, technology companies have irresponsibly operated targeted advertising by taking advantage of users' personal data without their consent. If a user searches for a product using Google's search engine service, an advertisement for the same product may appear on their Instagram feed shortly afterwards. Internet users are also likely to be familiar with variations of the statement "this website uses cookies for the best possible search experience." In this way, technology companies have gone beyond their roles as search engine service providers and social media outlets. Rather, they are shrewdly run billion-dollar corporations that depend heavily on advertising. For instance, in 2018, Facebook made more than $50 billion in advertising revenue, which amounted to 98.5 percent of its total revenues.[76] Targeted advertisements are transmitted to individuals by utilizing personal data collected by technology companies routinely and without the targets' consent.[77] How much a technology company knows about an individual determines how much money it can make.[78]

---

[73] Douglas MacMillan & Robert McMillan, *Google Exposed User Data, Feared Repercussions of Disclosing to Public*, WALL ST. J. (Oct. 8, 2018), https://on.wsj.com/2YgoEEq; Lily Hay Newman, *A New Google+ Blunder Exposed Data From 52.5 Million Users*, WIRED (Dec. 10, 2018, 2:19 PM), https://bit.ly/3AebTr9.

[74] MacMillan & McMillan, *supra* note 73.

[75] *Id.*

[76] Matthew Johnston, *How Facebook Makes Money: Advertising Dominates Revenue, but Growth Is Slowing*, INVESTOPEDIA, https://bit.ly/3izW8EY (last updated Jan. 12, 2020).

[77] *See* Louise Matsakis, *Facebook's Targeted Ads Are More Complex than It Lets On*, WIRED (Apr. 25, 2018, 4:04 PM), https://bit.ly/3a6bpJf.

[78] Joanna Glasner, *What Search Sites Know About You*, WIRED (Apr. 5, 2005, 2:00 AM), www.wired.com/2005/04/what-search-sites-know-about-you.

Despite greater scrutiny of platform conduct in recent years, many believe that targeted advertisements are becoming increasingly invasive. A survey of US internet users showed that as of mid-2018, 71 percent believed that online advertisements were more intrusive than they had been three years previously.[79] While research has shown that its effectiveness is reduced when users become aware that their information is being shared with third parties, targeted advertising has proven generally effective in increasing sales. Platforms therefore have a financial incentive to continue using targeted advertisements with minimal transparency.[80] To date, they have done so in concerning ways, as advertisers have not only used personal information to sell products, but also to launch or interfere with political campaigns[81] or to engage in socially divisive advertising, "where malicious advertisers incite social conflict by publishing ads on divisive societal issues of the day."[82]

Such conduct was most notably engaged in by Russia in the lead-up to the 2016 US presidential election. In 2018, the Democrat-led Permanent Select Committee on Intelligence released 3,517 Facebook advertisements from 2015 to 2017 that were all linked to the Internet Research Agency,[83] a company owned by a close ally of the Russian president.[84] The advertisers concerned focused primarily on swing states with tight races and took advantage of information made available by Facebook to send divisive advertisements to targeted audiences.[85] For instance, voters in Wisconsin received advertisements relating to gun rights around 72 percent more often than the national average,

[79] Melanie Mohr, *Ads are Becoming More Intrusive in 2019*, MEDIUM (Jan. 22, 2019), https://bit.ly/2YkTA71.
[80] Louise Matsakis, *Online Ad Targeting Does Work – As Long As It's Not Creepy*, WIRED (May 11, 2018), https://bit.ly/3mt5V0U.
[81] Stuart A. Thompson, *These Ads Think They Know You*, N.Y. TIMES (Apr. 30, 2019), https://nyti.ms/3mt6bwU.
[82] Felipe N. Riberio, *et al.*, *On Microtargeting Socially Divisive Ads: A Case Study of Russia-Linked Ad Campaigns on Facebook*, FAT* '19: PROCEEDINGS OF THE CONFERENCE ON FAIRNESS, ACCOUNTABILITY, AND TRANSPARENCY (2019), https://dl.acm.org/doi/abs/10.1145/3287560.3287580.
[83] *Id.*
[84] Scott Shane & Sheera Frenkel, *Russian 2016 Influence Operation Targeted African-Americans on Social Media*, N.Y. TIMES (Dec. 17, 2018), https://nyti.ms/3Iofkkt.
[85] Issie Lapowsky, *How Russian Facebook Ads Divided and Targeted US Voters Before the 2016 Election*, WIRED (Apr. 16, 2018).

and white voters received 87 percent of all advertisements relating to immigration.[86]

Adding to these social concerns, tax evasion or avoidance by technology companies is occurring more frequently and on a larger scale than ever before, with Apple being named one of the largest tax avoiders in the United States[87] and Amazon paying no income tax whatsoever.[88] The difference in tax rates between the United States and overseas jurisdictions has incentivized many US-based multinational companies to adjust their corporate structures to enjoy tax benefits. Apple, for example, has transferred large amounts of its profits to offshore subsidiaries in tax havens such as Ireland and the Channel Island of Jersey to avoid tens of billions of dollars in US taxes.[89] In 2016, the European Commission found that Ireland had given illegal state aid to Apple by levying an effective corporate tax rate of less than 1 percent on the firm, despite a prevailing Irish corporate tax rate of 12.5 percent.[90] Apple saved €13 billion in taxes because of that aid.[91]

Congress enacted the Tax Cuts and Jobs Act in 2017.[92] The act reduces the tax rate on money repatriated to the United States from 35 percent to 15.5 percent.[93] Amazon has been a beneficiary of these and other tax cuts.[94] Although it earned more than $11 billion in profits

---

[86] *Id.*

[87] *Apple "Among Largest Tax Avoiders in US" – Senate Committee*, BBC (May 21, 2013), www .bbc.com/news/business-22600984.

[88] Glenn Kessler, *Does Amazon Pay Any Taxes?*, WASH. POST (July 30, 2019), (highlighting Bernie Sanders' statement that "[r]ight now, 500,000 Americans are sleeping out on the street and yet companies like Amazon that made billions in profits did not pay one nickel in federal income tax"); Vanessa Barford & Gerry Holt, *Google, Amazon, Starbucks: The Rise of "Tax Shaming"*, BBC (May 21, 2013).

[89] Jesse Drucker & Simon Bowers, *The Paradise Papers: After a Tax Crackdown, Apple Found a New Shelter for Its Profits*, N.Y. TIMES (Nov. 6, 2017), www.nytimes.com/2017/11/06/ world/apple-taxes-jersey.html.

[90] David Meyer, *Apple Has Paid the $14.3 Billion It Owes the Irish Tax Authorities – But the Check Hasn't Cleared Yet*, FORTUNE (Sept. 19, 2018, 5:58 AM), https://bit.ly/3uQ6Hsv.

[91] *Ireland Forced to Collect Apple's Disputed €13Bn Tax Bill*, BBC (Dec. 5, 2017), www .bbc.com/news/business-42237312.

[92] Tax Cut and Jobs Act of 2017, Pub. L. No. 115-97, 131 Stat. 2054 (codified as amended at 26 U.S.C. § 1 (2018)).

[93] *What's in the Final Republican Tax Bill*, REUTERS (Dec. 20, 2017, 11:43 AM), https://reut .rs/3aaMNz2.

[94] Andrew Davis, *Why Amazon Paid No 2018 US Federal Income Tax*, CNBC (Apr. 4, 2019).

in 2018, it paid zero federal corporate income tax owing to the reduction in tax rates for corporations, carry-forward losses from previous years, an R&D tax credit, and stock-based employee compensation.[95] Furthermore, Amazon received a $129 million federal income tax rebate, which made its tax rate -1 percent.[96]

---

[95] *Id.*
[96] Laura Stampler, *Amazon Will Pay a Whopping $0 in Federal Taxes on $11.2 Billion Profits*, FORTUNE (Feb. 14, 2019, 3:34 PM).

5 FUNDAMENTAL CORPORATE RESPONSIBILITY

In the wake of the Cambridge Analytica data scandal discussed in Chapter 4, Facebook and other major technology companies were accused of being even more irresponsible than the financial institutions that caused the 2008 financial crisis.[1] The Federal Trade Commission (FTC) responded to the scandal by imposing a fine of roughly $5 billion on Facebook in July 2019 for mishandling private data, the largest fine ever issued by the FTC.[2] However, the FTC's response triggered heated debate over whether a fine was an effective deterrent. Facebook's stock price actually surged following the FTC's decision, which led to claims that the decision had served to increase Mark Zuckerberg's net worth.[3] Legislators pronounced that the FTC had "failed miserably" with this "inadequate" and "historically hollow" decision.[4]

Indeed, amid a crisis of responsibility, monetary fines – even staggering ones – are no cure. They are backward-looking, reactive, and ultimately inadequate for changing the behavior of today's tech behemoths. These firms have been the beneficiaries of lax statutory and regulatory arrangements, and are today among the most financially and politically powerful in the world. They are willing to spend lavishly in exchange for what they desire.

---

[1] Saqib Shah, *Banks Behind Financial Crash Were Better Behaved Than Facebook, Says Ex-Goldman Sachs President Gary Cohn*, SUN (Aug. 7, 2018) ("[B]anks were more responsible citizens in '08 than some of the social-media companies are today. And it affects everyone in the world. The banks have never had that much pull.").

[2] Cecilia Kang, *F.T.C. Approves Facebook Fine of About $5 Billion*, N.Y. TIMES (July 12, 2019).

[3] Nilay Patel, *Facebook's $5 Billion FTC Fine Is an Embarrassing Joke*, VERGE (July 12, 2019).

[4] *Id.*

How then should we deal with irresponsible technology companies? In my opinion, we need an affirmative vision of the nature and scope of the responsibilities that technology companies should accept. We must as a matter of urgency pose and seriously discuss this question: *What do technology companies owe the world?*

In this chapter, I put forward the idea of fundamental corporate responsibility as a lens through which to scrutinize technology companies and the ethical crises they have created. Reflecting the realities of the technology industry today, this tripartite responsibility would require technology companies to reciprocate for users' contributions, play a positive role, and confront the injustices created by technological development. Drawing on the ethical theories of reciprocity, role responsibility, and social justice, I discuss how and why these three fundamental responsibilities should be imposed upon technology companies.

A THE RESPONSIBILITY TO RECIPROCATE

1 Reciprocity

As an ethical norm, reciprocity requires that one should respond to a positive action by another by returning that action proportionately.[5] Aristotle used friendship, one of the most basic human relationships, to illustrate the importance of reciprocity. According to him, a positive friendship, two persons treat each other as equals and are willing to reciprocate each other's admiration and good deeds.[6] By contrast, a negative friendship develops without the intention to reciprocate because the two persons only care about their own utility or pleasure.[7] Central to reciprocity, therefore, is that people must assume responsibility to take positive action in return for others'

---

[5] *See* LAWRENCE C. BECKER, RECIPROCITY 3 (1986). Conversely, reciprocity also allows one to respond to a negative action from another – such as a harmful or hurtful action – with indifference or retaliation. *Id.*

[6] ARISTOTLE, NICOMACHEAN ETHICS bk. VIII, at 147, 149 (Roger Crisp ed. & trans., 2000) (c. 384 BCE) ("It is bad people who will tend to be friends for pleasure or utility ... But good people will be friends for each other's sake.").

[7] *Id.* at 149.

kindness.[8] Cicero regarded reciprocity as the bedrock of all ethical norms, emphasizing that "there is no more essential duty than that of returning kindness received; to omit the returning of kindness is impossible for a good man."[9]

Reciprocity is universally accepted and practiced because of its intrinsic value in stabilizing interpersonal relationships and societal institutions.[10] The ethos of reciprocity requires the recipient of a positive action to overcome his or her selfish impulses and consider how he or she can act in return in another's interest.[11] It provides the original positive actor with the expectation that kindness will ultimately be responded to positively.[12] Through the repetition of reciprocal actions, people become more willing to initiate positive deeds for others and respond to others' positive deeds.[13]

Reciprocity involves two specific responsibilities. First, people have the responsibility to appreciate positive actions done by others for them[14] by recognizing the benefits received and identifying ways in which those benefits have promoted their well-being. This process of appreciation motivates one to take reciprocal action. Indifference to others' positive actions will preclude any possibility of reflecting on the positive consequences of those actions.

Second, people have the responsibility to act in return for benefits received as a result of others' actions. Central to "[r]eciprocity is a moral idea situated between impartiality, which is altruistic, on the one side and mutual advantage on the other."[15] Reciprocation may involve

[8] See MARTHA C. NUSSBAUM, WOMEN AND HUMAN DEVELOPMENT: THE CAPABILITIES APPROACH 72 (2000).

[9] Marcus Tullius Cicero, De Officiis, in ETHICAL WRITINGS OF CICERO 32 (Andrew P. Peabody, trans., 1887).

[10] See Alvin W. Gouldner, The Norm of Reciprocity: A Preliminary Statement, 25 AM. SOC. REV. 161, 171–76 (1960); DAVID SCHMIDTZ, THE ELEMENTS OF JUSTICE 79 (2006) (arguing that reciprocity induces cooperation and "enables people to live together in mutually respectful peace").

[11] See, e.g., Gouldner, supra note 10, at 170.

[12] Id.

[13] See GEORG SIMMEL, THE SOCIOLOGY OF GEORG SIMMEL 387 (Kurt H. Wolff ed. & trans., 1950) (concluding that social equilibrium and cohesion only exist because of "the reciprocity of service and return service").

[14] See, e.g., SCHMIDTZ, supra note 10, at 76 ("The art of reciprocity is partly an art of graciously acknowledging favors.").

[15] JOHN RAWLS, JUSTICE AS FAIRNESS: A RESTATEMENT 77 (Erin Kelly ed., 2001).

a mathematical formula, for example, paying off a specific amount of debt owed to another party according to a contract between the parties.[16] More frequently, reciprocation takes the form of actions such as expressing appreciation verbally or in writing or providing assistance or care.[17]

2 Reciprocity and Technology Companies

How should technology companies deal with the ethics of reciprocity? In this section, I identify how users of technology companies' services have contributed to those companies' market successes. I further argue that technology companies should first take responsibility for appreciating users' contributions and then consider how they should reciprocate by proactively protecting users' interests.

The first contribution that users make is supplying content that is quantitatively and qualitatively essential to the rapid development and success of social media platforms. With the rise of Web 2.0, users have uploaded and disseminated an unprecedented amount of content on these platforms. As of January 2019, the number of active social media users had reached 3.48 billion.[18] A statistics report shows that every minute in January 2020, Facebook users posted 510,000 comments, updated 293,000 user statuses, and uploaded 136,000 photos.[19] As of May 2019,

---

[16] *See* SIMMEL, *supra* note 13, at 387 (commenting that "[a]ll contacts among men rest on the schema of giving and returning the equivalence").

[17] *See, e.g.*, IRIS MARION YOUNG, INCLUSION AND DEMOCRACY 30 (2000) ("The conditions of equal opportunity to speak and freedom from domination encourage all to express their needs and interests. The equality condition also requires a reciprocity such that each acknowledges that the interests of the others must be taken into account in order to reach a judgement.").

[18] Simon KEMP, DIGITAL 2019: ESSENTIAL INSIGHTS INTO HOW PEOPLE AROUND THE WORLD USE THE INTERNET, MOBILE DEVICES, SOCIAL MEDIA, AND E-COMMERCE 7 (2019), https://p .widencdn.net/kqy7ii/Digital2019-Report-en. Facebook's number of monthly active users increased from 100 million in the third quarter of 2008 to 2.45 billion in the third quarter of 2019. J. Clement, *Number of Monthly Active Facebook Users Worldwide as of 3rd Quarter 2019 (in Millions)*, STATISTA (Nov. 19, 2019), https://bit.ly/3AolI5W. In December 2010, the number of active monthly users of Instagram stood at 1 million; as of June 2018, it was 1 billion. Josh Constine, *Instagram Hits 1 Billion Monthly Users, Up From 800M in September*, TECHCRUNCH (June 20, 2018), https://techcrunch.com/2018/06/20/insta gram-1-billion-users.

[19] Dan Noyes, *The Top 20 Valuable Facebook Statistics*, ZEPHORIA, https://zephoria.com/top-15-valuable-facebook-statistics (last updated Jan. 2020). As of June 2016, Instagram users were contributing 95 million posts every day. Yasmeen Abutaleb, *Instagram's User Base Grows to More Than 500 Million*, REUTERS (June 21, 2016), https://reut.rs/3ahy2uc.

YouTube's two billion monthly active users[20] had uploaded more than 500 hours of video per minute.[21]

Users have also significantly enriched the quality of the content available on social media platforms, making that content much more attractive culturally. In many cases, the more directly that users engage with content, the more culturally significant it becomes. For instance, comments, likes, and other interactions between audiences and content creators have prompted video game commentary videos on YouTube to expand beyond mere demonstrations of gaming prowess into cultural artifacts, serving as "performances of identity, community conflicts and allegiances."[22] Video game commentary has become so important to attracting users that social media platforms are competing to become the primary host of such content.[23] In a similar vein, users' secondary creative content continues to grow in influence as a form of online expression owing to the increasing ease with which individuals can participate. The short-form video platform TikTok provides a notable example. Dance challenges have gone viral when viewed and built upon by users, becoming sufficiently influential to increase the cultural significance and value of the underlying works.[24] Such user conduct has even become a justification for the platform's controversial practices. For example, in response to complaints submitted to US senators calling for scrutiny of TikTok's use of musical works not covered by licensing agreements, the company argued that its platform and the viral meme culture it supports can provide value to artists.[25]

---

[20] Adam Warner, *Which Social Media Platform Has the Most Users? [2020 DISCUSSION]*, WEBSITE PLANET, www.websiteplanet.com/blog/social-media-platform-users (last visited Jan. 19, 2020).

[21] James Hale, *More Than 500 Hours of Content Are Now Being Uploaded to YouTube Every Minute*, TUBEFILTER (May 7, 2019), https://bit.ly/3Ar3wst.

[22] Hector Postigo, *The Socio-technical Architecture of Digital Labor: Converting Play into YouTube Money*, 18 NEW MEDIA & SOCIETY 332, 332–33, 337–39 (2014).

[23] *See, e.g.*, Kat Tenbarge, *Gamers Say They're Earning More Money on Facebook's Streaming Platform than on Twitch and YouTube*, BUSINESS INSIDER (Oct. 12, 2019), https://bit.ly /3iIGOGg.

[24] Mariel Soto Reyes, *TikTok Inks a Global Licensing Deal with Music Agency Merlin*, BUSINESS INSIDER (Jan. 27, 2020).

[25] Murray Stassen, *NMPA Calls For "Scrutiny" of TikTok, Says Platform Has "Consistently Violated US Copyright Law and the Rights of Songwriters and Music Publishers,"* MUSIC BUSINESS WORLDWIDE (Oct. 16, 2019), https://bit.ly/3Botoql.

More broadly, genuine user engagement and contributions have enabled social media platforms to operate and profit.

The second substantial user contribution is to technology companies' advertising revenues. Because of users' frequent usage of their services, internet advertising has become the major source of revenue for many of these companies,[26] rising in value to $107.5 billion in the United States in 2018.[27] Facebook's advertising revenue nearly doubled in just two years, rising from $8.63 billion in the fourth quarter of 2016 to $16.64 billion in the fourth quarter of 2018.[28] Google's parent company Alphabet revealed in a fourth-quarter earnings report that YouTube advertising generated $15 billion in 2019, accounting for roughly 10 percent of Google's entire revenue.[29] Initially, advertisers expressed concerns about displaying advertisements next to low-quality amateur content. However, as such content has continued to grow in quantity and importance, perceptions have changed. Many advertisers now choose social media outlets as their major advertising platforms because of their large audience share.[30]

A third positive user contribution is to technology companies' innovation capacities. For example, AI-powered applications require a vast amount of training data for their development. Apart from training datasets purchased from data brokers, huge amounts of training data can also be amassed from the Internet based on users' activities.[31] In late 2015, Google rolled out its Inbox Smart Reply feature, which provides automatic e-mail response suggestions.[32] Smart Reply uses AI to read incoming e-mails, understand the content, and then automatically generate up to three responses from which

---

[26] *See* JAMIE BARTLETT, THE PEOPLE VS TECH: HOW THE INTERNET IS KILLING DEMOCRACY (AND HOW WE SAVE IT) 12 (2018).

[27] *See* PwC, IAB INTERNET ADVERTISING REVENUE REPORT: 2018 FULL RESULTS 2 (2019).

[28] Amy Gesenhues, *Facebook Ad Revenue Tops $16.6 billion, Driven by Instagram, Stories,* MARTECH TODAY (Jan. 31, 2019).

[29] Nick Statt, *YouTube is a $15 Billion-a-Year Business, Google Reveals for the First Time,* THE VERGE (Feb. 3, 2020, 4:24 PM).

[30] *See* KEITH A. QUESENBERRY, SOCIAL MEDIA STRATEGY: MARKETING, ADVERTISING, AND PUBLIC RELATIONS IN THE CONSUMER REVOLUTION 8–9 (2015) (discussing social media's operation in user-centric modes and its profound influence over users).

[31] *See, e.g.,* James Vincent, *Google is Testing a New Way of Training its AI Algorithms Directly on Your Phone,* THE VERGE (Apr. 10, 2017).

[32] Arjun Kharpal, *Google's New Feature Will Reply to Emails for You,* CNBC (Nov. 3, 2015).

users can select.[33] The Smart Reply algorithm was trained on a corpus of 238 million e-mail messages,[34] messages that were presumably sourced from Gmail accounts.[35]

Similarly, facial recognition technologies take advantage of images contributed by users.[36] The photos that people store and share on social media platforms and image hosting sites provide face image data that train computers to recognize, identify, and analyze faces. When users tag friends in photos, these labeled faces can be used to train facial recognition AI. For example, Facebook used 4.4 million labeled images from more than 4,000 individuals to develop the facial recognition technology known as DeepFace.[37] In addition to improving the platform's own services, this technology has many other applications that Facebook could commercialize, including assisting in the investigation of crimes and being installed in home security systems.[38] In recognition of the potential of such technology, IBM extracted nearly a million photos from a dataset of the image-hosting site Flickr for its own facial recognition project.[39]

Despite these user contributions, the managers of technology companies may still argue that their companies have no responsibility to reciprocate because they have already made contributions to users by initiating their platform services or technologies to provide users with new experiences. Alternatively, these managers may contend that their companies fulfill their responsibility to reciprocate by regularly upgrading the quality of their platforms and technologies, thereby improving user experiences.

---

[33] *Id.*

[34] Anjuli Kannan et al., *Smart Reply: Automated Response Suggestion for Email*, KDD'16: PROC. 22ND ACM SIGKDD INT'L CONF. ON KNOWLEDGE DISCOVERY & DATA MINING, Aug. 2016, at 955, 962.

[35] *Id.*

[36] *See* FERNANDO IAFRATE, ARTIFICIAL INTELLIGENCE AND BIG DATA: THE BIRTH OF A NEW INTELLIGENCE 48 (2018).

[37] Yaniv Taigman et al., *DeepFace: Closing the Gap to Human-Level Performance in Face Verification, in* 2014 IEEE CONFERENCE ON COMPUTER VISION AND PATTERN RECOGNITION 1701, 1705 (2014).

[38] Tech Echelons Blog, *Deepface Unleashed: What Does the Facebook Do to Recognize Faces?*, TECHECHELONS, https://bit.ly/3lpK8Yo (last visited Jun. 1, 2020).

[39] Emily Price, *Millions of Flickr Photos Were Scraped to Train Facial Recognition Software*, FORTUNE (Mar. 12, 2019).

These arguments unduly downplay user contributions. Most technology companies are very different from conventional companies that manufacture and sell products such as food and clothing or offer services such as catering and transportation. Conventional companies serve *passive users* who consume products or services rather than produce or provide products or services themselves. Therefore, such companies thrive primarily through their own efforts.

By contrast, many technology companies thrive both through their own efforts and the contributions of their users. *Active users* play an indispensable role in the growth of these companies because they are directly or indirectly engaged in the development of online platforms and data-driven technologies. As discussed earlier in this section, users actively post, upload, and update content on social media platforms. Managers of technology companies such as YouTube may argue that they reciprocate adequately by paying users for sharing videos if they comply with the platform's guidelines and meet the viewership threshold.[40] However, there are problems with even this positive example. When YouTube's Content ID software flags copyright-protected material, YouTube offers the rights holders an opportunity to claim the uploader's share of advertising revenue rather than blocking the video in question.[41] Although this system protects the platform's interests in avoiding copyright litigation and ensuring that content remains available, it has often been applied at the expense of user interests. For instance, a user's video can be fully demonetized despite containing only a small amount of infringing material or falling under a copyright exception.[42] By preemptively freezing revenue without first conducting any fair use analysis, Content ID creates a presumption against the uploader.[43] The system has been criticized

[40] YouTube Help, *YouTube Partner Program overview & eligibility*, GOOGLE SUPPORT, https://support.google.com/youtube/answer/72851?hl=en (last visited May 31, 2020).

[41] YouTube Help, *How Content ID works*, GOOGLE SUPPORT, https://bit.ly/3ahXaRJ (last visited May 31, 2020).

[42] Henning Grosse Ruse-Khan, *Automated Copyright Enforcement Online: From Blocking to Monetization of User-Generated Content*, in TRANSITION AND COHERENCE IN INTELLECTUAL PROPERTY LAW, (Bruun et al. eds, forthcoming 2021), https://papers.ssrn.com/sol3/papers.cfm?abstract_id=3565071.

[43] Taylor B. Bartholomew, *The Death of Fair Use in Cyberspace: YouTube and The Problem with Content ID*, 13 DUKE LAW & TECHNOLOGY REVIEW 66, 77 (2015).

for enabling rights holders to "hijack" advertising revenue that they should be entitled to only in part, if at all.[44]

YouTube does warn against such over-claiming and suggests that copyright owners set minimum thresholds as to when Content ID should claim content.[45] Nonetheless, in aiming to ensure that content remains available, YouTube has facilitated abuses of its copyright monetization policy. For example, unless the rights holders making use of Content ID decide otherwise, the default response set by YouTube is to monetize the content worldwide.[46] Content creators are given an opportunity to dispute Content ID claims, but Google reported in 2018 that less than 1 percent of cases are disputed,[47] suggesting that the system is flawed and probably allows unfair claims to go unchecked in vast numbers. This is unsurprising given that YouTube's own economic interest lies in ensuring that Content ID is widely used for monetization rather than blocking; the company simply leaves it to copyright owners to stay within the boundaries of copyright law.[48] Such self-serving deference to copyright owners challenges the suggestion that the platform truly values content contributions by users and reciprocates for them.

Another consideration with respect to user content is that in their active engagement with social media, users also provide personal data such as addresses and preferences that are shared with other online platforms such as Amazon. Users have thus contributed a vast amount of information and images for the development of technologies by tech companies, such as AI and facial recognition.

All of these developments demonstrate that technology companies ought to take seriously their responsibility to reciprocate for users' contributions, no matter how financially successful and politically powerful those companies are. The content and data contributed by users have been crucial to their corporate development, and they need to consider what actions they can take to reciprocate.

---

[44] Andrea Katalin Tóth, *Regulation and AI in the Field of Algorithmic Copyright Enforcement*, in LAW 4.0 – CHALLENGES OF THE DIGITAL AGE 89, 91 (Glivantis & Király eds, 2019).

[45] YouTube Help, *Clean Up Incorrect Claims*, GOOGLE SUPPORT, https://support.google.com/youtube/answer/4352063 (last visited Jun. 03, 2020).

[46] YouTube Help, *Set Default Policies*, GOOGLE SUPPORT, https://support.google.com/youtube/answer/3369992 (last visited Jun. 03, 2020).

[47] Google, HOW GOOGLE FIGHTS PIRACY, 29 (2018), https://bit.ly/3ak1X4Z.

[48] *See* Ruse-Khan, *supra* note 42.

B THE RESPONSIBILITY TO PLAY A POSITIVE ROLE

1 Role Responsibility

While reciprocity-based responsibility is triggered by the positive deeds of others, role responsibility entails individuals or institutions spontaneously assuming certain roles in personal or social activities. Ethically, individuals take responsibility for the specific roles they have chosen to adopt. H. L. A. Hart explains role responsibility as follows:

> A sea captain is responsible for the safety of his ship, and that is his responsibility, or one of his responsibilities. A husband is responsible for the maintenance of his wife; parents for the upbringing of their children; ... a clerk for keeping the accounts of his firm. These examples of a person's responsibilities suggest the generalization that, whenever a person occupies a distinctive place or office in a social organization, to which specific duties are attached to provide for the welfare of others or to advance in some specific way the aims or purposes of the organization, he is properly said to be responsible for the performance of these duties, or for doing what is necessary to fulfil them. Such duties are a person's responsibilities.[49]

Responsibility, then, can be imposed on a person based on their roles, such as an individual occupying an official role as sea captain, husband, or clerk. These interpersonal roles place the person in a special position in relation to others whose interests might be affected by their actions, assigning them certain functions to perform or goals to fulfill.[50] The expectation is that the individual will take responsibility for performing the functions or fulfilling the goals attached to their role.[51]

---

[49] H. L. A. HART, PUNISHMENT AND RESPONSIBILITY: ESSAYS IN THE PHILOSOPHY OF LAW 212 (2d ed. 2008).

[50] See MEIR DAN-COHEN, RIGHTS, PERSONS, AND ORGANIZATIONS: A LEGAL THEORY FOR BUREAUCRATIC SOCIETY 38 (1986) (arguing that "at any given point in time and within a particular normative scheme, organizational behavior is amenable to analysis and interpretation in terms of the organization's instrumental nature, that is, in terms of its pursuit of some predetermined individual or social goals").

[51] See Robin Zheng, *What is My Role in Changing the System? A New Model of Responsibility for Structural Injustice*, 21 ETHICAL THEORY & MORAL PRAC. 869, 875 (2018) ("Performing a role ... is an ongoing process of making infinitely many tiny decisions about *how* to perform it, thereby calibrating one's behavior with another's expectations and behavior at

Role responsibility leads to two kinds of responsibilities in practice. First, there are *personal responsibilities* attached to specific roles, such as husband, wife, father, and mother, based on the intimate relationships that form such small-scale institutions as the family and marriage. Second, *professional responsibilities* arise from the specific roles that individuals choose to assume in larger institutions, such as companies and governmental agencies. Once an individual chooses a profession that confers upon him or her the authority to control people and resources, certain responsibilities are imposed within the bounds of that profession.[52]

Compared with personal responsibilities, professional responsibilities trigger accountability toward a greater number of people whose interests may be affected either directly or indirectly. For instance, a sea captain, as Hart points out, is responsible for the safety of a ship for the sake of its passengers. Following the ethos of role responsibility, the captain is expected to exercise due care and take prudent measures throughout the journey.[53] A judge serving on the bench is responsible for impartial adjudication of cases heard.[54] The judge must make every effort to fulfill this role responsibly, delivering a properly reasoned judicial decision for the parties involved.[55]

Moreover, while personal responsibilities serve only the interests of individuals in intimate relationships, professional responsibilities affect societal interests at large in the short and long term. For example, if most of the judges in a given country are corrupt, then their biased rulings or meddling in individual cases will ultimately undermine the societal interest in maintaining the rule of law. Similarly, if environmental regulators fail to take proactive actions to prevent certain factories from polluting the air or water, then such failure will ultimately erode the societal interest in environmental protection. If legislators

---

the same time that the other is calibrating their expectations and behavior with yours.") (emphasis in original).

[52] *See* Peter Cane, *Role Responsibility*, 20 J. ETHICS 279, 285 (2016) ("[A]person in authority may, in fact, be (or have been) capable of controlling the people and events complained of; and if the authority should have exercised control, this may provide a basis for imposing personal responsibility on the authority for what occurred. However, regardless of capacity to control, the authority may be role-responsible simply by virtue of the authority.").

[53] HART, *supra* note 49, at 212.

[54] *See, e.g.*, Lon L. Fuller, *The Forms and Limits of Adjudication*, 92 HARV. L. REV. 353, 354 (1978).

[55] *Id.*

take bribes from a food company to push for the passage of a new food law relaxing safety standards, then the societal interest in ensuring food safety will be jeopardized. These examples show that social roles require prudent decisions to be made in the public interest rather than in favor of any particular person or group.

Central to the fulfillment of role responsibility is the ability to engage in ethical deliberation. Hart emphasizes this deliberative function, pointing out that "[a] responsible person is one who is disposed to take his duties seriously; to think about them, and to make serious efforts to fulfill them. To behave responsibly is to behave as a man would who took his duties in this serious way."[56]

There are two key steps in conducting ethical deliberation with regard to role responsibility.[57] First, individuals in specific personal or professional roles must learn to consider the private or societal interests that might be affected by their performance of their roles. For instance, doctors need to be aware of their responsibility to receive adequate medical ethics education[58] because their failure to do so would negatively affect their capacity to tackle medical problems and protect their patients' interests in health. Second, those individuals must prudently consider how they should perform their personal or professional roles so as to promote the private or societal interests identified in the first step.[59] This process normally requires "care and attention over a protracted period of time."[60] Failure to meet role responsibilities can trigger legal liabilities or moral blame.[61]

2 Technology Companies' Role Responsibilities

What roles do technology companies play in contemporary society? In this section, I examine technology companies' important professional

---

[56] HART, *supra* note 49, at 213.

[57] *See* Haochen Sun, *Copyright and Responsibility*, 4 HARV. J. SPORTS & ENT. L. 263, 292–93 (2013) (discussing the role of moral deliberation).

[58] *See* ARISTOTLE, *supra* note 6, at 3 (pointing out that "the end of [the medical art] is health").

[59] *See, e.g.*, JUSTIN OAKLEY & DEAN COCKING, VIRTUE ETHICS AND PROFESSIONAL ROLES 74 (2001) (arguing that "a professional role is ... importantly determined by how well that role functions in serving the goals of the profession, and by how those goals are connected with characteristic human activities").

[60] HART, *supra* note 49, at 213.

[61] *Id.* at 215–22.

roles as information disseminators, collectors, and/or creators. Following the theory of role responsibility, I argue that managers should consider how their companies can play these roles in a positive manner.

Technology companies such as Facebook, Instagram, Twitter, and YouTube act as *information disseminators* by operating social media platforms.[62] These companies help to disseminate all variety of information, including e-commerce data, entertainment updates, and news.[63] Compared with conventional media outlets, social media platforms have three major advantages in disseminating information.

First, they allow users to disseminate information with unprecedented ease. As long as users are connected to the Internet, they can upload content to a platform whenever and wherever they wish.[64] Moreover, technology companies equip social media platforms with enhanced communication functionalities such as private messaging, voice calls, voice messages, and video calling. These functionalities have made social connection much more convenient, which in turn has accelerated the transmission of information.

Second, social media platforms offer unprecedented network effects in disseminating information by significantly amplifying the number of users who view or use information.[65] By increasing the ease of information access and dissemination and providing their services for free or at a low charge, social media platforms can build and expand their user base. Facebook, WeChat, and other platforms offer an extensive range of interactive functionalities allowing commercial entities to disseminate business information to an entire or partial network of users.[66] Platforms also have the ability to control which information will have the most significant reach. For example, Facebook employs algorithms that amplify posts sparking the most conversations and interactions. These algorithms are designed to

---

[62] *See, e.g.,* Esteban Ortiz-Ospina, *The Rise of Social Media,* Our World Data (Sept. 18, 2019), https://ourworldindata.org/rise-of-social-media (reporting that Facebook has 2.4 billion users out of the 3.5 billion people online).

[63] Jenny Force, *How Social Media Continues to Affect Society,* Sysomos (Aug. 23, 2016), https://bit.ly/3mEMW3D.

[64] Sam Hinton & Larissa Hjorth, Understanding Social Media 32 (2013).

[65] *See* Amitai Aviram, *Regulation by Networks,* 2003 BYU L. Rev. 1179, 1195 (2003).

[66] *See* Alex Gray, *Here's the Secret to How WeChat Attracts 1 Billion Monthly Users,* World Econ. F. (Mar. 21, 2018), https://bit.ly/3uTJ4PH.

maximize the amount of time users spend on the platform to further increase the reach of advertisements displayed alongside user content.[67]

Third, social media platforms have also facilitated the democratization of information dissemination. Traditional media outlets require content producers to conform to and gain acceptance from the established infrastructure. Within the traditional media, one must become a television anchor or journalist if one wishes to deliver news. Social media platforms have removed such barriers, allowing anyone to create content and disseminate it directly to the world.[68] By providing a direct communication channel to individuals, social media platforms have arguably helped previously untapped human capital and talent to emerge. Naturally, as talented personalities are discovered, the influence and importance of the platform they inhabit also grows. To use revenue as an indicator, in 2017, YouTube's revenue ($7.8 billion)[69] was more than quadruple that of the *New York Times* ($1.7 billion).[70] YouTube has recognized the value of its most popular personalities, frequently securing their future on the platform through exclusive streaming agreements.[71]

Given these advantages, a platform's failure to adequately assume responsibility for its role as an information disseminator can have serious consequences. For instance, Facebook has received widespread criticism for the way in which its post-amplifying algorithms optimize outrage, polarization, and disinformation.[72] In Myanmar, Facebook's reach was utilized by military personnel in 2018 to spread anti-Muslim

---

[67] *See* Paige Cooper, *How the Facebook Algorithm Works in 2020 and How to Make it Work for You*, HOOTSUITE (Jan. 27, 2020), https://blog.hootsuite.com/facebook-algorithm.

[68] *See, e.g.*, Alfred Hermida, *Social Journalism: Exploring How Social Media is Shaping Journalism*, in THE HANDBOOK OF GLOBAL ONLINE JOURNALISM 312 (Eugenia Siapera & Andreas Veglis eds., 2012).

[69] J. Clement, *Worldwide Net Advertising Revenues of YouTube from 2016 to 2020* (in Billion U.S. Dollars), STATISTA (May 7, 2019), https://bit.ly/3AqjYsO.

[70] *New York Times Revenue 2006-2019*, MACROTRENDS www.macrotrends.net/stocks/charts/NYT/new-york-times/revenue.

[71] *See, e.g.*, Gene Park, *PewDiePie, YouTube's Controversial but Popular Creator, Signs Exclusive Streaming Deal*, THE WASHINGTON POST. (May 5, 2020).

[72] *See, e.g.*, Jon Evans, *Facebook isn't Free Speech, it's Algorithmic Amplification Optimized for Outrage*, TECH CRUNCH. (Oct. 20, 2019), https://tcrn.ch/3Fwu4w3.

hatred and disinformation, which subsequently incited the ethnic cleansing of the country's Rohingya population.[73]

Technology companies also act as information collectors. They collect data on consumers through their shopping activities, communications, social media activities, and so on.[74] They analyze and then utilize datasets on consumers' locations, behaviors, preferences, and characteristics for a variety of purposes that are in their corporate interests. These interests may range from enhancing security or facilitating the effective dissemination of advertisements on their platforms to developing technologies such as AI and facial recognition. Technology companies may also collect data for sale to other parties, such as consumer scoring companies or credit rating agencies. The Cambridge Analytica scandal demonstrated how far-reaching the effects can be when a platform does not act responsibly with the information it has collected.

Technology companies also act as *information creators* by generating new intellectual property. In 2019, the top fifty recipients of registered patents were all technology companies. IBM topped this ranking with 9,262 patent applications approved by the US Patent and Trademark Office.[75] For many researchers, technology companies provide the means to create, operationalize, and commercialize their inventions. Therefore, they are willing to sign employee contracts that grant ownership of their employment-related inventions to those companies.

Technology companies fare so well as innovative information creators because they meet the three crucial factors required for innovation: (1) a recognized need, (2) competent people with relevant technology, and (3) financial support.[76] Technology companies have departments associated with each factor. The "need" in the case of technology companies refers to consumer needs, preferences, and desires. Market research personnel in technology companies are

---

[73] Paul Mozur, *A Genocide Incited on Facebook, With Posts From Myanmar's Military*, N. Y. Times (Oct. 15, 2018).

[74] Jack M. Balkin, *Free Speech in the Algorithmic Society: Big Data, Private Governance, and New School Speech Regulation*, 51 U.C. Davis L. Rev. 1149, 1156 (2018).

[75] IFI CLAIMS Patent Services, *2019 Top 50 US Patent Assignees*, www.ificlaims.com/rankings-top-50-2019.htm.

[76] *See* O. E. Barishnikova & M. N. Nevzorova, *Development of Innovation*, 6 Eur. J. Nat. Hist. 53, 53 (2015).

specialized in discovering unmet needs, while research and development departments are made up of people familiar with existing relevant
technologies who can create new technologies according to specifications discovered by the market research team. Financial support for
these projects is secured by the companies' finance departments.

Pursuant to the ethos of role responsibility, technology companies
should play their professional roles as information disseminators, collectors, and creators in positive ways. First, they should adequately
consider how these roles might affect their users' private interests, as
well as societal interests. Second, they should take actions that are
reasonably necessary to protect these interests. Failure to do either
should subject them to legal penalties and/or moral blame.

The information fiduciary approach proposed by Professor Jack
Balkin has received a lot of attention. Drawing on conventional fiduciary doctrine, Professor Balkin suggests that technology companies
should be deemed the fiduciaries of their users' private data, thereby
imposing heightened duties upon corporate managers in protecting
private data.[77] Akin to the information fiduciary approach, the ethos
of role responsibility supports the imposition of fiduciary duties upon
technology company managers. Acting as information collectors,
they should have a fiduciary duty to protect their users' private
interests in personal data. Both the role responsibility approach and
the information fiduciary approach require managers of technology
companies to fulfill these duties of their own volition, based upon their
own ethical deliberation. As Professor Jonathan Zittrain observes, the
information fiduciary approach "protects consumers and corrects
a clear market failure without the need for heavy-handed government
intervention."[78]

---

[77] Jack M. Balkin, *Information Fiduciaries and the First Amendment*, 49 U.C. DAVIS L. REV.
1183, 1209 (2016). Balkin describes the nature of the information fiduciary approach as
follows:

> An information fiduciary is a person or business who, because of their relationship
> with another, has taken on special duties with respect to the information they obtain
> in the course of the relationship. People and organizations that have fiduciary duties
> arising from the use and exchange of information are information fiduciaries
> whether or not they also do other things on the client's behalf, like manage an estate
> or perform legal or medical services.

[78] Jonathan Zittrain, *How to Exercise the Power You Didn't Ask For*, HARV. BUS. REV.: BIG IDEA
(Sept. 19, 2018), https://bit.ly/3iIsjSQ.

The role responsibility approach, however, draws on a different ethical theory and can address two theoretical and practical problems with the information fiduciary approach. First, the information fiduciary approach does not tackle the potential conflict between managers' duty to protect users' interests in personal data and their duty to maximize their shareholders' interests.[79] Such conflicts abound in reality. Technology companies' fiduciary duty to use personal data with due care conflicts with their motive to further their corporate interests in earning profits by hosting advertisements or selling datasets to other parties. Following the Cambridge Analytica scandal, Facebook CEO Mark Zuckerberg sought to convince users that the platform's future is privacy-focused.[80] However, critics have questioned how far Facebook is actually willing to go, suggesting that a stock price drop arising out of concerns that increased privacy will impede profits demonstrates that the two are mutually exclusive.[81] Such concerns are understandable, given that Facebook will be unable to redesign its privacy policy without also redesigning its business model. Currently, Facebook's primary source of income is a behavioral advertising model that generates value by collecting detailed information on users to offer efficient advertising on the platform.[82] Unless an alternative revenue stream can be found, the collection of user information will remain essential to maintaining Facebook's profitability.[83] How, therefore, can the information fiduciary approach win the hearts and minds of managers hired to serve shareholders' interests?

The role responsibility approach has the potential to address this problem by integrating role responsibility into the corporate decision-making process. It reimagines technology companies as social enterprises that prioritize serving their users' private interests and societal interests at large while promoting their shareholders' interests as a secondary

---

[79] *See* Lina M. Khan & David E. Pozen, *A Skeptical View of Information Fiduciaries*, 133 Harv. L. Rev. 497, 506 (2019) (suggesting that the information fiduciary approach "would also pose a threat to Facebook's bottom line and therefore to the interest of shareholders").

[80] Mark Zuckerberg, *A Privacy-Focused Vision for Social Networking*, Facebook (Mar. 7, 2019), https://bit.ly/3AqO3Zr.

[81] Kalev Leetaru, *Profits Versus Privacy: Facebook's Stock Collapse and its Empty "Privacy First" Promise*, Forbes. (Jul. 29, 2018), https://bit.ly/3iL8fPA.

[82] *See* Khan & Pozen, *supra* note 79, at 511–12.

[83] *Id.*

consideration. This approach still allows managers of technology companies to pursue the maximization of shareholder value, so long as it does not conflict with the company's priorities in serving both users' private interests and societal interests. From this perspective, role responsibility requires managers to adequately consider how their corporate operations might affect these interests as part of their initial decision-making process.[84] Moreover, technology companies' responsibility to reciprocate for users' contributions reinforces their responsibility because it also requires managers to take action to protect users' interests.

Second, the information fiduciary approach deals only with technology companies' role as information collectors, not their role as information disseminators and creators. The protection of personal data is indeed crucially important given the prevalence of data breaches. However, as I have shown, the roles of information disseminator and creator are also of crucial importance to individual users and society at large. They affect the flow of information, regulation of speech, and innovation. In contrast to the information fiduciary approach, the role responsibility approach does not single out the information collector role. Rather, it integrates the three roles and shapes them as the functions that technology companies must perform as social enterprises. It also requires technology companies to formulate broader strategies to fulfill the responsibilities arising from the three roles. Under this approach, if a technology company takes its information disseminator and creator roles seriously and fulfills its corresponding responsibilities, then it also puts itself in a very good position to perform its information collector role while protecting personal data.

3 The Responsibility to Protect Personal Data Effectively

Given the risk of privacy breaches caused by digital technologies, consumers are now more concerned about the protection of their personal

---

[84] See Erika George, *Corporate Social Responsibility and Social Media Corporations: Incorporating Human Rights Through Rankings, Self-Regulation and Shareholder Resolutions*, 28 DUKE J. COMP. & INT'L L. 521, 524 (2018)("Given the power and influence of private corporations to create platforms used by members of the public who share news, ideas, and often even personal information, it is important to better understand the ways in which human rights issues implicated by the policies and practices of social media companies.").

data than ever before. Such protection is of fundamental importance to the freedom and dignity of every individual. The unauthorized collection or disclosure of such data as home or email addresses, identification card numbers, banking information, and medical records may infringe an individual's right to privacy and cause serious emotional distress or financial harm. The widespread collection of big data has exacerbated the problem. The secretive collection of big data has become normalized in the digital world, making all consumers vulnerable.

The protection of personal data frequently triggers cross-jurisdictional issues, as technology companies face different legal standards across the globe.[85] For example, the US protection regime is grounded in consumer protection, encouraging fairness in the exchange of private data. By contrast, the EU framework adopts a rights-based approach to data protection by recognizing and protecting the fundamental right to privacy.[86]

Against this backdrop, I argue that technology companies should treat private data protection as a core part of their fundamental responsibilities. First, such treatment is mandated by technology companies' fundamental responsibility to reciprocate for users' contributions. As I have shown in Section 2, having collected personal data from their users, technology companies should appreciate users' contributions to their data reservoir and make every effort to protect those data effectively.

Second, role responsibility requires that technology companies play their professional role as data collectors well. This role gives them the authority to control personal data, which constitute one of the world's most valuable resources.[87] Their role responsibility then requires them

---

[85] Robert Levine, *Behind the European Privacy Ruling That's Confounding Silicon Valley*, N.Y. TIMES (Oct. 9, 2015) ("International data transfers are the lifeblood of the digital economy.").

[86] *See, e.g.*, James Q. Whitman, *The Two Western Cultures of Privacy: Dignity Versus Liberty*, 113 YALE L.J. 1151, 1157 (2004)(pointing out that "it has become common for Europeans to maintain that they respect a 'fundamental right to privacy' that is either weak or wholly absent in the 'cultural context' of the United States"); Paul M. Schwartz & Karl-Nikolaus Peifer, *Transatlantic Data Privacy Law*, 106 GEO. L.J. 115, 121 (2017) (finding that "the EU system protects the individual by granting her fundamental rights pertaining to data protection" and that "U.S. law protects the individual as a privacy consumer").

[87] *The World's Most Valuable Resource Is No Longer Oil, but Data*, ECONOMIST (May 6, 2017), https://econ.st/3alXuP6.

to recognize that their collection and further utilization of personal data may affect their users' private interests in dignity,[88] as well as the larger societal interests in data security.[89] Moreover, technology companies should consider how they can exercise their authority in utilizing personal data in ways that adequately protect both users' private interests and societal interests.

To legally fulfill these two responsibilities, I propose that technology companies should adopt the fundamental principles for data protection under the General Data Protection Regulation (GDPR),[90] which took effect in the European Union in May 2018.[91] The GDPR sets the world's highest standards of data protection, protecting EU residents' right to personal data and enforcing data collectors' duties.[92] It is applicable to any company that processes EU residents' personal data. My proposal would require technology companies to operate a two-tiered private data protection mechanism.

First, technology companies should comply with the GDPR in good faith if they collect private data belonging to those residing in the European Union. In that context, they are legally subject to regulation by the GDPR given its mandate of extraterritorial application.[93] When EU residents use Amazon, Facebook, WhatsApp, and Apple Pay, the relevant US technology companies process their personal data. If these companies made every effort to follow the GDPR to enhance data protection, they would prove their commitment to taking their EU users' right to privacy seriously. In demonstrating their ability to

---

[88] *See* Schmerber v. California, 384 U.S. 757, 767 (1966); Robert C. Post, *The Social Foundations of Privacy: Community and Self in the Common Law Tort*, 77 CAL. L. REV. 957,1008 (1989); Whitman, *supra* note 86, at 1161 .

[89] *See* Julie E. Cohen, *What Privacy Is For*, 126 HARV. L. REV. 1904, 1914 (2013)(using electronic voting as an example to show the importance of data security).

[90] Regulation (EU) 2016/679 of the European Parliament and of the Council of 27 April 2016 on the Protection of Natural Persons with Regard to the Processing of Personal Data and on the Free Movement of Such Data, and Repealing Directive 95/46/EC (General Data Protection Regulation), 2016 O.J. (L 119) 1.

[91] *The General Data Protection Regulation Applies in All Member States from 25 May 2018*, EUR-LEX (May 24, 2018), https://bit.ly/3DlmrH0.

[92] Lydia de la Torre, *GDPR Matchup: The California Consumer Privacy Act 2018*, IAPP (July 31, 2018), https://bit.ly/3myWooY.

[93] GDPR, art. 3(2) (prescribing that the GDPR "applies to the processing of personal data of data subjects who are in the Union by a controller or processor not established in the Union").

comply with the stringent data protection standards of the GDPR, they would further convince the international community that they are truly devoted to safeguarding the security of personal data.

Second, technology companies should consider adopting the GDPR as their internal privacy compliance guidelines. Although the GDPR is not legally applicable to technology companies collecting private data from users residing outside the European Union, these companies should still regard it as a model law for strengthening their protection of private data, proactively ensuring that their data protection measures live up to the GDPR's principles.[94] As they expand their businesses across the globe, technology companies need to tackle data protection in each country or region in which they process data. Data privacy laws vary significantly across countries, and some countries have no such laws. No international treaties have been adopted to govern data protection globally. In the face of such legal complexities, technology companies' adoption of the GDPR as their internal guidelines would ensure that their products or services are fully compliant with the most stringent data protection standards. This strategy would send the message to consumers around the world that they take personal data protection seriously and believe that everyone deserves the same high level of personal data protection.[95]

C THE RESPONSIBILITY TO CONFRONT INJUSTICES CREATED BY TECHNOLOGICAL DEVELOPMENT

1 Social Justice

All human beings are equal in dignity and freedom, and this status is legally recognized in both international human rights treaties and

---

[94] *See* Anupam Chander et al., *Catalyzing Privacy Law* 105 MINN. L. REV. 1733, 1758 (2021) ("The GDPR quintessentially targets compliance from an organizational perspective: it attempts to build up a particular kind of responsible corporate infrastructure, including internal positions and processes.").

[95] See Bryan Casey et al., *Rethinking Explainable Machines: The GDPR's "Right to Explanation" Debate and the Rise of Algorithmic Audits in Enterprise*, 34 BERKELEY TECH. L.J. 143, 187 (2019) (discussing the public relations benefits of following the GDPR).

national constitutions.[96] However, injustice is a part of every society. The unjust distribution of social resources that leads to income disparities continues to worsen.[97] Status injustices caused by racial, gender, and sexuality discrimination still exist in the United States and many other countries.

Against this backdrop, social justice is widely regarded as a fundamental value intended to minimize the impact of the unequal distribution of resources and status discrimination. For example, John Rawls has elevated social justice to the status of the "first virtue of social institutions."[98]

Social justice, by nature, centers on how to allocate responsibilities for distributing resources and social status. From this perspective, Rawls captures the essence of a responsibility-based notion of social justice as follows:

> This conception [of social justice] includes what we may call a *social division of responsibility*: society, the citizens as a collective body, accepts the responsibility for maintaining the equal basic liberties and fair equality of opportunity, and for providing a fair share of the other primary goods for everyone within this framework, while citizens (as individuals) and associations accept the responsibility for revising and adjusting their ends and aspirations in view of the all-purpose means they can expect, given their present and foreseeable situation.[99]

---

[96] For example, Article 1 of the Universal Declaration on Human Rights states that "[a]ll human beings are born free and equal in dignity and rights. They are endowed with reason and conscience and should act towards one another in a spirit of brotherhood." G.A. Res. 217 (III) A, Universal Declaration of Human Rights, art. 1 (Dec. 10, 1948).

[97] *See generally* THOMAS PIKETTY, CAPITAL IN THE TWENTY-FIRST CENTURY 430–32 (Arthur Goldhammer trans., 2014) (surveying the growing inequality in distribution of resources); Ilyana Kuziemko & Stefanie Stantcheva, *Our Feelings About Inequality: It's Complicated* N. Y. TIMES: OPINIONATOR (Apr. 21, 2013), https://nyti.ms/3oHBZAG ("Since the 1970s, income inequality in the United States has increased at a historic rate. In 1970, the richest 1 percent of Americans enjoyed 9 percent of total national pre-tax income. In 2011, by contrast, that share had risen to 19.8 percent.").

[98] JOHN RAWLS, A THEORY OF JUSTICE 3 (Harvard Univ. Press rev. ed. 1999) [hereinafter RAWLS, A THEORY OF JUSTICE]. Rawls also points out that "[a] theory however elegant and economical must be rejected or revised if it is untrue; likewise laws and institutions no matter how efficient and well-arranged must be reformed or abolished if they are unjust." *Id.*

[99] JOHN RAWLS, *Social Unity and Primary Goods*, *in* COLLECTED PAPERS 359, 371 (Samuel Freeman ed., Harvard Univ. Press 1999) (emphasis added).

This statement shows that central to social justice is the distribution of responsibilities among citizens. Thus, Rawls further argues that "the principles of social justice ... provide a way of assigning rights and duties in the basic institutions of society and they define the appropriate distribution of the benefits and burdens of social cooperation."[100]

The responsibility to promote social justice, in my opinion, involves tackling three forms of injustice: privatization-driven injustice, technology-driven injustice, and identity-driven injustice. The third form of injustice typically classifies people on the basis of race, gender, and/or sexuality, causing discriminatory harm to them. In the discussion that follows, I discuss the first two forms of injustice.

The responsibility to counter privatization-driven injustice arises because it causes the structural maldistribution of social resources.[101] Although the free market allows voluntary transactions of private property, it is still fraught with injustice due to the coercive power embedded in larger social structures.[102] The unequal distribution of private property is a fundamental source of coercive power in the marketplace. This power is not defensive, but rather offensive. It is not a means of shielding the property owner from unwarranted interference from others or the state, but the legal basis for coercing others to do things that the property owner wishes.[103]

Thus, the free market is by no means free of coercion. Rather, property-based coercive power still exists in the marketplace. Effective distributional policies require an analysis of how the legal system allocates coercive power. For instance, the rationale against the expansive privatization of natural resources by and large stems from the fact that the free market, despite its liberty-promoting function, results in coercion by creating the monopolization of resources.[104] It does so because while

---

[100] RAWLS, A THEORY OF JUSTICE, *supra* note 98, at 4.

[101] *See* IRIS MARION YOUNG, RESPONSIBILITY FOR JUSTICE 45 (2011).

[102] *See* Robert L. Hale, *Coercion and Distribution in a Supposedly Non-Coercive State*, 38 POL. SCI. Q. 470, 470 (1923).

[103] *Id.* at 472.

[104] *See, e.g.*, David Brodwin, *The Tragedy of Privatizing the Commons: Why Privatizing Our Shared Resources Doesn't Work.*, U.S. NEWS (Mar. 2, 2015), https://bit.ly/3oKc23M ("The concentration of rights creates an arms race that attracts capital and new technology to extract in ways that are ever more efficient (that's a good thing), but which are also ever more destructive to the future productivity of the commons ... Given our pay-to-play politics,

every person is an equal, nominal participant in the marketplace, the type or amount of resources that each individual controls differs from person to person. Therefore, bargaining power always varies from person to person when they negotiate deals in the marketplace, making it possible for people with stronger bargaining power to coerce others into following their commands.[105]

Technology-driven injustice is also problematic because of the pervasiveness of technology in contemporary society. Technological advancement in recent decades has offered solutions to many of humanity's problems. However, it has also caused increasing inequality, primarily in the two following ways.

First, public investment in the provision of access to technological benefits causes injustice. Despite significant advancements in technology, a large portion of the world's population is denied the benefits offered because investment has prioritized developing high-end technology over ensuring universal access to fundamental technologies. For example, nearly 1 billion people lack access to electricity. To overcome this problem, as much as 65 percent of new investment would need to be directed at off-grid technology.[106]

Unequal access to broadband technology has magnified pre-existing social problems and widened the divide between rich and poor.[107] A recent United Nations report revealed that more than half the world's population lacks access to the Internet and its advantages.[108] For instance, in the United States, access to technology is a determining factor in the knowledge divide between rich and poor youth.[109] In Africa, only 17.8 percent of households have internet access, meaning that most of the 250 million school children affected by the COVID-19 pandemic have been unable to continue

once rights get concentrated, it's all too easy for the new owners to hijack the regulatory and legislative process.").

[105] *See, e.g.,* Hale, *supra* note 102, at 472.

[106] Practical Action, *Technology Justice: A Call to Action,* PRACTICAL ACTION PUBLISHING 9 (2016), https://bit.ly/2YzUfBu.

[107] *See, e.g.,* Daniele Selby, *Millions of Students in the US Lack Access to Technology and High-Speed Internet,* GLOBAL CITIZEN (Sept. 14, 2018), https://bit.ly/3mBUB2A.

[108] Ray Downs, *UN: Majority of World's Population Lacks Internet Access,* UPI (Sep. 18, 2017, 9:06 PM), https://bit.ly/3am02wW.

[109] Meghan Murphy, *Technology as a Basic Need: The Impact of the Access Gap in Poverty,* 1776 (Apr. 2, 2015), https://bit.ly/3F2ubPT.

their education online, unlike their counterparts in wealthier countries.[110] This low rate of access will also compound Africa's less than 1 percent contribution to the world's digital economy, which now constitutes around 15 percent of global GDP.[111]

Second, inappropriate use of technologies has caused a wide array of unintended consequences, exacerbating injustice across the globe. Technology is generally used in a way that prioritizes short-term goals over sustainability and the preservation of natural resources. Examples abound in energy, agriculture, and manufacturing. Despite knowledge that dramatic reductions in CO_2 emissions must be made to keep global warming under 2°C, fossil fuels continue to be used extensively, and in 2016 the fossil fuel industry was still receiving subsidization as high as $5 trillion per year worldwide.[112] In commercial agriculture, high yields are prioritized at the expense of the genetic diversity offered by traditional food crops, and in the United States, 80 percent of all antibiotics in use are fed to livestock, creating an ideal environment for drug-resistant bacteria to develop.[113] Notwithstanding the negative environmental impacts and depletion of resources, products are designed and manufactured for short-term use, with planned obsolescence being justified on the grounds that long-lasting products slow innovation.[114] For instance, manufacturers of mobile devices, including Apple and Samsung, have faced criticism and fines for intentionally slowing down older devices to ensure that they are suitable only for short-term use.[115] With the ubiquity of smartphones and tablets worldwide, this practice is having a significant detrimental impact on mineral resources, including cobalt, gold, silver, palladium, and tin, particularly in developing countries.[116]

[110] Addis Ababba, *COVID-19: Africa in Urgent Need of Affordable Broadband Internet*, ALL AFRICA (Jun. 10, 2020), https://allafrica.com/stories/202006110005.html.
[111] *Id.*
[112] Practical Action, *Technology Justice, supra* note 106, at 16.
[113] *Id.*, at 15–18
[114] W. C. Satyro, J. B. Sacomano, J. C. Contador, & R. Telles, *Planned Obsolescence or Planned Resource Depletion? A Sustainable Approach*, 195(10) JOURNAL OF CLEANER PRODUCTION 744, 745 (2018).
[115] Antonio G, *Planned Obsolescence of Mobile Phones*, MEDIUM (Dec. 13, 2019), https://bit.ly/3uRcWfM.
[116] Kat George, *The Tech Industry Has a Serious Sustainability Problem – And it's Going Unchecked*, HUCK (Mar. 27, 2019), https://bit.ly/3oHAF0G.

Moreover, the inappropriate use of technologies can negatively affect the distribution of social resources, especially in the labor market. Theoretically, all rational individuals, upon being replaced by automation, will simply acquire new skillsets to make themselves employable again in the labor market.[117] However, this phenomenon is not observed in reality. Statistics show that significant numbers of workers displaced due to technological developments are simply not able to find new jobs.[118] The apparent winners capturing the economic benefits of technological innovation are the managers and owners of technology companies and other entities that apply productivity-boosting technologies.[119] Wealth ends up concentrated in the hands of these individuals through technology's replacement of the labor force,[120] thereby exacerbating existing wealth inequality, making a small minority richer and the poor even more impoverished.

A poignant example of the relationship between technology and injustice can be found in Silicon Valley, where tech giants that have accumulated immense wealth are located just twenty minutes away from possibly the largest camp of homeless people in the United States, thus demonstrating that booms no longer lift all boats.[121] Increased efficiency, productivity, and economic gains from technological advancement are not being enjoyed by all. Instead, the high wages enjoyed by those employed in the technology industry have driven up the cost of living in the region, while wealth is not being proportionally redistributed to the community.[122]

---

[117] *How Will Automation Affect Jobs, Skills, and Wages?*, McKinsey & Co., https://mck.co/3iJ4muC.

[118] *See* Andrew Yang, The War on Normal People: The Truth About America's Disappearing Jobs and Why Universal Basic Income Is Our Future xiii (2018).

[119] Cynthia Estlund, *What Should We Do After Work? Automation and Employment Law*, 128 Yale L.J. 254, 287 (2018).

[120] David Rotman, *Technology and Inequality*, MIT Tech. Rev., Nov.–Dec. 2014, at 52, 56 ("As machines increasingly substitute for labor and building a business becomes less capital-intensive – you don't need a printing plant to produce an online news site, or large investments to create an app – the biggest economic winners will not be those owning conventional capital but, instead, those with the ideas behind innovative new products and successful business models.").

[121] *Id.* at 54; Alexia Fernández Campbell et al., *How Silicon Valley Created America's Largest Homeless Camp*, Atlantic (Nov. 25, 2014).

[122] *See* Campbell et al., *supra* note 121.

2 Social Justice and Technology Companies

Based on the discussion in Section 1, I argue that technology companies have a fundamental responsibility to confront the injustices created by technological development. This responsibility should legally and ethically motivate them to counter both privatization-driven and technology-driven injustices.

With respect to privatization-driven injustice, technology companies have to deal with the conflict between their intellectual property rights and the public's enjoyment of the benefits of technological progress.[123] Given that technology companies can significantly affect the distribution and enjoyment of these benefits, the Venice Statement on the Right to Enjoy the Benefits of Scientific Progress and its Applications highlights the responsibility of corporations, noting that "the right to enjoy the benefits of scientific progress and its applications may create tensions with the intellectual property regime, which is a temporary monopoly with a valuable social function that should be managed in accordance with a common *responsibility* to prevent the unacceptable prioritization of profit for some over benefit for all."[124]

As information creators, technology companies have exercised their intellectual property rights irresponsibly, causing privatization-based injustice. Technology that should have made it easier for the public to access and use copyrighted works has in many instances made it significantly more expensive and difficult to do so. For example, developments in CD and DVD technology were followed by copy protection software that was criticized for preventing users from making fair use of works stored on those media despite such conduct being legal under copyright law.[125] The rise of streaming platforms initially provided users with a broad range of cheap, high-quality alternatives to piracy, but copyright owners are increasingly limiting the availability of works to their own platforms, making it more expensive to attain the

---

[123] *See* LAURENCE R. HELFER & GRAEME W. AUSTIN, HUMAN RIGHTS AND INTELLECTUAL PROPERTY: MAPPING THE GLOBAL INTERFACE 234–37 (2011).

[124] UNESCO, THE RIGHT TO ENJOY THE BENEFITS OF SCIENTIFIC PROGRESS AND ITS APPLICATIONS 15 (2019), https://unesdoc.unesco.org/ark:/48223/pf0000185558.

[125] *Comments on Rulemaking on Exemptions on Anticircumvention*, COPYRIGHT.GOV (last accessed Jun. 13, 2020), www.copyright.gov/1201/2003/comments/index.html.

broad access previously offered.[126] The irresponsible exercise of copyright has involved two important stages.

First, the copyright-based industry makes every effort to lobby legislatures to adopt laws that provide increasingly stringent protection of copyright.[127] As a result, the legal protection of technological measures has entitled copyright holders to lock up information, copyright terms have been retroactively extended to place more works under proprietary control, and databases have been afforded stronger legal protection to fence off public access.[128] At the same time, the recent expansion of copyright protection has severely jeopardized the public interest accommodations in copyright law and significantly narrowed copyright limitations.[129]

Second, fueled by the expansion of copyright protection, many copyright holders have exercised their rights irresponsibly.[130] As the commercial value of copyrights has grown, corporations have taken possession of copyrights over a rapidly increasing number of works.[131] Most corporations are profit-maximizing entities and are thus inclined to resort to aggressive copyright protection strategies. For example, the scope of copyright rights is routinely exaggerated to prevent members of the public from using copyrighted works in ways that the fair use doctrine would permit.[132] Copyright owners have also abused the software designed to help them discover infringing uses of their protected works. In addition to abusing the monetization feature of YouTube's Content ID, copyright owners have been able to profit from the use of work in the public domain. For example, major labels have claimed public domain songs on YouTube, and as recently as

---

[126] Katherine Trendacosta, *Welcome to the Streaming Wars*, SLATE (Feb. 21, 2020). Following the success of Netflix, a number of companies, including Disney, CBS, HBO, and Warner Bros., have launched their own independent streaming platforms.

[127] *See* Louis Menand, *Crooner in Rights Spat: Are Copyright Laws Too Strict?*, NEW YORKER (Oct. 13, 2014).

[128] *See* Sun, *supra* note 57, at 272–78.

[129] *Id.* at 279.

[130] *Id.* at 269–78.

[131] At present, copyrights are largely concentrated in the hands of big media, including copyright-based entertainment, publishing, communications, and software industries. *Id.* at 273.

[132] *See* JASON MAZZONE, COPYFRAUD AND OTHER ABUSES OF INTELLECTUAL PROPERTY LAW 12 (2011).

January 2020, an entertainment company owned by a subsidiary of WarnerMedia used the system to claim ownership of the numbers "36" and "50."[133] Many copyright owners "only speak in terms of the *advantage* of property rights, and never [of] the *burdens* that necessarily go with property ownership."[134]

Oftentimes, the irresponsible exercise of intellectual property rights causes serious harm to the public interest in knowledge creation and diffusion. The marketing practice adopted by Elsevier, the world's largest academic publisher, is a case in point. Despite its profit margins being higher than those of top technology companies, including Apple, Google, and Amazon,[135] Elsevier charges exorbitantly high prices for subscriptions to individual journals and for the purchase of individual articles. A top mathematics journal published by Princeton University Press charges $0.13 per page. In sharp contrast, the top-ten Elsevier journals cost $1.30 per page or more.[136] Many prominent universities and academics have already come into conflict with Elsevier over its unreasonably high subscription fees.[137] Negotiations between the University of California (UC) and Elsevier for a new journal subscription contract broke down after UC's subscription expired in December 2018,[138] resulting in access to Elsevier's journal articles being cut off for approximately 350,000 UC researchers and students.[139]

Technology companies thus have a responsibility to deal with technology-driven injustice. While rapid technological advancement has offered remarkable benefits for humanity, it has also created new problems of social injustice. Against this backdrop, technology companies

---

[133] *See*, Timothy Geigner, *YouTube Streamer Hit With Demonetization Over Copyright Claims to Numbers "36" and "50"*, TECH DIRT (Jan. 24, 2020), https://bit.ly/3oIbfA8.

[134] WILLIAM PATRY, MORAL PANICS AND THE COPYRIGHT WARS 123 (2009).

[135] Stephen Buranyi, *Is the Staggeringly Profitable Business of Scientific Publishing Bad for Science?*, GUARDIAN (June 27, 2017). ("In 2010, Elsevier's scientific publishing arm reported profits of £724m on just over £2bn in revenue. It was a 36% margin – higher than Apple, Google, or Amazon posted that year.").

[136] *The Cost of Knowledge*, https://bit.ly/2YD3dhp.

[137] *See, e.g.*, Sarah Zhang, *The Real Cost of Knowledge*, ATLANTIC (Mar. 4, 2019).

[138] Gretchen Kell, *Why UC Split with Publishing Giant Elsevier*, U.C. (Mar. 6, 2019), https://bit.ly/3iILSdC.

[139] Diana Kwon, *University of California Loses Access to New Content in Elsevier Journals*, SCIENTIST (July 12, 2019), https://bit.ly/3BqzxCn.

should explore the extent to which the new technologies they develop might negatively affect societal interests at large and group interests in particular, and then take their own actions to tackle these problems or support related governmental measures.

As a first step, technology companies should consider how their newly developed technologies might, for example, negatively affect equality in the job market. Technologies such as automation and AI are transforming labor markets and gradually resulting in job losses.[140] The jobs lost are typically middle-class jobs that require repetitive and predictable work,[141] such as administrative, clerical, or production positions.[142] The resulting change in socioeconomic class composition is increasing the wealth disparity between rich and poor.[143] It is also creating a larger supply of available low-skill, low-paid labor, thereby depressing wages and further exacerbating income and wealth inequality.[144] As an example, increased productivity resulting from technology could mean that a firm that once required five accountants now needs only three to manage the same workload. As AI and automation-related technologies improve, the same firm may require only one accountant or none at all.[145] Increased productivity may ultimately result in a hypercompetitive labor market with the increased stakes bringing it closer to a winner-takes-all situation.[146]

Technology companies should also consider how the design of their newly developed technologies is likely to negatively affect group interests. Those who are marginalized or possess less wealth are typically not the primary target groups of the companies providing new technology-based products because they typically lack sufficient buying power.[147] As a result, the members of these groups are ignored in the

---

[140]   OXFORD ECON., HOW ROBOTS CHANGE THE WORLD: WHAT AUTOMATION REALLY MEANS FOR JOBS AND PRODUCTIVITY 19–21 (2019); Estlund, *supra* note 119, at 269.

[141]   OXFORD ECON., *id.* at 23.

[142]   Rotman, *supra* note 120, at 56–58.

[143]   *Id.*

[144]   *Id.*

[145]   *See, e.g.,* Jay Wacker, *How Much Will AI Decrease the Need For Human Labor?*, FORBES (Jan. 18, 2017).

[146]   Estlund, *supra* note 119, at 280.

[147]   For example, an increasing number of software and mobile apps require an uninterrupted internet connection to function. *See List of Technology Design Decisions That Marginalize People*, GEEK FEMINISM WIKI, https://bit.ly/3oHsMIQ (last visited Jan. 26, 2020). This is technologically and financially infeasible in poor countries in which the information

design of new technologies, further marginalizing them and limiting their access to certain technologies.[148] Even well-meaning initiatives can unintentionally exclude marginalized groups. Accordingly, when assisting a government project to increase the accessibility of a public service by transferring that service online so that anyone can access it at any time, a technology company should closely examine how particular groups of people are likely to be affected. Without such scrutiny, the upgrade could unintentionally disadvantage the illiterate or visually impaired, among other groups, making a service that was once accessible to them inaccessible.

Given their size and influence, technology companies must also constantly assess their role in addressing identity-driven injustices. An important starting point would be to ensure internal diversity, as modern technology directly affects individuals of all classes. However, a lack of diversity has long been a serious problem in the technology sector. For example, as of June 2020, only 3 percent of employees at the five biggest technology firms in the United States were black.[149] Similarly, despite efforts to increase representation, the number of women working in technology has remained largely unchanged in the past ten years.[150] This lack of diversity has made it increasingly difficult to create objective and identity-neutral products, as underlying employee bias is hard to separate from the decision-making algorithms currently being developed.[151] Human error, prejudice, and misjudgment can enable bias to become embedded in these algorithms at any stage of their development, and existing societal and historical patterns in training data can lead to discriminatory results unless steps are taken to correct them.[152] Unfortunately, technology companies have to date

technology and communication infrastructure is significantly inadequate and the cost of an Internet connection is beyond the affordability of the general public. *Id.*

[148] *See id.*

[149] *Beyond the Pale: Will Silicon Valley Face up to its Diversity Problem?*, THE ECONOMIST (Jun. 20, 2020), https://econ.st/3mv0UVG.

[150] Jenny Little, *Ten Years On, Why Are There Still So Few Women in Tech?*, GUARDIAN (Jan. 2, 2020), https://bit.ly/3Bhusfs.

[151] S. U. NOBLE, ALGORITHMS OF OPPRESSION: HOW SEARCH ENGINES REINFORCE RACISM 2 (2018).

[152] David Leslie, *Understanding Artificial Intelligence Ethics and Safety: A Guide for the Responsible Design and Implementation of AI Systems in the Public Sector*, THE ALAN TURING INSTITUTE 13–14 (2019), https://bit.ly/3Bppeyc.

taken insufficient steps to counter these problems, thus failing in their responsibility to counter identity-driven injustice.

One effect of these failings is that developments in AI have reinforced stereotypes and discriminatory views. For example, Google has made multiple errors in attempting to break new ground in image recognition technology. When insufficiently trained algorithms led to Google Photos identifying some black people as gorillas, Google responded by simply blocking the software from identifying gorillas.[153] More recently, in a viral experiment Google's Vision AI labeled a thermometer in the hand of a black person as a gun, but as a monocular when held in a white hand.[154] These problems are also evident in some of Google's most established and influential technologies. For instance, Google Search autosuggestions have previously been found to include sexist ideas such as "women should: stay at home, be slaves, be in the kitchen, not speak in church,"[155] and pornographic results were frequently displayed when searching for "black girls."[156] Although some have defended Google Search results for simply reflecting users' beliefs, such a defense would prevent minorities from influencing the way in which they are represented in search engines and ignores the fact that algorithms prioritizing the generation of clicks and promotion of paid advertisements are responsible for driving results to the top of the page.[157]

Furthermore, by offering such technology for public sector use, companies have helped to reinforce systemic bias and contributed to racial profiling. For example, a study by ProPublica suggested that the privately developed recidivism prediction software COMPAS wrongly labels black defendants as high risk at almost twice the rate of white defendants after taking into account such loaded factors as whether the subject's parents had ever been jailed or imprisoned.[158] The use of AI in

---

[153] James Vincent, *Google "Fixed" its Racist Algorithm by Removing Gorillas From its Image-Labelling Tech*, THE VERGE (Jan. 12, 2018), https://bit.ly/2WOvXCO.

[154] Nicholas Kayser-Brill, *Google Apologizes After its Vision AI Produced Racist Results*, ALGORITHM WATCH (Apr. 7, 2020), https://algorithmwatch.org/en/story/google-vision-racism/.

[155] NOBLE, *supra* note 151, at 15.

[156] *Id.* at 17–18.

[157] *Id.* at 16–24.

[158] *See* Julia Angwin, Jeff Larson, Surya Mattu & Lauren Kirchner, *Machine Bias*, PROPUBLICA (May. 23, 2016), https://bit.ly/3Bm4esr.

law enforcement has faced similar criticism, as it makes use of historical police data colored by racism, countering claims that data-driven approaches can be used to avoid racially biased policing.[159] Owing to the difficulties of identifying people of color outlined above, the suitability of facial recognition software for use in policing must also be questioned. However, in 2019 Amazon refused to stop selling its facial recognition software to law enforcement despite public concern about potential racial bias.[160] This concern has proved justified, as studies have shown that facial recognition software has difficulty accurately identifying individuals with darker skin colors, meaning that such individuals are more likely to be unjustifiably investigated, stopped, arrested, or incorrectly labeled as a match for a suspect.[161] Only following the recent Black Lives Matter protests in the United States and elsewhere have Amazon and several other technology companies begun to reconsider their sale of facial recognition software to law enforcement.[162]

Due to the influence they have attained, internet platforms must also take steps to address the discriminatory conduct of their users. Disinformation and abuse are two activities that can cause identity-driven injustice. It has been suggested that, given the scale of Facebook, if as little as 1 percent of its content consisted of fake news and if that content reached only a minority of users, it would still be sufficient to, for example, sway marginal election results.[163] This reach is significant, as in many cases fake news has been used to target vulnerable minority groups. For instance, refugees and migrants are frequently the target of disinformation campaigns involving accusations of criminal actions and terrorism.[164] Similarly, online abuse, often facilitated by

[159] A. G. Ferguson, The Rise of Big Data Policing: Surveillance, Race, and the Future of Law Enforcement 131–32(2017).

[160] Zak Doffman, *Amazon Refuses to Quit Selling "Flawed"' and "Racially Biased" Facial Recognition*, Forbes (Jan. 28, 2019), https://bit.ly/3oI5enc.

[161] Fabio Bacchini & Ludovica Lorusso, *Race, Again: How Facial Recognition Technology Reinforces Racial Discrimination*, 17(3) J. Info. Comm. & Ethics Soc'y 321, 324 (2019).

[162] Kori Hale, *Amazon, Microsoft & IBM Slightly Social Distancing From the $8 Billion Facial Recognition Market*, Forbes (Jun. 15, 2020), https://bit.ly/3iIIK1k.

[163] Irini Katsirea, *"Fake News": Reconsidering the Value of Untruthful Expression in the Face of Regulatory Uncertainty*, 10 Journal of Media Law 159, 168 (2018).

[164] Soraya Sarhaddi Nelson, *With Huge Fines, German Law Pushes Social Networks to Delete Abusive Posts*, NPR (Oct. 31, 2017).

the anonymity some platforms offer, has been found to disproportion-ately target women and minority groups.[165] Social media platforms have faced criticism over inaction in the face of these problems.[166] In response to a recent resurgence of public discourse on the matter, Mark Zuckerberg declared that Facebook did not want to be the "arbiter of truth of everything that people say online."[167] Although many would agree that private companies should not determine what content is permitted to appear online, the aforementioned Facebook-incited eth-nic cleansing campaign in Myanmar demonstrates the potential sever-ity of identity-driven injustices when platforms do not take at least some responsibility for tackling disinformation.

SUMMARY

The three fundamental corporate responsibilities that I have put for-ward in this chapter form a matrix of legal and ethical guidance for the benevolent behavior of technology companies. First, the responsibility to reciprocate for users' contributions is the base of this matrix, urging technology companies to take immediate action to appreciate and compensate such contributions by protecting users' private data effect-ively. Second, the responsibility to play a positive role constitutes a major pillar of the matrix, encouraging corporate managers' ethical deliberations about how their companies can fulfill their responsibilities in accordance with their three professional roles. Third, the responsi-bility to confront the injustices created by technological development acts as the beacon of light flashing on top of the matrix.[168] It is the

---

[165] *See, e.g.,* HM Government, *Online Harms White Paper,* UK HOME OFFICE (Apr., 2019), https://bit.ly/3iIK2cW.

[166] *See, e.g., Statement On The Code Of Practice Against Disinformation: Commission Asks Online Platforms To Provide More Details On Progress Made,* EUROPEAN COMMISSION (Feb. 28, 2019), https://bit.ly/3lmBXfM.

[167] Tom McCarthy, *Zuckerberg Says Facebook Won't Be Arbiters of Truth After Trump Threat,* GUARDIAN (May 28, 2020).

[168] Professor Purdy regards the responsibility for social justice as the highest aspiration because it requires "embracing both our creative ethical capacity and our sense of responsibility to make sense of and do justice, in every sense of that word" to society at large. Jedediah Purdy, *Our Place in the World: A New Relationship for Environmental Ethics and Law,* 62 DUKE L.J. 857, 932 (2013).

highest responsibility that technology companies should aspire to after they have fulfilled the first two responsibilities.

The ethical theories of reciprocity, role responsibility, and social justice have been conventionally utilized to justify personal responsibility. Here, I have applied them to justify corporate responsibility because the doctrine of piercing the corporate veil teaches that persons who control a company should be held responsible for any wrongdoing committed in their company's name.[169]

Piercing the veil of technology companies, it is their managers and shareholders who should bear the three fundamental corporate responsibilities. To fulfill them, they must learn how to manage the relationship between their institutions and society. From this perspective, what is required is an ethical educational process in which managers and shareholders learn how to become responsible members of a technological society.[170]

---

[169] *See, e.g.*, Broward Marine, Inc. v. S/V Zeus, No. 05-23105, 2010 WL 427496, at *6 (S.D. Fla. Feb. 1, 2010) (deciding to pierce the corporate veil and finding that the company's dominant shareholder should be personally liable for the torts of his company); Ocala Breeders' Sales Co. v. Hialeah, Inc., 735 So. 2d 542, 543–44 (Fla. Dist. Ct. App. 1999) (piercing the corporate veil to pursue the personal liability of corporate officers).

[170] As Hannah Arendt reminds us, "men, not Man, live on the earth and inhabit the world." HANNAH ARENDT, THE HUMAN CONDITION 7 (2d ed. 1998). No human being lives alone in the world. Rather, human beings live together in a common world, from birth to death.

6 PATENT RESPONSIBILITY

In March 2020, even after the World Health Organization (WHO) declared COVID-19 a pandemic, Labrador Diagnostics attempted through "the most tone-deaf IP suit in history"[1] to block testing for coronavirus that used its patents. In June 2020, Gilead Sciences shocked the international community by pricing its patented medicine remdesivir at $3,120 per course of treatment for COVID-19 patients with private insurance in the United States. Thereafter, the company was vehemently accused of overcharging in "an offensive display of hubris and disregard for the public,"[2] which also led to serious concerns that global efforts to contain the pandemic were effectively at the mercy of medical patent owners.[3] Since December 2020 when the first COVID-19 vaccine was approved by the US Food and Drug Administration, vaccine inequity has ravaged the globe. As of September 2021, a mere 3 percent of people in low-income countries had been vaccinated with at least one dose, in stark contrast to high-income countries' 60 percent.[4] Due to the overly high prices charged

---

[1] Timothy B. Lee, *Firm Wielding Theranos Patents Asks Judge to Block Coronavirus Test*, ARS TECHNICA (Mar. 17, 2020) ("As Stanford patent scholar Mark Lemley puts it, 'this could be the most tone-deaf IP suit in history.'").

[2] *See, e.g.*, Peter Maybarduk, *Gilead's Remdesivir Price Is Offensive*, PUB. CITIZEN (June 29, 2020); David Lazarus, *Is Gilead Ripping Us Off with a COVID-19 Treatment Topping $3,000?*, L.A. TIMES (June 29, 2020).

[3] For example, the Institute for Clinical and Economic Review warned that "Gilead has the power to price remdesivir at will in the U.S., and no governmental or private insurer could even entertain the idea of walking away from the negotiating table." *See* Gina Kolata, *Remdesivir, the First Coronavirus Drug, Gets a Price Tag*, N.Y. TIMES (June 29, 2020).

[4] *See COVID Vaccines*, UN NEWS (Sept. 19, 2021), https://news.un.org/en/story/2021/09/1100192.

by pharmaceutical companies, governments around the world have paid "between 4 and 24 times more than they could be for COVID-19 vaccines."[5] Although Pfizer/BioNTech sold their COVID-19 vaccines to the African Union at their lowest reported price of $6.75 per dose, this charge is nearly the same as Uganda's health expenditure per citizen in a whole year.[6]

Indeed, this tragic sequence of events emerging in the COVID-19 pandemic clearly shows that pharmaceutical companies have sought to capitalize on their patents and maximize private commercial interests at the expense of public interests.[7] What drives pharmaceutical companies to prioritize private interests in their patents over the COVID-19 containment? In this chapter, I first examine the negative effects of Gilead's high-priced patented medicine and other major pharmaceutical companies' absence from the Open COVID Pledge and COVID-19 Technology Access Pool designed to share patented technologies in the public interest. Their performance during the COVID-19 pandemic has exposed problems with patent law's downplaying of patent holder responsibilities. Patent law in the United States encourages the irresponsible exercise of patent rights through its asymmetric allocation of rights and responsibilities. It protects a bundle of strong exclusive rights that entitle patent holders to set product prices as high as they wish. Yet it imposes very weak responsibilities upon them, setting a low patent information disclosure threshold and enfeebling experimental use and compulsory licensing as limitations on patent rights. The asymmetry in patent law has emboldened patent holders to abuse their rights and legitimized governmental condoning of such exploitation.

I further argue that Chapter 5's conception of tripartite fundamental corporate responsibilities provides a constructive means of tackling patent holders' irresponsibility. Drawing on this conception, I propose that US patent law should be reformed to require technology companies to assume three new responsibilities for the patents they hold. First,

---

[5] Anna Marriott and Alex Maitland, *The Great Vaccine Robbery* 1 (Jul. 29, 2021).

[6] *See* Oxfam, *Vaccine Monopolies Make Cost of Vaccinating the World Against COVID at Least 5 Times More Expensive Than It Could Be Published* (Jul. 29, 2021).

[7] *See* Brook Baker, *Drug Companies are Running Scared: Let's Make Them Run Faster,* HEALTH GAP (Mar. 30, 2020).

they should be required to reciprocate for public contributions to the creation of their patents by faithfully disclosing sufficient patent information and taking proactive measures to benefit the users of patents developed with public funding. Second, they should be encouraged to take their innovator role seriously, accommodating the invocation of limitations on their patent rights by the public. Third, they should be made to confront injustices caused by patent protection. For example, they could address the unaffordability of patented medicines by cooperating with the government to implement compulsory licensing orders so as to provide lower-priced patented drugs to curb public health crises.

A PATENTS, PHARMACEUTICAL COMPANIES, AND COVID-19

A broad-spectrum antiviral medication researched as a potential treatment first for hepatitis C and then for Ebola, remdesivir has also been found effective in treating COVID-19.[8] Following its patent filing in 2014, remdesivir developer Gilead Sciences decided to pursue broad protection to preclude competitors from producing and selling the medicine.[9] The company also applied for the designation of remdesivir as an orphan drug in March 2020.[10] Orphan status was granted by the Food and Drug Administration (FDA),[11] allowing Gilead to enjoy a seven-year market exclusivity period.[12]

In June 2020, Gilead announced its decision to price remdesivir at $520 or $390 per vial and $3,120 or $2,340 per treatment course for

---

[8] Gilead, *Development of Remdesivir*, https://bit.ly/3lwr1fv.

[9] Anders Heebøll-Nielsen & Michael Bech Sommer, *What Patent Protection Does Gilead's COVID-19 Treatment Remdesivir Have?*, Lexology (Apr. 30, 2020), ("By filing three PCT applications, Gilead obviously had a clear strategy to obtain broad protection, and their strategy can be inferred from the patent registers.").

[10] Kao-Ping Chua & Rena M. Conti, *Policy Implications of the Orphan Drug Designation for Remdesivir to Treat COVID-19* (Aug. 17, 2020), https://bit.ly/3lrW5gq.

[11] Lee Fang & Sharon Lerner, *Coronavirus Treatment Developed by Gilead Sciences Granted "Rare Disease" Status, Potentially Limiting Affordability*, The Intercept (Mar. 23, 2020), https://bit.ly/30i8cob.

[12] *See* Federal Food, Drug, and Cosmetic Act, 21 U.S.C. § 360cc. In March 2020, after public criticism, Gilead submitted a request to the FDA to rescind remdesivir's orphan drug designation.

US patients with private insurance and government-sponsored insurance, respectively.[13] The company argued that such prices were below the drug's value and necessary to help maintain future innovation capacity.[14] Later that month, the US government bought more than 500,000 treatment courses at a reported price of around $3,200 each.[15]

Gilead's pricing decisions have drawn fierce criticism for a number of reasons. First, experts have pointed out that remdesivir is not expensive to produce. One study estimated that it could be produced for only a few dollars per treatment course, and an approved manufacturer in India announced that it would price its generic equivalent at just $71 per vial.[16] Although private companies by nature seek to maximize revenue, in the circumstances of a pandemic it is difficult to frame Gilead's conduct as anything other than exploitation, as governments and hospitals have been left with no option but to accept its terms.[17]

Second, public funding worth at least $70.5 million was contributed to remdesivir's development.[18] Even though they are effectively stakeholders in remdesivir, US citizens receive no financial benefit from their stake and must pay whatever Gilead charges.[19]

Third, Gilead's price announcement was timed to maximize profits. Research into the effects of remdesivir on COVID-19 was still ongoing, leading to speculation that Gilead was hoping to maximize profits before any data challenging the drug's efficacy could be published.[20] Moreover, with countries around the world concurrently

---

[13] An Open Letter from Daniel O'Day, Chairman & CEO, Gilead Sciences, GILEAD SCIENCES (June 29, 2020) [hereinafter An Open Letter], https://bit.ly/3AzZaPI.

[14] Id. ("We also balanced that with our longer-term responsibilities: to continue with our ongoing work on remdesivir, to maintain our long-term research in antivirals and to invest in scientific innovation that might help generations to come.").

[15] Barbara Mintzes & Ellen 't Hoen, The US Has Bought Most of the World's Remdesivir: Here's What It Means for the Rest of Us, THE CONVERSATION (July 3, 2020), https://bit.ly /3luzXBW.

[16] Vidya Krishnan, How Secret Deals Could Keep a COVID-19 Drug Out of Reach for Millions, L.A. TIMES (July 1, 2020).

[17] Rohan Chalasani, The US Is Paying Way Too Much for Remdesivir, WIRED (July 17, 2020).

[18] The Real Story of Remdesivir, PUBLIC CITIZEN (May 7, 2020), www.citizen.org/article/the-real-story-of-remdesivir.

[19] See Lazarus, supra note 2.

[20] Id.

working on a vaccine, Gilead potentially had only a limited period in which to generate profits from remdesivir.[21]

Last but not least, the special licensing agreements that Gilead has entered into with a number of developing countries may jeopardize attempts to combat COVID-19 elsewhere. Critics have noted that such agreements prevent generic drugs from being distributed in dozens of countries, making low-cost alternatives unavailable to nearly half the world's population.[22] The countries excluded by the agreements include some of the hardest hit, including the US, Brazil, Russia, Britain, and Peru, leading many to argue that Gilead was intended to exploit the pandemic by charging the most desperate countries higher prices for access to the brand-name version of the drug.[23]

Although Gilead's aggressive patent strategies have caused public outcry, other pharmaceutical companies have followed in its footsteps. In May 2020, NellOne Therapeutics announced that it had filed a provisional patent application for use of the NELL1 signaling protein for the treatment of tissue damage and inflammation caused by COVID-19.[24] In the same month, Annovis Bio filed a patent application in the US for a method of inhibiting, preventing, or treating COVID-19 neurological injuries.[25] In June 2020, the Salzman Group filed a provisional patent application for the preventative and therapeutic use of a compound in relation to COVID-19-caused pneumonia and acute lung injury.[26] Quite a number of other pharmaceutical companies have filed patent applications for medicines that can treat or alleviate COVID-19 symptoms.[27]

---

[21] *Id.*

[22] Krishnan, *supra* note 16.

[23] *Id.*

[24] Press Release, NellOne Therapeutics Inc., *NellOne Therapeutics Files COVID-19 Treatment Patent*, PR NEWSWIRES (May 18, 2020).

[25] Press Release, *Annovis Bio Files Patent Application for Method of Inhibiting, Preventing, or Treating Neurological Injuries Due to Viral and Other Infections Including COVID-19*, ANNOVIS (May 27, 2020).

[26] Press Release, *Kalytera Announces Filing of Provisional Patent Protecting Use of R-107 for Treatment of Coronavirus and COVID-19 Associated Pneumonia*, KALYTERA (June 2, 2020), https://kalytera.co/news/r-107-provisional-patent.

[27] *See, e.g.,* Press Release, *Sunshine Biopharma Files a Patent Application for a New Coronavirus COVID-19 Treatment*, SUNSHINE BIOPHARMA INC. (June 1, 2020).

Pharmaceutical companies have also filed for patent protection for other COVID-19-related innovations, ranging from vaccines, personal protection equipment, testing methods, and portable ventilators to pandemic management platforms. In addition, patent litigation associated with COVID-19 has been proposed or launched. For instance, Labrador initiated a lawsuit in the United States in March 2020 in an attempt to block COVID-19 testing that uses its patents.[28] In the same month, volunteers in Italy who produced 3D-printed valves for use in ventilators were threatened with legal action by the patent owner of the ventilator valves if they continued to manufacture them without permission.[29]

In response to the pandemic, an international group of scientists, engineers, lawyers, and entrepreneurs launched the Open COVID Coalition.[30] Its primary concern is that intellectual property rights are unduly impeding efforts to contain the COVID-19 pandemic[31] by limiting access to the relevant research and manufacturing technologies.[32] To address this concern, the coalition created the Open COVID Pledge (OCP) in April 2020.[33] The OCP grants a "non-exclusive, royalty-free, worldwide, fully paid-up license" to pledgors' patents and other IP rights.[34]

International organizations have also called for expeditious scientific and technical cooperation at the global level.[35] In April 2020, the UN Committee on Economic, Social and Cultural Rights stated that "[i]f a pandemic develops, sharing the best scientific knowledge and its applications, especially in the medical field, becomes crucial to mitigate the impact of the disease, and to expedite the discovery of effective treatments and vaccines."[36] Subsequently, the World Health Organization (WHO)

---

[28] *See* Lee, *supra* note 1.
[29] Chloe Kent, *Covid-19: Start-Up That Saved Lives With 3D-Printed Valve May Face Legal Action* (Mar.18, 2020), https://bit.ly/3oRZJSI.
[30] *About,* OPEN COVID PLEDGE (updated July 29, 2020), https://opencovidpledge.org/about.
[31] Mark A Lemley, *Stanford's Mark Lemley on Effort to Make IP Available to End COVID-19 Pandemic,* STAN. L. SCH. (Apr. 1, 2020), https://stanford.io/3DuOvHX.
[32] *Id.*
[33] *Id.*
[34] OCL-P v1.1, OCL-PC v1.1, Open COVID Pledge (Apr. 17, 2020), https://opencovid pledge.org/v1-1-ocl-p.
[35] Katrina Perehudoff & Jennifer Sellin, *COVID-19 Technology Access Pool (C-TAP): A Promising Human Rights Approach,* HEALTH & HUM. RTS. J. (June 4, 2020), https://bit.ly/3BwBugl.
[36] U.N., Econ. & Soc. Council, Comm. on Econ., Soc. & Cultural Rts., Statement on the Coronavirus Disease (COVID-19) Pandemic and Economic, Social and Cultural Rights 5, U.N. Doc. E/C.12/2020/1 (Apr. 17, 2020).

launched the COVID-19 Technology Access Pool (C-TAP) in
May 2020 to accelerate and broaden global access to vaccines, treatments,
and diagnostics. The WHO outlined five priorities for C-TAP in order to
create "a one-stop shop for scientific knowledge, data and intellectual
property to be shared equitably by the global community."[37] They
include ensuring transparency in the publication of clinical trial results;
tying public research funds to affordable and equitable distribution; and
licensing patents from promising discoveries to the established and UN-
backed Medicines Patent Pool so that they can be produced at scale by
generic manufacturers.[38]

However, major pharmaceutical companies have failed to react
to the global call for responsibility. For the purpose of containing
the pandemic, the OCP and C-TAP urge patent holders to responsibly share their patented technologies in the public interest by
altering their dedication to exclusive rights protection. As the key
institutions in bringing an end to the pandemic, the major pharmaceutical companies have yet to take part in either initiative. The
OCP has engaged many other companies, including IBM,
Facebook, and Uber,[39] and has obtained over 250,000 pledged
patents.[40] However, none of the major pharmaceutical companies
has pledged patents to the OCP,[41] resulting in a gridlock that has
led some commentators to urge these companies to take the initiative to do so.[42] Since its inception, the C-TAP has not yet started
to function because "no technology or treatments have been
shared."[43] No pharmaceutical companies had voluntarily joined

[37] *International Community Rallies to Support Open Research and Science to Fight COVID-19,*
WORLD HEALTH ORG. (May 29, 2020), https://bit.ly/2YAtfkY.

[38] *See id.*

[39] *See* Charlotte Kilpatrick, *Tech Companies Promote Benefits of Open Covid Pledge,* Sept.24
2020, https://bit.ly/3DyzTaO.

[40] *See* Michael S. Horikawa, *The Open COVID Pledge: Don't Say "I Do" Till You Think It
Through,* https://bit.ly/3F2VBFi.

[41] *Id.* ("However, the Pledge has not yet seen wide adoption in certain key industries. For
example, it does not appear that the Open COVID Pledge has been embraced by the
pharmaceutical or medical device industries.").

[42] *Id.* (cautioning that "it is especially important for companies to carefully consider the
impacts of being an early (or sole) adopter in an industry").

[43] Michael Safi, *WHO Platform for Pharmaceutical Firms Unused Since Pandemic Began,*
GUARDIAN (Jan. 22, 2021).

the C-TAP as of March 2021.[44] Worse still, some of them have even condemned it as "nonsense" and "dangerous."[45]

B THE ASYMMETRY BETWEEN STRONG PATENT RIGHTS AND WEAK RESPONSIBILITIES

When announcing remdesivir prices, Gilead's CEO emphasized the responsibility of his company six times.[46] However, as revealed above, Gilead has in reality attempted to maximize the economic value of patent rights while minimizing its corresponding responsibilities. One consequence is that health advocacy groups and the medical humanitarian organization Doctors Without Borders have urged the Indian government to rescind its remdesivir patents.[47]

In this section, I argue that by creating asymmetry between rights and responsibilities, patent law has facilitated irresponsible acts by technology companies like Gilead. While the law protects strong patent rights, it imposes very weak responsibilities upon patent holders and lacks effective legal mechanisms to enforce them.

1 Strong Patent Rights

Patent law grants the rights to make, use, sell, offer for sale, or import a patented invention for the term of the patent.[48] These rights are protected as a bundle of very strong exclusive rights in terms of their nature and scope. Patents, according to leading jurists such as Justice Story, are private property rights entitling patentees to "absolute enjoyment and possession."[49] The Supreme Court supports this

---

[44] Selam Gebrekidan and Matt Apuzzo, *Rich Countries Signed Away a Chance to Vaccinate the World* ("Not a single vaccine company has signed up [for the C-TAP].").

[45] Sarah Newey, *WHO Patent Pool for Potential Covid-19 Products Is "Nonsense", Pharma Leaders Claim*, TELEGRAPH (May 29, 2020).

[46] *See An Open Letter*, *supra* note 13("In making our decision on how to price remdesivir, we considered the full scope of our responsibilities.").

[47] Zeba Siddiqui, *Health Groups Ask India to Rescind Gilead's Patents for COVID-19 Drug Remdesivir*, REUTERS (May 14, 2020).

[48] 35 U.S. C. § 154 (a)(1).

[49] *Ex parte* Wood, 22 U.S. 603, 608 (1824) (stating that patent law "intended to give [a patentee] the absolute enjoyment and possession").

characterization.[50] Patent rights safeguard the value of patents[51] and penalize free-riders who make unauthorized use of them.[52] The scope of patent rights is generally broader than that of the rights protected by other intellectual property laws.[53] Through the doctrine of equivalents, patent law prohibits the production and sale of non-exact copies that are functionally equivalent to the invention concerned.[54] Judge Learned Hand championed the cause of this doctrine as being "to temper unsparing logic and prevent an infringer from stealing the benefit of the invention."[55]

This structure of strong patent rights is predominantly justified by utilitarian theory.[56] Given the nonrivalrous and nonexclusive nature of intellectual property as a public good, absent any way of extracting value from the supply of a public good or preventing free riding, market players have little incentive to produce that public good, a situation that, over time, results in undersupply, harming innovation and industrial progress.[57] Therefore, inventors should be rewarded with strong patent rights over their inventions in order to incentivize the disclosure of those inventions.[58] This approach can equally be conceptualized or

---

[50] *See* United States v. Am. Bell Tel. Co., 167 U.S. 224, 243 (1897) (ruling that "a patent was issued to the telephone company . . . [and] was the property of the telephone company"). In Oil States Energy Servs., LLC v. Greene's Energy Grp., LLC, the Supreme Court ruled that a patent should be deemed "a public franchise" granted by the USPTO. But it also stated that this opinion did not contradict established case law that regards patents as private properties. See 138 S. Ct. 1365, 1375 (2018).

[51] *Wood*, 22 U.S. at 608 (ruling that "[t]he inventor has . . . a property in his inventions; a property which is often of very great value.").

[52] *See* Lowell v. Lewis, 15 F. Cas. 1018, 1019 (C.C.D. Mass. 1817).

[53] *See* Colleen Chien, *Contextualizing Patent Disclosure*, 69 VAND. L. REV. 1849, 1851 (2016) ("Patent law provides protection that is in many ways stronger and broader than trade secrecy or copyright: it can be enforced against independent inventors and non-exact copies.").

[54] Warner-Jenkinson Co. v. Hilton Davis Chem. Co., 520 U.S. 17, 38 (1997) (ruling that the doctrine centers on the question about "substantially the same function in substantially the same way to obtain the same result") (quoting Machine Co. v. Murphy, 97 U.S. 120, 125(1878)).

[55] Royal Typewriter Co. v. Remington Rand, Inc., 168 F.2d 691, 692 (2d. Cir. 1948).

[56] *See* Dan L. Burk & Mark A. Lemley, *Policy Levers in Patent Law*, 89 VA. L. REV. 1575, 1597 (2003) ("To a greater extent than any other area of intellectual property, courts and commentators widely agree that the basic purpose of patent law is utilitarian: We grant patents in order to encourage invention.").

[57] *See* Dan L. Burk, *Law and Economics of Intellectual Property: In Search of First Principles*, 8 ANN. REV. L. & SOC. SCI. 397, 400 (2012).

[58] *See* Fritz Machlup & Edith Penrose, *The Patent Controversy in the Nineteenth Century*, 10 J. ECON. HIST. 1, 25–26 (1950).

framed as a social contract whereby the disclosure of knowledge is exchanged for patent protection.[59] The Supreme Court has elaborated as follows.

> The patent laws promote [technological] progress by offering a right of exclusion for a limited period as an incentive to inventors to risk the often enormous costs in terms of time, research, and development. The productive effort thereby fostered will have a positive effect on society through the introduction of new products and processes of manufacture into the economy, and the emanations by way of increased employment and better lives for our citizens. In return for the right of exclusion – this "reward for inventions," – the patent laws impose upon the inventor a requirement of disclosure.[60]

According to this view, patent rights serve economic policy because the more new inventions are made publicly available, the better the promotion of technological progress and knowledge growth. Central to the realization of such policy is incentivizing invention through the granting and protection of strong patent rights.

Apart from this incentive-oriented utilitarianism, strong patent rights are also justified by the conventional wisdom that invention emerges from an inventor's sole individual contribution.[61] This traditional narrative envisions lone inventors relying on their own labor, talents, and ideas to develop extraordinary inventions and advance industrial progress.[62] The lone inventor narrative is reflected in both the philosophical foundations and distinct features of patent law.[63] By requiring protectible inventions to be both novel and non-obvious,

---

[59] *Id.* at 26. The emphasis is on the intermediate element of information and knowledge, rather than innovation. Simultaneously, this is often understood in combination with the economic incentive to innovate. In other words, the economic reward incentivizes (or rewards) both the disclosure of information and the innovation.

[60] Kewanee Oil Co. v. Bicron Corp., 416 U.S. 470, 480 (1974).

[61] *See* Mark A. Lemley, *The Myth of the Sole Inventor*, 110 MICH. L. REV. 709, 710 (2011) ("[T]he very theory of patent law is based on the idea that a lone genius can solve problems that stump the experts, and that the lone genius will do so only if properly incented by the lure of a patent.").

[62] *See* Christopher A. Cotropia, *The Individual Inventor Motif in the Age of the Patent Troll*, 12 YALE J.L. & TECH. 52, 54–55.

[63] *See id.* ("The patent system has traditionally taken the individual inventor motif to heart and seen patents as a vehicle to both fuel individual inventors and protect them from large corporations.").

patent law presupposes that a given invention would not have been invented (or disclosed) without the issue of a patent to the inventor.[64] To provide an economic incentive for innovation, there is a need to identify individuals to whom exclusive rights can be granted.[65] Therefore, patent law presumes that the source of an invention or innovation is a discrete and identifiable inventor.[66] This presumption is a practical consequence of the property rights approach that patent law takes to incentivize innovation, whereby exclusive property rights are granted to individuals who have been incentivized to invent by the lure of a patent. Alternatively, it can be said that property rights are granted to individuals who are best placed to engage in private ordering.[67] The presumptions of patent law as to the source of innovation are fueled by a belief that a given invention would not have been invented but for the entirely original idea of a single creator.[68]

2 Weak Patent Responsibilities

While patent law protects strong exclusive rights, it imposes two categories of weak legal responsibilities upon patent holders. It first requires them to take responsibility for the sufficient disclosure of technical information. By carving out limitations on patent rights such as experimental use and compulsory licensing, patent law also imposes upon patent holders a responsibility to accommodate the public's unauthorized uses of their inventions within the ambit of these limitations. However, both responsibilities are weakly legislated and enforced in practice, as the following discussion reveals.

a Disclosure
A bundle of patent rights is granted in exchange for patent holders' public disclosure of inventions that might otherwise remain trade

[64] *See* Lemley, *supra* note 61, at 736.
[65] *See* Peter Lee, *Social Innovation*, 92 WASH. U. L. REV. 1, 27 (2014).
[66] *See id.* at 26.
[67] Edmund W. Kitch, *The Nature and Function of the Patent System*, 20 J.L. & ECON. 265, 269 (1977).
[68] *See* Cotropia, *supra* note 62, at 57–58 (pointing out that "one of the main goals of the patent system should be to assist, and in some ways protect, the individual inventor").

secrets.[69] Therefore, patent disclosure is "the *quid pro quo* of the right to exclude."[70] The Patent Act establishes three independent conditions for the sufficient disclosure of the invention contained within a patent: a written description of the invention, enablement, and best mode.[71] Where necessary for understanding, the patent specification must contain drawings of the subject matter, and it must conclude with one or more claims describing the subject matter considered by the applicant to constitute the invention.[72] Failure to meet these requirements could lead the courts or USPTO to invalidate the patent. Through requiring patent holders to supply the relevant technical information, the disclosure responsibility benefits society at large.[73] First, disclosure facilitates cumulative invention. Second, it clarifies the boundaries of an invention, enabling others to invent a non-infringing alternative.[74]

However, many patent holders irresponsibly avoid making a sufficient disclosure of information when filing patent applications. One way in which they do so is through language that is difficult to decipher. The patentees of information technology inventions, for instance, are notorious for producing patents that contain very little information about the nature of technical solutions,[75] thereby creating an "indeterminate zone of potential ... infringement for third parties to traverse."[76] The Supreme

---

[69] *See, e.g.*, Brenner v. Manson, 383 U.S. 519, 534 n.21 (1966) ("As a reward for inventions and to encourage their disclose, the United States offers a ... monopoly to an inventor who refrains from keeping his invention a trade secret.").

[70] J.E.M. Ag Supply, Inc. v. Pioneer Hi-Bred Int'l, Inc., 534 U.S. 124, 142 (2001) (quoting Kewanee Oil Co., v. Bicron Corp, 416 U.S. 470, 484 (1974)).

[71] 35 U.S.C. § 112 (2006).

[72] Lisa L. Ouellette, *Do Patents Disclose Useful Information?*, 12 HARV. J.L. & TECH. 545, 550 (2012).

[73] Sinclair & Carroll Co. v. Interchemical Corp., 325 U.S. 327, 331 (1945) ("[The patent law's] inducement is directed to disclosure of advances in knowledge which will be beneficial to society; it is not a certificate of merit, but an incentive to disclosure."); Bonito Boats, Inc. v. Thunder Craft Boats, Inc., 489 U.S. 141, 151 (1989) ("'In consideration of [the fulfillment of] disclosure and the consequent benefit to the community, the patent is granted.'") (quoting United States v. Dubilier Condenser Corp., 289 U.S. 178, 186 (1933)).

[74] *See* Alan Devlin, *The Misunderstood Function of Disclosure in Patent Law*, 23 HARV. J.L. & TECH. 401, 407–08 (2012).

[75] *See* Ben Klemens, *The Rise of the Information Processing Patent*, 14 B.U. J. SCI. & TECH. L. 1, 35 (2008) (concluding that "patents on software and other information-processing technologies [are] virtually useless for disclosure purposes").

[76] Devlin, *supra* note 74, at 410.

Court conceded in *Brenner v. Manson*[77] that the patent system has resulted in "the highly developed art of drafting patent claims so that they disclose as little useful information as possible – while broadening the scope of the claim as widely as possible."[78]

Furthermore, there is a wealth of important information that is necessarily absent from patent documents. Some commentators have pointed out the importance of subsequent ancillary disclosures, licensing agreements, and post-grant challenges, for example, which can enhance the technical teaching within a patent document.[79] More specifically, it has been suggested that the enablement doctrine's failure to adequately consider validating follow-on research favors patents "grounded in early, irreproducible data."[80] Therefore, the doctrine's narrow and retrospective focus on the patent document has ultimately led inventors to disclose the minimum information necessary to obtain patent protection.[81] One survey of nanotechnology researchers found that 86 percent of those who do not read patents simply do not believe that patents contain useful information.[82]

b Experimental Use

In *Whittemore v. Cutter*, Justice Story stated, in dicta, that "it could never have been the intention of the legislature to punish a man, who constructed … a machine merely for philosophical experiments, or for the purpose of ascertaining the sufficiency of the machine to produce its described effects."[83] Although not binding, this opinion influenced the creation of the experimental use defense,[84] which was recognized in 1890 in § 898 of The Law of Patents for Useful Inventions.[85] Subsequent court decisions have contributed to the belief that academic research is broadly exempted from patent infringement liability.[86]

---

[77] 383 U.S. 519 (1966).
[78] *Id.* at 534.
[79] *See* Chien, *supra* note 53, at 1869–77.
[80] Jacob S. Sherkow, *Patent Law's Reproducibility Paradox*, 66 DUKE L.J. 845, 911 (2017).
[81] *See id.* at 847–49.
[82] *See* Ouellette, *supra* note 72, at 571.
[83] Whittemore v. Cutter, 29 F. Cas. 1120, 1121 (C.C.D. Mass. 1813).
[84] Kris J. Kostolansky & Daniel Salgado, *Does the Experimental Use Exception in Patent Law Have a Future?*, COLO. LAW. (Jan. 2018), at 32, 36.
[85] *Id.*
[86] *Id.*

The experimental use exception encourages experimentation and innovation that might otherwise be stifled by patent law's granting of limited monopolies to inventors.[87] Although monopolies provide an incentive for the investment of time and money in innovation, they would undermine patent law's broader goal of promoting the progress of science and useful arts if they prevented researchers from applying a patented invention in new and useful areas.[88] The experimental use defense has helped to alleviate this strain on innovation, and has proved useful for research institutions.[89]

However, the Federal Circuit has overseen the weakening of the experimental use defense of patent infringement.[90] Limitation of the defense began with the introduction of the Bolar exemption in the Hatch-Waxman Act.[91] The Federal Circuit had previously opposed Bolar's testing of a patented drug in preparation for FDA approval of its generic drug, as it was obviously commercial in nature. Congress, however, hoping to foster a generic drug industry, introduced a specific exception for drug research in this context.[92] Despite Congress's approval of experimentation in the Hatch-Waxman Act, the Federal Circuit proceeded to take a narrow approach to the experimental use exception, increasingly finding commercial intent in academic research not relating to drugs.[93]

For instance, in *Embrex, Inc. v. Service Engineering Corp.*, the Federal Circuit held that an academic scientist's attempt to invent around a patent for a chick inoculation method was not protected by

This widespread belief was also buttressed by the 1935 District of Colorado case *Ruth v. Stearns-Roger Manufacturing Co.* This was the first case that examined the experimental use exception in the context of academic research. In *Ruth*, the defendant sold parts for a patented inflation device to the Colorado School of Mines. The district court found the defendant liable for contributory patent infringement, but ruled that Colorado School of Mines' use was exempt from infringement because it used the flotation device as an instrument in conducting research.

(citing Ruth v. Stearns-Roger Manufacturing Co., 13 F. Supp. 697, 713 (D. Colo. 1935)).

[87] *Id.* at 36.

[88] *Id.*

[89] *Id.*

[90] *See* Rochelle Cooper Dreyfuss, *Reconsidering Experimental Use*, 50 AKRON L. REV. 699, 702–04 (2016).

[91] *Id.*

[92] Dreyfuss, *supra* note 90, at 702–03.

[93] *Id.*

the exception as the intent was ultimately commercial.[94] The most notable limitation of the experimental use exception came in *Madey v. Duke University*.[95] In this case, researchers at a nonprofit university had used a patented laser technology in the belief that pure academic research and teaching were exactly what the experimental use exception was designed to protect.[96] The Federal Circuit disagreed, holding that the researchers' use of the laser during teaching was in keeping with Duke University's commercial goal of attaining sufficient status to attract students and lucrative research grants.[97] Although this decision has not eliminated the experimental use exception entirely, many now consider the exception to be essentially useless for research universities and suggest that its demise could significantly inhibit innovation.[98]

The clause "or otherwise available to the public" added to § 102 has two potential interpretations. The first is that it has no impact upon what amounts to public use. Proponents of this view argue that Congress has reenacted the term "public use," which creates a strong presumption that the language continues to have the same meaning it had previously.[99] The second interpretation is that the categories of prior art listed in § 102, including public use, must now be "available to the public," implying a requirement of public knowledge.[100] In nonbinding statements, the USPTO and Federal Circuit appear to support the latter interpretation. For example, the 2011 America Invents Act (AIA) guidelines state that, in the view of the USPTO, the clause means that secret use does not qualify as prior art, and, in dicta, in *Helsinn* the Federal Circuit suggests that the AIA's legislative history indicates an intent to narrow the scope of public use.[101] Accordingly, some commentators have questioned whether the additional clause will render the experimental use exception less important and lead to its erosion.[102]

[94] 216 F.3d 1343, 1346, 1349 (Fed. Cir. 2000) (per curiam).
[95] 307 F.3d 1351 (Fed. Cir. 2002).
[96] *See* Dreyfuss, *supra* note 90, at 703.
[97] *Id.* at 703–04.
[98] Kostolansky & Salgado, *supra* note 84, at 37.
[99] *Id.* at 34.
[100] *Id.*
[101] Helsinn Healthcare S.A. v. Teva Pharmas. USA, Inc., 855 F.3d 1356, 1368–69 (Fed. Cir. 2017);*see* Kostolansky & Salgado, *supra* note 84, at 35.
[102] *Id.*

However, the AIA did not revive the experimental use defense,[103] owing in part to an absence of data suggesting that research has been impeded by the exception's limitation, although that may be the result of researchers ignoring patents or patentees ignoring scientists.[104] It is mostly the result of opposition from the biotechnology industry. At the time of the AIA's enactment, biomedical research discoveries concerned basic information on living organisms such as their genetic sequence and metabolic pathway, and there was concern that a broad exception would interfere with the ability to earn revenue from the licensing of innovations.[105]

c Compulsory Licensing

In patent law, compulsory licensing entitles a governmental agency to authorize the third-party manufacturer of a patented product or the practice of a patented process without the consent of the patent owner in exchange for adequate remuneration.[106] Grounds previously asserted for compulsory licensing worldwide include circumstances of national emergency, vital public health needs, strong societal interest in access to an invention, abuse of economic power by a patent owner, and a situation in which multiple patents are blocking a potential new technology.[107]

The potential for compulsory licensing is recognized in US patent law, which allows the government to use a patented invention for any reason and allows patent holders to sue only to recover reasonable compensation.[108] However, the US patent system has generally proved hostile to the application of this provision.[109] The Bayh-Dole Act also provides the government with "march-in rights," which in theory allow third parties to apply for compulsory licenses of patented inventions

---

[103] *See* Dreyfuss, *supra* note 90, at 701 (pointing out "the AIA's failure to revive this defense legislatively").

[104] *Id.* at 706.

[105] *Id.* at 707.

[106] *See* Margo A. Bagley, *The Morality of Compulsory Licensing as an Access to Medicine Tool,* 102 MINN. L. REV. 2463, 2465 (2018).

[107] Justin Culbertson & Jason J. Jardine, *Compulsory Patent Licensing in the Era of Pandemic,* INT'L. BAR ASS'N (June 30, 2020), https://bit.ly/2YMSPDH.

[108] *See* Sapna Kumar, *Compulsory Licensing of Patents During Pandemics,* SSRN 1, 8 (2020), https://ssrn.com/abstract=3636456.

[109] *See* Culbertson & Jardine, *supra* note 107.

created using government funds.[110] This form of compulsory license may be granted on reasonable terms where such action is necessary to meet health or safety needs.[111]

During a public health crisis, such as the current COVID-19 pandemic, compulsory licenses can be used by a country to ensure the provision of lifesaving drugs to its citizens.[112] If the patent owner produces insufficient quantities of such a drug or selling it at a price a government cannot reasonably afford, then that government can grant compulsory licenses enabling third parties to produce it. The Bayh-Dole Act's "march-in rights" serve a similar purpose. The act aims to incentivize innovation by allowing universities to partner with private companies in the production of patented inventions, and also protects the public against the non-use or unreasonable use of inventions that have received public funding.[113] Like compulsory licensing generally, such protection provides an important tool for the government when faced with unreasonable drug costs. Although compulsory licensing has traditionally been used by low-income countries, in response to COVID-19, higher-income countries, including various EU member states, Canada, and Israel, are using or looking into the use of compulsory licensing as a tool to aid the production of drugs.[114]

The United States, however, remains opposed to compulsory licensing. First, patent owners have framed it as the "theft" of intellectual property rights. Compulsory licensing is "morally wrong"[115] because it triggers stealing of patents and forces patent owners to bear costs of such "theft". Second, patent owners take the view that compulsory licenses destroy innovation by removing the monopoly incentive. However, pharmaceutical companies base their innovation on the needs of the most developed countries, which are highly unlikely to use compulsory licenses in any case.[116] Third, patent owners

---

[110] 35 U.S.C. § 203(a).

[111] *Id.*

[112] World Trade Organization, Declaration on the TRIPS Agreement and Public Health of 14 November 2001 ¶ 5.b, WTO Doc. WT/MIN(01)/ DEC/2, 41 I.L.M. 755 (2002).

[113] *See* Kumar, *supra* note 108, at 13.

[114] *Id.* at 4, 26–29.

[115] Bagley, *supra* note 106, at 2474.

[116] *Id.* at 2474 (pointing out that it has been argued that "compulsory licenses will harm innovation and society will not get the new drugs it needs").

frequently cite a study claiming that developing countries get better drug prices from international procurement markets than from compulsory licensing.[117]

Hence, the United States has also avoided making use of compulsory licensing during previous public health crises. In response to fears of potential anthrax attacks in the early 2000s, the government considered using the statute to secure Bayer's ciprofloxacin antibiotic at a cost lower than the prices offered to it by Bayer.[118] It was only able to negotiate a better price after Canada issued a compulsory license to a domestic company, creating a threat to Bayer.[119] In 2016 and 2018, the government outright opposed calls for use of the § 1498 compulsory license in response to suggestions made by several scholars and elected officials that it should be used to lower the cost of hepatitis C antiviral drugs and other drugs covered by Medicare and Medicaid.[120]

Making use of the Bayh-Dole Act's "march-in rights" to obtain a compulsory license is difficult in part because of the complex and lengthy administrative process involved. This includes a fact-finding hearing that affords the patent owner an opportunity to appear with counsel and provide witnesses to oppose the license-seeker, and the license cannot proceed until the patent owner has exhausted all appeals.[121] Despite third-party requests, the government has not exercised its march-in rights to issue any compulsory licenses thus far.[122] For example, a shortage of Genzyme's Fabrazyme beginning in 2009 led to drug rationing that resulted in disability and death for patients with Fabry disease.[123] Despite such harm to consumers and

---

[117] *See* Reed F. Beall, Randall Kuhn, & Amir Attaran, *Compulsory Licensing Often Did Not Produce Lower Prices for Antiretrovirals Compared to International Procurement*, 34 HEALTH AFFS. 493, 500 (2015).

[118] *See* Kumar, *supra* note 108, at 10.

[119] *Id.* at 10.

[120] *See, e.g.*, Amy Kapczynski & Aaron S. Kesselheim, *"Government Patent Use": A Legal Approach to Reducing Drug Spending*, 35 HEALTH AFFS. 791, 792 (2016) (proposing that the federal government should utilize § 1498 to lower the price of hepatitis C drugs).

[121] Kumar, *supra* note 108, at 13–14.

[122] *Id.* at 13 ("To date, however, the government has never directly exercised its march-in rights.")

[123] *See* Andrew Pollack, *Genzyme Drug Shortage Leaves Users Feeling Betrayed*, N.Y. TIMES (Apr. 15, 2010), https://perma.cc/J975-SJPH.

the pharmaceutical company in question repeatedly missing production targets, the Obama administration resisted compulsory licensing on the grounds that it would take too long to approve another manufacturer.[124]

Internationally, the US approach has contributed to resistance to compulsory licensing issued by other countries. Compulsory licenses are permitted under Article 31 of the Agreement on Trade-Related Aspects of Intellectual Property Rights (TRIPS Agreement)[125] provided that they "do not unreasonably conflict with a normal exploitation of the patent and do not unreasonably prejudice the legitimate interests of the patent owner."[126] However, when South Africa passed legislation to lower the cost of medicines through compulsory licensing during the peak of the AIDS epidemic, trade group Pharmaceutical Research and Manufacturers of America asked the US Trade Representative to place the country on the Special 301 Watch List on the grounds that the legislation violated the TRIPS Agreement.[127] The US backed down only after a public outcry and support for South Africa from the EU and WHO, among others.[128] The US government's resistance to international compulsory licensing not only limits its own patent system's ability to effectively balance the incentive of monopoly rights against public health interests, but also the ability of the TRIPS Agreement to do so regionally and internationally.

C CREATING PATENT RESPONSIBILITIES

How can we reshape patent law into a legal system capable of requiring patent holders to assume adequate responsibility? Drawing on Chapter 5's tripartite conception of fundamental corporate responsibilities, I put forth

[124] *See* Kumar, *supra* note 108, at 36–37.
[125] Agreement on Trade-Related Aspects of Intellectual Property Rights art. 31, Apr. 15, 1994, Marrakesh Agreement Establishing the World Trade Organization, Annex 1C, 1869 U.N.T.S. 213999 (1994) [hereinafter TRIPS Agreement], https://perma.cc/C27A-6G8X.
[126] *Id.* at art. 30.
[127] *See* Kumar, *supra* note 108, at 14–15.
[128] *Id.* at 15 ("President Clinton issued an executive order stating that the U.S. government will not seek the revocation of any policy of a sub-Saharan African country that expands access to HIV/AIDS drugs for impacted areas.").

in this section three major responsibilities that should be imposed on patent holders to promote innovation in the public interest.

1 Responsibility to Reciprocate

The ethical norm of reciprocity, as I discuss in Chapter 5, requires that we return the positive actions of others proportionately, overcoming our selfish impulses to consider how we can act in return in their interest. Based on reciprocity, I argue in the two following sections that patent holders should assume two major responsibilities: the *ex ante* responsibility to reciprocate the grant of patent rights by faithfully fulfilling the patent disclosure requirement and the *ex post* responsibility to reciprocate public funding for their innovations by lowering the prices of their patented products or their amount of patent royalties.

Redefining the nature of the patent disclosure requirement is a sensible way of dealing with the major problems with that requirement. Conventionally, patent law has treated insufficient disclosure as a legal basis for rejecting or invalidating the grant of a patent. Accordingly, the law places the inadequate disclosure burden of proof on the patent examiner rather than on the patent applicant to show adequate disclosure.[129] A 2003 report by the Federal Trade Commission summarizes the major problem with that rule for the burden of proof:

> The *ex parte* nature of the [examination] proceeding leaves the examiner on his or her own to evaluate and challenge applicants' assertions. Because the courts have placed the burden on the PTO to demonstrate grounds for rejecting a patent, rather than on the applicant to demonstrate that it meets the statutory criteria, difficulties in assembling responsive evidence work in favor of patent applicants.[130]

The conventional characterization of patent disclosure has therefore rendered patent examiners and courts reluctant to reject or

---

[129] *See* Sean B. Seymore, *The Presumption of Patentability*, 97 MINN. L. REV. 990, 1015 (2013) (contending that the nature of patent disclosure has actually required examiners to make affirmative rejections, which creates a presumption of patentability that they must rebut in order to reject patent applications).

[130] FED. TRADE COMM'N, TO PROMOTE INNOVATION: THE PROPER BALANCE OF COMPETITION AND PATENT LAW AND POLICY 8 (2003), https://bit.ly/3iRbO6O.

invalidate patents on the ground that they lack an enabling disclosure.[131] In addition, confusingly drafted and scientifically limited patents offer little help to researchers hoping to put the information therein into practice. In a survey of nanotechnology researchers looking to patents for technical information, 60 percent indicated that they found useful information, but only 38 percent that the information found was reproducible.[132] This outcome is significant because "[w]hen specifications fail to teach how protected technologies operate, they subvert the disclosure function of patent law."[133]

Following the ethical norm of reciprocity, I argue that patent disclosure should be redefined as an *ex ante* responsibility that patent holders should faithfully fulfill in return for the grant of patent rights and others' contributions to innovation. First, the patent holder should bear the burden of proving sufficient disclosure in judicial proceedings challenging a USPTO denial of a patent application. The court could order the patent holder to supply evidence showing that the written description and extra specifications filed with the PTO constituted sufficient information disclosure by demonstrating that they provide information in sufficient detail that a "person having ordinary skill in the art" (PHOSITA) will be able to practice the invention.[134] To meet this enablement responsibility, the patent holder must explain how a PHOSITA would be able to make and use the invention without "undue experimentation."[135]

Second, the patent holder needs to prove that he or she has disclosed information in the best mode possible; that is, he or she has described the best way of making the invention that he or she knew of at the time of the application.[136] More specifically, the patent holder should demonstrate possession of the best mode for practicing the

---

[131] *See* Chien, *supra* note 53, at 1862–63 ("[A]ccording to a study of patent applications, of all grounds of rejection, enablement was the least used ground for rejection among bioinformatics applications and the second-to-least used by examiners among data-processing applications. Based on an analysis of published district court decisions from 2008 to 2009, enablement and written description were among the least asserted grounds for invalidity during litigation.").

[132] *See* Ouellette, *supra* note 72, at 560–62, 576.

[133] *See* Devlin, *supra* note 74, at 411.

[134] Chien, *supra* note 53, at 1856.

[135] *Id.*

[136] *Id.* at 1857.

invention and disclose it to the PTO to enable a PHOSITA to practice it.[137] Although patents may no longer be invalidated for a failure to disclose the best mode under the AIA, best mode disclosure is still considered a requirement for receiving a patent.[138]

Third, Congress should enforce the *ex ante* responsibility for information disclosure by introducing new civil liabilities for patent holders who willfully withhold disclosable patent information. At present, the only legal consequence for a failure to disclose is revocation of the registered patent. Absent other penalties, patent holders may still have a financial incentive to disclose insufficient patent information in the hope that the patent examiners will be unable to detect it. For instance, patent holders could withhold patent information in order to accumulate a portfolio of patents and exclude competitors in the marketplace.[139] The introduction of civil penalties such as fines for fraudulent acts would likely deter the willful nondisclosure of patent information by patent holders.

In addition to their *ex ante* responsibility for disclosure, patent holders should also assume an *ex post* responsibility for the public funding they have received. A great deal of public funding has supported essential research, especially the development of life-saving drugs. In the case of the Ebola vaccine, for example, Canadian government scientists were responsible for its development from the laboratory bench to a commercial grade product ready for clinical trials, whereas private companies waited for an Ebola outbreak to undertake this process.[140] A number of pharmaceutical companies, including AstraZeneca, Johnson & Johnson, and Moderna, have received public funding to develop COVID-19 vaccines.

A major problem with public funding is that many patent holders fail to reciprocate in the form of benefits to the public. This chapter has revealed that despite public funding support, Gilead overcharges for its patented medicine remdesivir. In addition, the company also charges

---

[137] *Id.*

[138] *See* Ouellette, *supra* note 72, at 552.

[139] Devlin, *supra* note 74, at 427-430.

[140] *See* Matthew Herder, Janice E. Graham & Richard Gold, *From Discovery to Delivery: Public Sector Development of the rVSV-ZEBOV Ebola Vaccine*, J.L. & THE BIOSCIENCES 3–4 (2020) ("Public sources contributed over 73% (USD$758.8 million) of the USD$1.035 billion allocated to Ebola and other filovirus research from 1997 to 2015.").

$20,000 for a one-year course of the patented drug Truvada, approved to prevent HIV infection, even though it too was developed with government funding.[141] In response to such irresponsible pricing, experts have urged the government to reconsider its support for pharmaceutical companies given that so many patented medicines developed using public funding still "remain unaffordable for millions of Americans."[142]

Similar practices have been seen with respect to patents developed by US universities with the support of public funding. Before 1980, patents resulting from publicly funded research were owned by the US government.[143] The 1980 Bayh-Dole Act, however, triggered a significant increase in patent applications by universities because it entitles US universities to elect to retain title to inventions arising from federally funded research or contract programs and to license them to firms under certain conditions.[144] The act was intended to motivate increased investment in the development of patent inventions into commercial products and to encourage technology transfers,[145] as commercial opportunities are seen as a sustainable way of maintaining high-quality, profitable research and innovation at universities in the long run.[146]

Greater protection of patents has also increasingly emboldened universities to launch patent litigation. From 2000 to 2009, universities joined their licensees in suing another party for patent infringement in 139 cases. In another fifty-one cases, universities brought patent infringement suits on their own.[147] Instead of using patents in the public interest to reciprocate for public funding, many universities

---

[141] *See* Donald G. McNeil Jr. and Apoorva Mandavilli, *Who Owns H.I.V.-Prevention Drugs? The Taxpayers, U.S. Says*, N.Y. TIMES (Nov. 8, 2019), https://nyti.ms/3DmO9Dk.

[142] *Id.*

[143] Adam Hayes, *When Universities Patent Their Research*, IP WATCHDOG, https://bit.ly/3iR0VC4.

[144] *See id.*

[145] *See* Charles R. McManis & Sucheol Noh, *The Impact of the Bayh-Dole Act on Genetic Research and Development, in* PERSPECTIVES ON COMMERCIALIZING INNOVATION 436–37 (F. Scott Kieff & Troy A. Paredes eds., 2012).

[146] Peter Lee, *Patent and the University*, 63 DUKE L.J.1, 32 (2013).

[147] *Id.* at 42. Universities participating in lawsuits are in a significant upward trend. There were only eleven lawsuits filed by the universities while there were eight cases of universities' participation in 2000. The figure rose to forty-three such lawsuits and twenty-two such cases in 2012 respectively. *See* Jacob H. Rooksby, *Innovation and Litigation: Tensions*

have adopted overly litigious tactics, which effectively makes them patent trolls aiming to extract large damage awards.

A positive way to deal with this dilemma would be to rely on the ethical norm of reciprocity to impose *ex post* responsibility on patent holders. Such responsibility would require patent holders to pro-actively reciprocate for public funding. First, inventions developed through public funding should be deemed social innovations devoted to promoting the public interest. Second, given the social innovation status of such inventions, patent holders should reduce the prices of their patented products or the amount of royalties they receive for licensing those patents. For example, pharmaceutical companies that have received public funding for COVID-19 vaccine development ought to make those vaccines available at a relatively low price. Doing so would make the vaccines available to as many people as possible, and would also induce other vaccine developers to follow suit.

To enforce this responsibility to reciprocate, the government should require patent holders to agree to assume it when submitting funding applications. If patent holders then fail to fulfill the responsi-bility faithfully, the government can demand repayment or even sue them for their misuse of public funding.

2 Innovators' Role Responsibility

As shown in Chapter 5, another ethical norm, role responsibility, requires individuals to take *personal responsibility* for the specific roles they choose to adopt, be it sea captain, husband, or clerk. These interpersonal roles put the individual into a special position in relation to others whose interests are affected by the performance of certain assigned functions or the fulfillment of assigned goals.[148] Role respon-sibility gives rise to *professional responsibilities* owing to the specific roles individuals choose to serve in larger institutions such as companies and governmental agencies. Once an individual chooses a profession that confers upon him or her the authority to control people and resources,

---

between *Universities and Patents and How to Fix Them*, 15 Yale J.L. & Tech. 312, 338 tbl.1. (2013).

[148] H. L. A. Hart, Punishment and Responsibility: Essays in the Philosophy of Law 212 (2d ed. 2008)

certain responsibilities are then imposed on him or her within the bounds of that profession.

As innovators, patent holders should assume a role responsibility to promote innovation in the public interest. As Chapter 5 has shown, technology companies play the role of innovators by generating new intellectual properties. In 2019, the top fifty recipients of registered patents were technology companies. For example, IBM topped the ranking, with 9,262 patent applications approved by the USPTO.[149] Technology companies are the most forceful drivers of innovation because they have institutional capacities to recognize market needs and recruit competent people for research and development (R&D),[150] as well as the departments to nurture these capacities. Market researchers specialize in discovering unmet consumer needs, preferences, and desires. Research and development personnel are familiar with existing related technologies, and are able to create new ones to meet these identified needs, preferences, and desires.

However, many technology companies have not adequately fulfilled their responsibilities associated with their COVID-19-related innovations and patents even at the tipping points of the pandemic. In this chapter, I shift from the pandemic periods of crisis management responsibilities to consider patent holders' responsibilities under the normal circumstances of innovation. I argue many technology companies have also failed to scrutinize their responsibilities required by the social nature of innovation. Responding to the fact that innovation is by nature a social process, we must challenge the conventional focus of patent law on the protection of patent holders' rights and call for a patent law reform intended to impose greater responsibilities on patent holders.

The process of innovation has a distributional dimension, which tackles how the benefits of technological progress should be distributed

---

[149] IFI CLAIMS Patent Services, *2019 Top 50 US Patent Assignees*, www.ificlaims.com /rankings-top-50-2019.htm (updated Jan. 8, 2020).

[150] *See* O. E. Barishnikova & M. N. Nevzorova, *Development of Innovation*, 6 EUR. J. NAT. HIST. 53, 53 (2015)("Information technology and changing business processes and management style can produce a work climate favorable to innovation.").

fairly in a society. Innovations have both market and social value.[151] Traditionally, markets determine, on the basis of ability to pay, access to innovations and the kinds of innovations that are developed and distributed.[152] Patent law allocates resources to innovations of high market value, irrespective of their social value,[153] and rewards market actors for developing potentially profitable rather than socially beneficial inventions. The law legally enables patent holders to distribute technological benefits as they wish through voluntary market transactions. They have the exclusive rights to permit others to use their patented technologies contingent on royalties.[154] Researchers are prevented from using results and data generated by companies undertaking R&D until patents are filed.[155] At the same time, for companies that draw upon the public domain in the R&D process, even where there is no intention to file a patent, relationships between commercial entities are characterized by confidentiality and secrecy.[156] Hence, the extent to which members of the public can use a technological benefit often hinges upon how much they can pay the patent holder concerned.

The rise of social innovation, however, challenges patent law's market value-oriented distribution of technological benefits. Social innovation serves the public interest by increasing social value and inducing social and behavioral changes.[157] Social value can be defined as "the creation of benefits or reduction of costs for society ... in ways

---

[151] See Lee, *supra* note 65, at 26 ("Although innovation in the patent paradigm focuses on individual inventors, social innovation reveals that many creations arise more collectively from communal efforts.").

[152] See Margaret Chon, *Intellectual Property and the Development Divide*, 27 CARDOZO L. REV. 2821, 2823 (2006).

[153] See Amy Kapczynski, Samantha Chaifetz, Zachary Katz, & Yochai Benkler, *Addressing Global Health Inequalities: An Open Licensing Approach for University Innovations*, 20 BERKELEY TECH. L.J. 1031, 1051 (2005).

[154] See ROBERT P. MERGES, JUSTIFYING INTELLECTUAL PROPERTY, at xi (2011) (IP rights let inventors "leverage their creative work, turning their effort into saleable assets. This not only enhances their income, it buys freedom.").

[155] Jonathan Alan King, *Protecting Public Health Requires COVID-19 Treatments to Be Patent-Free*, TRUTHOUT (May 19, 2020), https://bit.ly/3v8MTRh.

[156] See id.

[157] See Lee, *supra* note 65, at 8–11; Carol Yeh-Yun LIN & JEFFREY CHEN, THE IMPACT OF SOCIETAL AND SOCIAL INNOVATION: A CASE-BASED APPROACH 64 (2018) (arguing that social innovation's goal is to produce actions that are "socially valuable and good for many").

that go beyond the private gains and general benefits of market activity."[158] In many ways, innovations traditionally covered by patent law do offer social value beyond the private value they offer to their creators. For instance, pharmaceuticals save lives, computers increase productivity, learning, and creativity, and cars simultaneously provide independence and promote contact between people who live apart.[159] They can be considered social innovations because, with regard to the motives underlying their creation, they are intended to social value and the public interest.[160] Public interests encapsulate substantive human needs and includes social welfare, public health, and safety.[161] It is the motivation to serve the public interest rather than purely obtain financial gain that distinguishes social innovations from normal commercial activities.

Examination of examples of social innovation reveals that in addition to being social in that they serve the public good, many are also social in that they arise collectively from communal efforts.[162] This is certainly the case when describing innovation at high levels of abstraction such as in feminism or environmentalism and in broad technological fields such as semiconductors.[163] It is also true in the case of more specific innovations. For example, although Aaron Beck and Albert Ellis are recognized for their role in developing cognitive behavioral therapy, the field has much broader origins, and its development owes a lot to the merger of behaviorism and the cognitive revolution.[164] Similarly, in the field of microfinance, Grameen Bank founder Muhammad Yunus alone is often credited, when in reality he would best be described as the articulator of a communal innovation.[165]

---

[158] James A. Phills Jr. et al., *Rediscovering Social Innovation*, STAN. SOC. INNOVATION REV., Fall 2008, at 34, 39 (2018).

[159] *Id.*

[160] *Id.*

[161] *See id.*, at 36 (defining social innovation as "[a] novel solution to a social problem that is more effective, efficient, sustainable, or just than existing solutions and for which the value created accrues primarily to society as a whole rather than private individuals"); Lee, *supra* note 65, at 9.

[162] *See* Lee, *supra* note 65, at 26–27.

[163] *See id.* at 28.

[164] *See id.* at 27–28.

[165] *Id.*

The COVID-19 pandemic has demonstrated the crucial importance of social innovation. By developing medicines and vaccines in the public interest, such innovation tackles the serious problems with the profit-driven, patent-oriented pharmaceutical industry. While for-profit private companies assert that strong patent protection offers the most effective incentive for pharmaceutical innovation[166] and leads to the development of new medicines to cure life-threatening diseases,[167] in reality these claims pose two serious problems.

One problem is that private pharmaceutical companies have largely failed to develop medicines and vaccines for deadly infectious diseases that create only limited market demand. When innovation is driven by the market, as in a pandemic, private companies frequently fail to act quickly enough because, until the pandemic has created sufficient demand, directing resources toward the development of vaccines is antithetical to market incentives.[168] The case of Ebola shows how obstructive the market approach can be to the creation of social value. After Canada's National Microbiology Laboratory had developed and produced in 2005 a vaccine for Ebola that was highly effective in animals, a small private company licensed it for $200,000, failing to take the vaccine any further before sublicensing it to Merck for $50 million in 2014 after the Ebola outbreak in Africa. Not only was the company's involvement unnecessary but it ultimately slowed down development of the vaccine, with Merck receiving approval for its vaccine only in 2019. [169]

Furthermore, despite patent rights frequently being cited by pharmaceutical companies as the necessary incentive for producing lifesaving drugs, the patent protection system has failed to drive

---

[166] *See* Tom Wilbur, *IP Explained: Myth vs. Fact About Strong Patent Protections in the Biopharmaceutical Industry*, PhRMA: The Catalyst (May 2, 2019), https://onphr.ma /3BzavRl (broadly claiming that strong patent protection "is the most effective tool to reward and incentivize innovation").

[167] *See* Mark Grayson, *5 Reasons Why Biopharmaceutical Patents Are Different*, PhRMA: The Catalyst (Sept. 10, 2015), https://onphr.ma/3FzXMR0.

[168] Ana Santos Rutschman, *IP Preparedness for Outbreak Diseases*, 65 UCLA L. Rev. 1200, 1222 (2018)("Even today, during the inter-outbreak period following the largest and most lethal Ebola pandemic in recorded history, it is not clear that the vaccines currently in advanced clinical development will have a 'clear commercial market.'").

[169] *See* Juliana Broad, *Coronavirus and Ebola Show We Can't Leave Vaccine Development to Big Pharma*, Truthout (Mar. 9, 2020), https://bit.ly/3iQJ0vq.

effective research on infectious diseases such as coronaviruses.[170] Although emerging viruses present significant scientific challenges, in 2019, prior to the outbreak of COVID-19, there were only six active coronavirus clinical trials.[171] Had the potential risk-driven companies to increase their coronavirus research, the medical community would likely have been better placed to address the challenges of the pandemic. However, market-oriented pharmaceutical companies do not proactively invest research effort in medical treatments and vaccines likely to yield low profits. Instead, they pursue only the most lucrative avenues of research. Some pharmaceutical companies have openly admitted that researching vaccines is not in their interest. Instead, they have chosen to fund treatments for chronic conditions, with cancer drugs being a favorite, as they command a high price despite often providing only marginal therapeutic improvements.[172]

By contrast, social innovation driven by nonprofit public institutions has contributed tremendously to deadly infectious disease responses, primarily in the form of funding and grants. A recent report on the Ebola vaccine found that it was "almost entirely researched and developed using public money."[173] Following the COVID-19 pandemic outbreak, the US government launched Operation Warp Speed with the aim of delivering over 300 million doses of a safe and effective vaccine by January 2021 through public investment in vaccine development, manufacturing, and distribution capabilities.[174] Examples of this public investment include $456 million in funds for Johnson & Johnson, $955 million for Moderna, and up to $1.2 billion for AstraZeneca for their respective vaccine candidates.[175] The US National Institutes of Health has issued over 1,500 grants for research into COVID-19.[176]

---

[170] *See* Zain Rizvi, *Blind Spot: How the COVID-19 Outbreak Shows the Limits of Pharma's Monopoly Model*, Pub. Citizen (Feb. 19, 2020), www.citizen.org/article/blind-spot.

[171] *Id.*

[172] *Id.*

[173] *See* Broad, *supra* note 169.

[174] U.S. Dep't of Defense, and Human Services, *Coronavirus: Operation Warp Speed*, https://bit.ly/3v1Uykb.

[175] Berkeley Lovelace Jr. & Nate Rattner, *Coronavirus Vaccine Frontrunner Pfizer Delivers Key Trial Data*, CNBC (Nov. 9, 2020), https://cnb.cx/3mMOBEl.

[176] Search Results, NIH Rsch. Portfolio Online Reporting Tools (2020), https://bit.ly/3mFGsBy (last visited Apr. 5, 2021).

3 The Responsibility to Confront Injustices Created by Patent Protection

As noted in Chapter 5, social justice is widely regarded as a fundamental value intended to minimize the impacts of the unequal distribution of resources and status discrimination. It is regarded as the "first virtue of social institutions."[177] By nature, social justice centers on how responsibilities for distributing resources and social status should be allocated.

Strong patent protection can cause two major social injustices in enjoying the benefits of technological progress. It first gives rise to the concern that technology companies have not adequately fulfilled their social justice responsibility to promote affordable access to technological benefits accrued from inventions. With the set of strong exclusive rights, patent holders can maximize their profits by charging prices as high as possible, so long as their inventions have viable market demands from those who are financially capable.[178] Their patent power, however, exclude those who are financially unable to afford their inventions from benefiting from the technological progress they created. Pharmaceutical inventions epitomize this worsening social injustice, which frequently causes matters of life or death. For instance, most patented medicines developed for curing cancers are too expensive for many patients. In just over a decade, prices of such life-saving medicines have virtually doubled in the US[179] Eleven of the twelve

---

[177] JOHN RAWLS, A THEORY OF JUSTICE 3 (Harvard Univ. Press rev. ed. 1999) [hereinafter RAWLS, A THEORY OF JUSTICE]. Rawls also points out that "[a] theory however elegant and economical must be rejected or revised if it is untrue; likewise laws and institutions no matter how efficient and well-arranged must be reformed or abolished if they are unjust." *Id.*

[178] *Report of the United Nations Secretary-General's High-Level Panel on Access to Medicines: Promoting Innovation and Access to Health Technologies* 21 (2016) ("IP rights confer patent monopolies on the right holder, who in turn often charges whatever price the market will bear."); Alexandra E. Blasi, *An Ethical Dilemma: Patents & Profits v. Access & Affordability*, 33 J. OF LEGAL MED. 115, 117 (2012).

[179] *Report of the United Nations Secretary-General's High-Level Panel on Access to* Medicines, *id.* at 21.

cancer medicines approved by the US Food and Drug Administration in 2012 were each "priced above US$ 100,000 per year."[180]

Another major social injustice that technological companies have not made efforts to correct is the development of technologies for those neglected population. Given the profits-driven incentives created by strong patent protection, pharmaceutical companies typically invest in the research and development of new medicines that can yield high market returns.[181] However, most of them do not develop medicines for neglected diseases that affect comparatively small proportions of the relevant populations. It has been revealed that patenting of medicines for neglected diseases is quite limited. The total number of filed patents for cardiovascular diseases or cancer is at least 200 times larger than neglected diseases.[182]

The ongoing COVID-19 pandemic has also exposed the conflict between patent protection and social justice. Private pharmaceutical companies cannot guarantee universal affordable access to medicines and vaccines for deadly infectious diseases. The control granted by patents allows companies to set exorbitant prices, delay competition, and, in the process, minimize the role of taxpayer investments in the development of important medical treatments.[183] The privatized nature of US pharmaceutical production slows down development in pursuit of private financial interests at the expense of the clear public interest in fast and affordable access to essential medicine.[184]

The COVID-19 pandemic is likely to result in further conflict between private patent owners and national governments attempting to secure the drugs and treatments necessary to protect their citizens. To promote social justice by guaranteeing equal access to

---

[180] *Id.* at 21.

[181] *Id.* at 8.

[182] Folahanmi Tomiwa Akinsolu et al., *Patent Landscape of Neglected Tropical Diseases: An Analysis of Worldwide Patent Families*, 13 GLOB. HEALTH 1, 11 (2017) ("The gap between patenting NTDs and cardiovascular diseases/cancers is striking; the number of filed patents for cardiovascular diseases or cancer is at least 200 times larger than NTDs.").

[183] *See* Rizvi, *supra* note 170.

[184] King, *supra* note 155.

COVID-19-related drugs and vaccines, countries have utilized compulsory licensing. A few developed countries have revised their laws concerning compulsory licensing. Canada has long been a proponent of compulsory licensing, but until recent legislation was introduced circumstances constituting public health-related national emergencies were relatively narrow.[185] However, after amendments introduced by the COVID-19 Emergency Response Act, a compulsory license may be issued if the application includes a confirmation that the Chief Public Health Officer believes there to be a public health emergency of national concern.[186] Germany has traditionally been opposed compulsory licensing, largely because it is home to two of the world's largest pharmaceutical companies, but has softened its approach in recent years.[187]

Other developed countries have issued compulsory licensing orders. In March 2020, Israel issued a compulsory license to import generic versions of AbbVie's antiretroviral drug Kaletra, after the Ministry of Health determined that it could be a possible treatment for patients with COVID-19.[188] Following the decision AbbVie made a commitment to "take all steps necessary to remove any potential barriers" for generic manufacturers, a process that includes dedicating their intellectual property rights to the public.[189] Though the decision did not involve the introduction of any new legislation, it so far amounts to the strongest action taken yet by any government of a developed country.[190] It has been suggested AbbVie's swift and dramatic response could be to dissuade governments from feeling compelled to take similar action in the case of future global health crises.[191]

Patent holders should assume a responsibility to cooperate with the government in reducing the tension between social justice and patent protection. Specifically, they should provide reasonable support for

[185] *See* Kumar, *supra* note 108, at 25–26.
[186] Patent Act, R.S.C. 1985, c P-4 §§ 19.4(1), 19.4(2) (Can.), amended by COVID-19 Emergency Response Act, S.C. 2020, c 5 § 51 (Can.).
[187] *See* Kumar, *supra* note 108, at 28–29.
[188] Hilary Wong, *The Case for Compulsory Licensing During COVID-19*, J. GLOB. HEALTH, www.jogh.org/documents/issue202001/jogh-10-010358.htm.
[189] Ed Silverman, *AbbVie Will Allow Generic Copies of Its HIV Pill in Israel After the Government Approved a License*, STAT NEWS (Mar. 20, 2020), https://bit.ly/2YBQk70.
[190] *See* Kumar, *supra* note 108, at 28–29.
[191] See *id.* at 26.

governmental schemes to achieve universal and affordable access to patented medicines essential to protecting public health.[192] To this end, I argue that as patent holders of medical inventions, pharmaceutical companies should assume, among others, two major social justice responsibilities. One is to take proactive actions to share the benefits of the patented medical inventions through schemes such as technology transfer and medical donations. The other is to accept compulsory licensing legally issued to contain public health crises as their responsibility to promote universal and affordable access to medicines and vaccines.

With respect to the first social justice responsibility, the US government should require pharmaceutical companies to devote resources to sharing the benefits of their patented medical inventions. I refer to this requirement as the Patent Philanthropy Initiative.[193] According to the initiative, for each patent it acquires from the USPTO a pharmaceutical company would be required to make a corresponding contribution to a domestic or global social welfare program. A pilot initiative program could be administered by the USPTO with each pharmaceutical company required to contribute 1 percent of its annual post-tax profits from sales of its patented products. Pharmaceutical companies would be allowed to take various actions to fulfill this responsibility. For instance, they may transfer technology to a company located in a developing country to boost production and distribution of medicines for neglected diseases. They may donate medical products and equipment to a not-for-profit organization or a developing country in dire need of them. Alternatively, they may deploy staff to train and boost the knowledge and skills of medical professionals in low-income regions in the US or developing countries.

The COVID-19 pandemic has demonstrated the potential efficacy of the proposed initiative. Despite global calls that patent rights concerning COVID-19 vaccines be waived, many leaders and experts have

---

[192] *See* Ruth L. Okediji, *Does Intellectual Property Need Human Rights?*, 51 N.Y.U. J. INT'L L. & POL. 1, 43, 35 (2018) (arguing that "access to medicines remains a key and growing challenge in virtually all countries" and "medicines need to be available for all and not only for those who can afford them").

[193] For detailed discussion about this initiative, *see* Haochen Sun, *Patent Philanthropy*, 54 CORNELL INT'L L.J. (forthcoming 2022).

pointed out it is more effective and urgent to capitalize on direct technology transfer associated with production of vaccines and donation of manufacture ingredients and equipment to ramp up the availability of vaccines in developing countries around the world. [194] In response to public health crises, the Patent Philanthropy Initiative would encourage pharmaceutical companies to increase technology transfer and donation of manufacture ingredients and equipment to boost the production and distribution of vaccines as well as medicines. After containment, the initiative would further promote in the long term the medical capacities of low-income regions in the US and developing countries.

The USPTO should require each pharmaceutical company to submit an annual report detailing the nature, scope, and effects of its actions taken in fulfillment of the responsibility attached to each of its medical inventions. I suggest that the USPTO should review those reports every five years with a panel consisting of its own administrators, independent patent experts, auditing professionals, and public interest activists. The panel would decide whether a relevant pharmaceutical company has met its responsibility to devote 1 percent of its annual post-tax profits from sales of its patented products to social welfare programs. If the panel finds that a company has failed to fulfill the responsibility, it will make recommendations to the USPTO on expeditious actions the company should take to mitigate its shortcomings. Every ten years, the USPTO should conduct a comprehensive review of the Patent Philanthropy Initiative, studying its efficacy and how it should be improved with new measures to boost social welfare and safeguards to protect pharmaceutical companies' interests. Therefore, the initiative would continue creating dynamic schemes reflective of social and technological developments.

[194] *See* Matthew Kavanagh & Madhavi Sunder, *Poor Countries May Not Be Vaccinated Until 2024: Here's How to Prevent That,* WASH. POST (Mar. 10, 2021) (arguing that "the covid-19 pandemic necessitates both a temporary intellectual property waiver from the WTO and a bold effort to share [technology to make COVID-19 vaccines]"); Ruth L. Okediji, *With a Covid-19 Vaccine Patent Waiver Likely, Time to Rethink Global Intellectual Property Rules Opinion,* CNN (May 7, 2021) ("[A]ccess to patents alone does not translate into optimal short or long-term ease of access to medicines. . . . There is a need for technology transfer related to the vaccine patents.").

Moreover, pharmaceutical companies should responsibly cooperate with the government to contain public health crises.[195] When they do so, the government should guarantee that any compulsory licensing order will provide fair compensation to affected pharmaceutical companies. For example, 28 USC § 1498 entitled the patent holder to claim "compensation," when his or her patent was subject to a compulsory license. But the law does not make clear the nature of compensation. The government should make clear that *fair* compensation should be provided to the patent holder. The Spanish patent regime includes an especially aggressive provision allowing the state to take ownership of patents in circumstances of public interest and, in recognition of the severity, it is stated that compensation received by patent owners will be *fair*.[196]

There are many different perspectives on what amounts to *fair* compensation, especially between governments and pharmaceutical companies. For example, past government compulsory license royalty rates have ranged from 0.5 to 4 percent, whereas pharmaceutical companies have tended to reach agreements for royalties ranging from 4 to 5 percent.[197] Several royalty systems have been established across the globe which could provide a framework for the US to consider. For instance, the United Nations Development Program's 2001 Guidelines set a base royalty rate of 4 percent which can be increased or decreased by up to 2 percent based on special factors such as whether the product is particularly innovative or whether the government has contributed to research and development.[198] Similarly, the Japanese Patent Office's 1998 Guidelines set a base rate of 2 to 4 percent which can be increased by 2 percent, creating a range of 0 to 6 percent.[199] A completely different approach is provided by the Tiered Royalty Method which, instead of calculating the royalty from generic product sales in the license issuing

[195] *See* MADHAVI SUNDER, FROM GOODS TO A GOOD LIFE: INTELLECTUAL PROPERTY AND GLOBAL JUSTICE 187 (2012) (arguing that compulsory licensing is designed to "correct a moral failure, not a market failure").

[196] *Compulsory License and New Provisions Affecting IP Holders During the Coronavirus Crisis in France and Globally*, CLIFFORD CHANCE (Apr. 2020), https://bit.ly/3iPitP0.

[197] Monika Shailesh, *Fair Remuneration for Compulsory Licensing*, MONDAQ (Aug. 3, 2017), https://bit.ly/3BLrn7T. ("For example Malaysia set a royalty rate of 4%; Mozambique establishes a 2% royalty; Zambia set a 2.5% royalty; and Indonesia arrived at 0.5% royalty.").

[198] *Id.*

[199] *Id.*

country, bases the royalty rate on the price of the product in the high income country where the product is patented, therefore more adequately sharing the actual cost of research and development.[200]

As a public policy matter, compulsory licensing for public health should be legally recognized because it can deter pharmaceutical companies from pricing their essential medicines at rates that are too high for the general public. Studies have shown that antibiotics protected by patents will often have a higher price than those unprotected.[201] However, other studies have shown that compulsory licenses are capable of countering this to provide dramatically lower drug costs. For example, in Brazil a compulsory license for the AIDS drug Efavirenz was issued in 2007. The patent owner Merck responded by offering a 30 percent price reduction but Brazil refused with the intention of proceeding with the compulsory license with a 1.5 percent royalty rate.[202] Ultimately Brazil did not proceed with the compulsory license as the chosen manufacturer lacked the capability to produce the drug. But the case demonstrates that the issuing of compulsory licenses can encourage patent owners to respond by lowering their prices.[203]

SUMMARY

The legal powers that patent law grants technology companies far exceed the responsibilities they have assumed. As this article reveals, this asymmetry of rights and responsibilities jeopardizes global efforts to develop medicines, vaccines, and testing methods necessary to contain the COVID-19 pandemic.

This chapter thus urges a correction to this long-existing asymmetry. It proposes that patent law be reformed to require patent holders to reciprocate for public contributions, fulfill their innovator role

---

[200] *Id.*

[201] *Review of Existing Research on Patents and Access to Medical Products and Health Technologies*, THIRTY-FIRST SESSION WIPO STANDING COMMITTEE ON THE LAW OF PATENTS 2 (2019), www.wipo.int/edocs/mdocs/scp/en/scp_31/scp_31_5.pdf.

[202] Eric Bond & Kamal Saggi, *Compulsory Licensing, Price Controls, and Access to Patented Foreign Products* 5 (Vanderbilt University Department of Economics Working Papers, Paper No. 12-00006, 2012).

[203] *Id.*

responsibility, and confront the injustices created by patent protection. The chapter also offers suggestions for how patent doctrines such as the disclosure requirement and compulsory licensing scheme could be reshaped to effectively enforce these responsibilities.

In conclusion, proper enforcement of technology companies' responsibilities, as Chapters 4, 5 and 6 demonstrate, would create three avenues for better protecting the public interest through the development and application of technology. First, the concept of fundamental corporate responsibility as applied to technology companies reveals public interests that deserve stronger protection. These relate to users' contributions to the development of technology by companies, the role responsibility of technology companies, and technology companies' responsibility to promote social justice in the enjoyment of technological benefits.

Second, examination of the nature and scope of technology companies' responsibilities affords a new legal status to technology-related public interests. The concept of fundamental corporate responsibility seeks to ensure that technology companies ethically fulfill their responsibilities to the public, thereby paving the way for the legislature, the judiciary, and the administration to renew legal rules to enforce such responsibilities in the public interest. The potential translation of these responsibilities into law would entitle members of the public to take legal action against technology companies that fail to perform their legal responsibilities.

Third, similar to the function of the right to technology, fundamental corporate responsibility would drive a social process of deliberating the nature and scope of technology-related public interests and means of effectively protecting them. As long as social media and pharmaceutical companies continue to innovate, new problems that affect the protection of technology-related public interests will emerge. Therefore, it is vital to maintain a robust, open-ended discourse on the nature and scope of technology companies' responsibilities to protect the public interest.

ACKNOWLEDGMENTS

The research projects that form the basis for this book started many years ago. Along the way, many colleagues and friends have provided comments, suggestions, and assistance for which I owe them a great debt of gratitude. I am fortunate to have experienced their unwavering support, tremendous wit, and steadfast dedication to research as they have joined me on an intellectually fascinating academic journey.

I began to explore initial ideas for this book through projects on copyright and the public interest. William "Terry" Fisher and George Wei provided very insightful comments on my early research papers on this topic and encouraged me to pursue further studies, while Terry's courses and theoretical work on intellectual property helped reveal to me my academic path. James Boyle, Jedediah Purdy, and Laura Underkuffler offered support and encouragement as I furthered my research, James sharing me ways to achieve quality research output, Jed leading me to engage more critically with political thought relevant to my academic writings, and Laura's work on property law broadening my perspective on the relationship between private ownership and social welfare.

While working on copyright, I saw through the lens of public health crises, specifically the HIV/AIDS epidemic and COVID-19 pandemic, how patents have become more closely intertwined with the public interest. I also saw that the pervasive use of digital technologies poses formidable challenges to public interest protection, from unequal access to the Internet to personal data breaches. Big data and advances in artificial intelligence technologies have exacerbated these challenges and made more urgent the problem of how to fairly distribute the benefits of technological progress.

These developments prompted me to undertake this book project on technology and the public interest. Many other colleagues and friends have since offered their support and encouragement at conferences, lectures, and talks, and also on private occasions such as tennis games, hikes, vacations, and meals. They have helped me see that when "academics never stop talking about their work," this can be a spiritually healthy lifestyle. For helpful comments and conversations, I am grateful to Douglas Arner, Graeme Austin, Shyamkrishna Balganesh, Barton Beebe, Lionel Bently, Robert Burrell, Cora Chan, Albert Chen, Anne Cheung, Michael Cheung, Anupam Chander, Rochelle Dreyfuss, Jeanne Fromer, Hualing Fu, Dev Gangjee, Daniel Gervais, Mitu Gulati, Michael Handler, Xin He, Reto Hilty, Calvin Ho, Michael Hor, Sonia Katyal, Ariel Katz, Kimberly Krawiec, David Law, Alice Lee, Peter Lee, Daryl Lim, Kung-Chung Liu, Mark Lemley, David Llewelyn, Robert Merges, Wee Loon Ng-Loy, Ruth Okediji, Frank Pasquale, Jerome Reichman, Pamela Samuelson, Martin Senftleben, Christopher Sprigman, Madhavi Sunder, Alec Stone Sweet, David Tan, Rebecca Tushnet, Scott Veitch, Marco Wan, Ying Xia, Anna Wu, Po Jen Yap, Christopher Yoo, Simon Young, Peter Yu, Angela Zhang, Taisu Zhang, Yun Zhao, and Diane Zimmerman.

Portions of this book are adapted from articles I have published in law reviews. These are: "Reinvigorating the Human Right to Technology," 41 *Michigan Journal of International Law* 279 (2020); "The Fundamental Right to Technology," 47 *Hofstra Law Review* 445 (2020); "Bridging the Digital Chasm through the Fundamental Right to Technology," 28 *Georgetown Journal on Poverty Law & Policy* 75 (2020); "Corporate Fundamental Responsibility: What do Technology Companies Owe the World?" 74 *University of Miami Law Review* 898-963 (2020); and "Patent Responsibility," 17 *Stanford Journal of Civil Rights and Civil Liberties* 321 (2021). I am also grateful to the editors of these law reviews for meticulously editing my articles.

My final thanks go to my parents. Their tremendous care and unconditional love have supported my academic career and enriched every moment of my life. In particular, I owe enormous gratitude to my mother. She is my soulmate and life mentor, and her wisdom, courage, humor, and indefatigable energy are the source of all the happiness of my family.

INDEX

CPSIA information can be obtained
at www.ICGtesting.com
Printed in the USA
BVHW042217120422
634087BV00008B/60

9 781108 403481